D1453126

THE USES OF THE PAST FROM HEIDEGGER TO RORTY
Doing Philosophy Historically

In this book Robert Piercey asks how it is possible to do philosophy by studying the thinkers of the past. He develops his answer through readings of Martin Heidegger, Richard Rorty, Paul Ricoeur, Alasdair MacIntyre, and other historically minded philosophers. Piercey shows that what is distinctive about these figures is a concern with *philosophical pictures* – extremely general conceptions of what the world is like – rather than specific theories. He offers a comprehensive and illuminating exploration of the way in which these thinkers use narrative to evaluate and criticize these pictures. The result is a powerful and original account of how philosophers use the past.

ROBERT PIERCEY is an Associate Professor of Philosophy at Campion College, University of Regina.

THE USES OF THE PAST FROM HEIDEGGER TO RORTY

Doing Philosophy Historically

ROBERT PIERCEY

Campion College, University of Regina

CAMBRIDGE
UNIVERSITY PRESS

CAMBRIDGE UNIVERSITY PRESS
Cambridge, New York, Melbourne, Madrid, Cape Town, Singapore, São Paulo, Delhi

Cambridge University Press
The Edinburgh Building, Cambridge CB2 8RU, UK

Published in the United States of America by Cambridge University Press, New York

www.cambridge.org
Information on this title: www.cambridge.org/9780521517539

First published 2009
Printed in the United Kingdom at the University Press, Cambridge

A catalog record for this publication is available from the British Library

Library of Congress Cataloging in Publication data
Piercey, Robert
The uses of the past from Heidegger to Rorty: doing philosophy historically / Robert Piercey.
p.   cm.
Includes bibliographical references.
ISBN 978-0-521-51753-9
1. Philosophy, Modern – 20th century.
I. Title.
B804.P555   2009
190.9′04–dc22
2008048862

ISBN 978-0-521-51753-9 hardback

For Anna, of course

Contents

Acknowledgments

Parts of this book were originally published elsewhere. An early version of Chapter 1 appeared in *Review of Metaphysics* 56. Part of Chapter 6 was first published, in somewhat different form, in *Philosophy Today* 51. Another article based on Chapter 6 will appear in a forthcoming issue of *American Catholic Philosophical Quarterly*. I'm grateful to all of these journals for letting me reuse this material. In addition, early versions of some parts of the book were presented as lectures to the Canadian Philosophical Association, the Memorial University Philosophy Colloquium, and the Philosophical Association of Religiously Affiliated Colleges. Thanks to all who attended these sessions for their stimulating comments.

My work on this book was funded by grants from Campion College, from the University of Regina, and from the Humanities Research Institute. I'd like to thank the people who helped me take advantage of this assistance: Benjamin Fiore, S.J., Samira McCarthy, and Nicholas Ruddick. I'm grateful to several other people at Campion who helped this project along in a variety of ways: Suzanne Hunter, Chris Riegel, Katherine Robinson, and Stacey Sallenback. Special thanks to Sarah Gray, my tireless research assistant and a true *débrouillard*.

I'm indebted to all those who commented on drafts of the book, or who discussed the ideas in it with me. They include: Michael Bowler, Scott Cameron, Gary Foster, Morny Joy, Christopher Lawn, David Pellauer, David Scott, John Scott, Michael Tilley, and Henry Venema. I'm particularly grateful to Hilary Gaskin and two anonymous readers for Cambridge University Press for their many helpful suggestions. And as always, I'd like to extend a very special thanks to Gary Gutting and Steve Watson – not just for their insights into the philosophical issues discussed in this book, but for sharing their time, their energy, and their immense practical wisdom.

Most of all, I'm grateful to Anna. She knows why.

Abbreviations

The following abbreviations will be used for frequently cited titles:

AV   Alasdair MacIntyre, *After Virtue*, 2nd edn. Notre Dame: University of Notre Dame Press, 1984.

BT   Martin Heidegger, *Being and Time*, trans. John Macquarrie and Edward Robinson. San Francisco: Harper Collins, 1962.

CI   Paul Ricoeur, *The Conflict of Interpretations*, ed. Don Ihde. Evanston: Northwestern University Press, 1974.

ET   Martin Heidegger, *The Essence of Truth*, trans. Ted Sadler. New York: Continuum, 2002.

FS   Paul Ricoeur, *Figuring the Sacred: Religion, Narrative, and Imagination*, trans. David Pellauer, ed. Mark Wallace. Minneapolis: Fortress Press, 1995.

ID   Martin Heidegger, *Identity and Difference*, trans. Joan Stambaugh. New York: Harper and Row, 1969.

KRV   Immanuel Kant, *Critique of Pure Reason*, trans. Norman Kemp Smith. London: Macmillan, 1927.

N1   Martin Heidegger, *Nietzsche, Volume I: The Will to Power as Art*, trans. David Farrell Krell. San Francisco: Harper Collins, 1991.

N2   Martin Heidegger, *Nietzsche, Volume II: The Eternal Recurrence of the Same*, trans. David Farrell Krell. San Francisco: Harper Collins, 1991.

N3   Martin Heidegger, *Nietzsche, Volume III: The Will to Power as Knowledge and as Metaphysics*, trans. David Farrell Krell. San Francisco: Harper Collins, 1991.

N4   Martin Heidegger, *Nietzsche, Volume IV: Nihilism*, trans. David Farrell Krell. San Francisco: Harper Collins, 1991.

OAA   Paul Ricoeur, *Oneself as Another*, trans. Kathleen Blamey. Chicago: University of Chicago Press, 1992.

TA   Paul Ricoeur, *From Text to Action*, trans. Kathleen Blamey and John Thompson. Evanston: Northwestern University Press, 1991.

TN1   Paul Ricoeur, *Time and Narrative*, Volume I, trans. Kathleen McLaughlin and David Pellauer. Chicago: University of Chicago Press, 1984.

TN3   Paul Ricoeur, *Time and Narrative*, Volume III, trans. Kathleen McLaughlin and David Pellauer. Chicago: University of Chicago Press, 1988.

TRV   Alasdair MacIntyre, *Three Rival Versions of Moral Enquiry*. Notre Dame: University of Notre Dame Press, 1990.

WJ   Alasdair MacIntyre, *Whose Justice? Which Rationality?* Notre Dame: University of Notre Dame Press, 1988.

Introduction: The uses of the past

Quine is said to have joked that "there are two sorts of people interested in philosophy, those interested in philosophy and those interested in the history of philosophy."[1] Though we might bristle at Quine's joke, it makes a straightforward point: that there is a difference between trying to solve contemporary philosophical problems and trying to understand the philosophers of the past. Doing philosophy and studying its history are separate enterprises, and they must be carefully distinguished.[2] During the last several decades, however, doing so has become more difficult, as it has become common for philosophers to speak of a third enterprise that must be distinguished both from doing philosophy and from studying its history. This enterprise is called *doing philosophy historically*. Doing philosophy historically involves more than just doing philosophy, since not every attempt to solve philosophical problems does so by engaging with thinkers from the past. We can try to solve philosophical problems in non-historical ways – through conceptual analysis or the study of ordinary language, for example. Doing philosophy historically also involves more than simply studying the history of philosophy, since not every attempt to understand the thinkers of the past is also an attempt to solve contemporary philosophical problems. We can try to understand what Aristotle or Aquinas said without asking whether what they said is true, rational, or relevant to our own concerns. Doing philosophy historically is a hybrid: an attempt to gain philosophical understanding *through* or *by means of* an engagement with philosophy's past. It takes the study of history to be a philosophical method, and a method that offers a kind of illumination that is

---

[1] Quoted in Alasdair MacIntyre, "The Relationship of Philosophy to its Past," in *Philosophy in History*, ed. Richard Rorty, J. B. Schneewind, and Quentin Skinner (Cambridge: Cambridge University Press, 1984), 39–40.
[2] Of course, many philosophers have maintained that these enterprises are ultimately *not* distinct, and that it is impossible to do philosophy properly without studying its past. Charles Taylor calls this view "the historical thesis about philosophy," and attributes it to Hegel and Heidegger, among others. See Charles Taylor, "Philosophy and its History," in *Philosophy in History*, 18. Both the historical thesis and Taylor's view of it are discussed at length in Chapter 3.

difficult or perhaps impossible to gain in any other way. This much seems clear. But the matters of what it means to do philosophy historically, and of what sort of illumination this enterprise offers, are much less clear.

This book asks what it means to do philosophy historically. It explains what we are doing when we try to do philosophy by engaging with its past. The book describes how this enterprise differs from doing philosophy in a non-historical way, on the one hand, and from traditional scholarship in the history of philosophy on the other. I want to show that doing philosophy historically differs from these enterprises in a number of ways. It has a distinctive *object*: it studies a different sort of thing than they do. It also employs a distinctive *method* and has a different set of *goals*. The aim of this book, then, is to understand the nature of the activity that we call doing philosophy historically, and to describe this activity's distinguishing features. But the book will not just study this activity in the abstract. It will also look closely at some examples of this activity. It will conduct a series of case studies of figures who *do* philosophy historically: Alasdair MacIntyre, Martin Heidegger, and Paul Ricoeur. Each, I argue, embodies a different strategy for doing philosophy historically. Each has a distinctive approach to the business of learning philosophical lessons by engaging with the thinkers of the past. As a result, each has something important to teach us about this enterprise: how it works in practice, what challenges it faces, and what is involved in doing it well. I hope that, by drawing attention to the importance of this enterprise for MacIntyre, Heidegger, and Ricoeur, I will shed new light on an important but neglected side of their work, and thus help to see these figures in a new way.

THE HISTORY OF A LABEL

There is nothing new about the practice of doing philosophy historically. For as long as there have been philosophers, they have looked to earlier thinkers for help in answering their own questions. And for as long as there have been philosophers, they have found it useful to advance their views through discussions of their predecessors. Aristotle is a classic example. In Book One of the *Metaphysics*, he begins his inquiry into the first principles of things by surveying what earlier thinkers have said about the topic. This survey is not just a sign of respect or a rhetorical device. Aristotle's survey of his predecessors helps shape his own views, and his conclusions emerge from his discussion of them.[3]

---

[3] For example, Aristotle's insistence on "distinguishing the many senses in which things are said to exist" emerges from his discussion of the difficulties in Plato's ontology. See Aristotle, *Metaphysics*, trans. W. D. Ross, in *The Complete Works of Aristotle*, Volume II, ed. Jonathan Barnes (Princeton: Princeton University Press, 1984), 1568–1569.

Another well-known example is Aquinas. Not only does Aquinas's "sacred doctrine" seek to fuse two extant bodies of knowledge (Aristotelianism and Christian revelation); he often presents his own views through commentaries on earlier thinkers. But while the practice of doing philosophy historically is not new, recent decades have seen a surge in the use of the label. Since the mid 1980s, there has been a sharp increase in the number of books and articles that talk about "doing philosophy historically," and that try to distinguish this enterprise from related ones. Peter Hare, for example, has edited a collection of essays entitled *Doing Philosophy Historically*;[4] recent books by Richard Campbell,[5] Bernard Dauenhauer,[6] and Jorge Gracia[7] also use the label extensively. The practice that these philosophers describe is not new, but their interest in talking about and understanding it seems to be.

There seem to be several reasons for this surge in interest. One is that recent decades have seen the publication of a number of influential books that cannot be comfortably labeled either "philosophy" or "history of philosophy." These books often look like pieces of traditional historical scholarship: attempts to understand and explain the views of important figures in the history of philosophy. On closer inspection, however, they prove to be less concerned with explaining the figure's views accurately than with using the figure to advance an original agenda. Jonathan Bennett's book *A Study of Spinoza's* Ethics[8] and Henry Veatch's book *Aristotle: A Contemporary Introduction*[9] are two well-known examples of this tendency. They are not simply studies in the history of philosophy; nor are they simply non-historical pieces of original philosophy. They contain elements of both, and as a result, they have been described as attempts to "do philosophy historically." A similar reception has greeted a number of works of so-called "continental" philosophy. During the 1970s and 1980s, a number of French and German works that used historical studies to advance original views appeared in English translation for the first time. Examples include Heidegger's lectures on Nietzsche and Derrida's deconstructive readings of figures such as Plato and Hegel.[10] Like Bennett's and Veatch's work,

---

[4] Peter Hare (ed.), *Doing Philosophy Historically* (Buffalo: Prometheus Books, 1988).
[5] Richard Campbell, *Truth and Historicity* (Oxford: Oxford University Press, 1992).
[6] Bernard Dauenhauer (ed.), *At the Nexus of Philosophy and History* (Athens: University of Georgia Press, 1987).
[7] Jorge Gracia, *Philosophy and its History* (Albany: SUNY Press, 1992).
[8] Jonathan Bennett, *A Study of Spinoza's* Ethics (Cambridge: Cambridge University Press, 1984).
[9] Henry Veatch, *Aristotle: A Contemporary Introduction* (Bloomington: Indiana University Press, 1974).
[10] Chapter 5 gives a more detailed discussion of Heidegger's lectures on Nietzsche. On Derrida's readings of Plato and Hegel, see, for example, Jacques Derrida, *Margins of Philosophy*, trans. Alan Bass (Chicago: University of Chicago Press, 1982).

these texts are not simply pieces of original philosophy, nor are they simply scholarly studies in the history of philosophy. They advance original philosophical claims, but they do so by engaging with earlier thinkers. So English-speaking readers have come to describe them as books that "do philosophy historically." These developments may not be the only reasons for the surge of interest in this label, but they seem to have contributed to its popularity.

But while this label is now widely used, its meaning is far from clear. Many philosophers acknowledge that this enterprise exists, but few give explicit, detailed accounts of what it is and how it works. Even philosophers who write about the enterprise rarely try to define it. Those who do give definitions tend to give vague ones. Hare, for example, defines it as the view that posing philosophical questions and studying philosophy's past are both instrumentally valuable as well as intrinsically so.[11] Each activity is worth doing for its own sake, but each also helps us to do the other better. Doing philosophy makes us better at understanding the work of earlier thinkers; learning about these thinkers in turn makes us better philosophers.[12] But while this definition seems true enough, it is frustratingly vague. *How* does doing philosophy help us understand the thinkers of the past? How does knowing about the philosophers of the past make us better philosophers? Hare does not answer these questions. But until we do, we will not understand what it means to do philosophy historically. Another problem is that the label "doing philosophy historically" is used in a wide variety of ways, some of which have little in common. Gracia, for example, uses it to refer to any attempt to derive assistance for one's own philosophical work from the thinkers of the past. This includes strategies as diverse as treating the past as "a source of inspiration,"[13] or as "a source of information and truth,"[14] or even as a source of "therapy."[15] Campbell, by contrast, uses the term more narrowly. He defines it as the search for "self-recognition"[16] in the past. In studying past philosophers, "one recognizes elements of one's own way of thinking in the past, and recognizes them *as one's own*."[17] We thereby come to understand ourselves and our thoughts better. No doubt there is a great deal that is true here. But again, the question of just how historical insight helps to make us better philosophers remains unanswered. If the term "doing philosophy historically" is to be of any value, we need to move

---

[11] Hare, "Introduction." *Doing Philosophy Historically*, 14
[12] Hare, "Introduction." *Doing Philosophy Historically*, 14.   [13] Gracia, *Philosophy and its History*, 140.
[14] Gracia, *Philosophy and its History*, 146.   [15] Gracia, *Philosophy and its History*, 148.
[16] Campbell, *Truth and Historicity*, 10.   [17] Campbell, *Truth and Historicity*, 10.

beyond the current discussions. We need to explain what this enterprise is, and precisely how it differs from related ones. We need to understand its goals, its methods, and its distinctive value. Finally, we need to study the enterprise in action, by looking closely at its practitioners. This book will try to do all of these things.

This book can be divided into two parts, a theoretical part and a practical part. The first three chapters present the theory. Chapter 1 gives a general account of what it means to do philosophy historically. It argues that in order to see how history can help us philosophize, we must understand the special kind of instruction that historical inquiry offers. History, I claim, helps us understand the natures of things that are essentially developmental. Studying what a thing *has* done shows us what it *can* do. Accordingly, I argue that doing philosophy historically involves tracing the development of what might be called *philosophical pictures*: extremely general conceptions of what the world is like and how we fit into it. Chapter 1 also explains what pictures are, and how they differ from the philosophical theories with which we tend to be more familiar.

Chapter 2 adds detail to this account. It explains *how* we do philosophy historically: how we learn about a picture's capabilities by tracing its development. It argues that we do so by constructing a specific sort of narrative, one that triggers a shift in our way of seeing the philosophers of the past. I make sense of this shift by drawing on the notion of "seeing as." Chapter 2 further argues that the narratives we construct while doing philosophy historically are a sort of argument, and that their construction is a rational pursuit, as well as a pursuit that aims at truth. This pursuit does, however, show that our views of argumentation, rationality, and truth need to be broadened.

Chapter 3 asks whether it is *necessary* to do philosophy historically. It connects this question to a longstanding debate about how philosophy is related to its past. Over the past two centuries, many philosophers have claimed that their discipline is inherently historical, but they have had a difficult time explaining what this means. I propose that their claims are best seen as reminders of the importance of doing philosophy historically. In addition to proposing detailed answers to specific theoretical questions, philosophers should be concerned with the development of our more general pictures of reality. Chapter 3 contends that there is good reason to think that doing philosophy historically is necessary – even though it turns out to be remarkably difficult to advance a formal argument for this claim.

Having sketched the theory, I turn to the case studies. Each of the next three chapters examines a figure who does philosophy historically, and who illustrates a specific way of engaging in this enterprise. Chapter 4 deals with Alasdair MacIntyre, who adopts what I call a *critical* approach to doing philosophy historically. MacIntyre traces the development of a picture called the enlightenment project, a picture that he thinks involves an untenable way of understanding morality and practical reason. MacIntyre also uses historical study to develop an alternative to the enlightenment project. Chapter 4 examines MacIntyre's critique of the enlightenment project in *After Virtue, Whose Justice? Which Rationality?*, and *Three Rival Versions of Moral Enquiry*. It contends that we cannot understand MacIntyre's project unless we see that its key arguments are historical through and through.

Chapter 5 deals with Martin Heidegger, who adopts what I call a *diagnostic* approach to doing philosophy historically. Whereas MacIntyre sets out to criticize a picture that governs our thinking, Heidegger seeks to discover the true natures of several pictures that are deceptive. Heidegger contends that the West has long been dominated by a group of related pictures that he calls Platonism, metaphysics, and onto-theology. He further argues that these pictures have never been properly understood, and that as a result, their effects have gone unnoticed. Chapter 5 examines Heidegger's use of the diagnostic approach in his readings of Plato, Nietzsche, and Hegel. It argues that these readings should not be seen as pieces of conventional scholarship in the history of philosophy, since Heidegger is less concerned with the theories these philosophers advance than with the pictures of reality they articulate.

Chapter 6 discusses Paul Ricoeur, who does philosophy historically in a way that is *synthetic*. Rather than criticizing or diagnosing, Ricoeur fuses the resources of two pictures that he finds attractive but problematic: those articulated in the work of Kant and Hegel. The result is what Ricoeur calls his post-Hegelian Kantianism, an approach to philosophy that tries to remedy the limitations of both thinkers by reading them in light of each other. Chapter 6 examines Ricoeur's use of the synthetic approach in his discussions of the self, the world, and God. His work on these topics uses the past to advance a contemporary agenda, offering an especially clear example of how history can help us philosophize.

Finally, in a concluding section entitled "Consequences," I ask what all of this shows about philosophy. What can we learn about the discipline from the fact that it may be done historically? I argue that this fact teaches us something important about the relation between philosophy and the rest of the humanities, and about the standards of excellence used to assess philosophical work. It also shows something important about philosophy's value and its place in the wider culture. In short, seeing that philosophy is the sort of thing that may be done historically helps deepen our understanding of the discipline as a whole.

Let me add a word about the status of this book. The book distinguishes three enterprises: philosophy, the history of philosophy, and doing philosophy historically. It explains what the third enterprise is, and how it differs from the other two. But what status does the explanation itself have? To which enterprise does it belong? First and foremost, this book is a piece of philosophy. It asks a specific question, and it answers that question by constructing an equally specific theory. In some ways, it is a very conventional piece of philosophy, since it tries to clarify the meaning of a concept: the concept "doing philosophy historically." It may seem odd that a discussion of doing philosophy historically does not itself proceed historically. I hope this fact will seem less strange once I have explained how the enterprise differs from other sorts of philosophical work. For now, suffice it to say that engaging in an activity is clearly not the same thing as understanding that activity through philosophical reflection. We do not find it strange that the philosophy of religion is not itself a part of religion, or that the philosophy of biology is not a part of biology. By the same token, it is one thing to do philosophy historically, and another to explain what it *means* to do so. This book is engaged in the latter enterprise.

But in other ways, matters are not so simple. This book does not simply try to clarify a concept or solve a philosophical problem. It also contains elements of the other activities I have mentioned: studying the history of philosophy, and doing philosophy historically. It engages in history of philosophy to the extent that it tries to situate itself, however cursorily, with respect to the past. At the beginning of this introduction, I noted that philosophers since Aristotle have studied earlier thinkers in the hope of advancing their own agendas. I also noted that philosophers have become much more interested in this practice during the last several decades, but that they have not given a satisfactory account of its nature. These are all straightforward historical claims, claims that could appear in any conventional history of philosophy. Similar claims appear later in the book. In Chapter 3, for example, I ask whether it is necessary to do philosophy historically. I suggest that it is, but note that the only really compelling argument we could give for this claim would be a sweeping historical narrative. I do not give such a narrative myself, though my position seems to call for one. In this respect as well, my project is closely connected with traditional historical scholarship, even as it seeks to do something quite different. There is a larger lesson here. If a book such as this one can belong primarily to one enterprise while containing elements of the other two, then the boundaries separating these activities cannot be perfectly sharp. This does not mean there are no important differences among doing philosophy, studying its history, and doing philosophy historically. But in practice, these activities may intermingle. A particular work may contain elements of all three.

There is a final respect in which this book blurs the lines between activities. One of the book's central claims is that when we do philosophy historically, we seek to trigger a change in our way of seeing thinkers from the past. The information we have about these thinkers may not change. What changes is what we see them *as*. I would be happy if this book triggered a similar change in the way we look at philosophy. I would like to persuade my readers to see philosophy as concerned with more than the solutions to highly technical problems, and to see the history of philosophy as more than a repository for outdated views. The methods of this book may be primarily philosophical. But its goal – or at any rate, its hope – is to broaden our conception of what philosophy is.

CHAPTER I

Doing philosophy historically

This chapter explains what it means to do philosophy historically. It gives an account of this enterprise's goals and methods, one that distinguishes it both from the practice of philosophy more narrowly construed and from the study of the history of philosophy. It also investigates the value of this activity. It explains what kind of illumination it offers, and why this illumination is worth seeking. To this end, I first examine a number of current views about what is involved in doing philosophy historically, and explain why I find them inadequate. Next, I raise the question of what kind of understanding is gained through the study of history – any kind of history. I do so by drawing on John Herman Randall's discussion of the "genetic method."[1] I then extend Randall's discussion of the genetic method to the case of philosophy, and explain how a study of past philosophy might teach philosophical lessons. Finally, since my discussion relies heavily on the notion of a *philosophical picture*, I end the chapter by clarifying this notion's meaning and defending its use.

CURRENT VIEWS

It is not difficult to describe the enterprise of doing philosophy historically in very general terms. Imagine two ideal types: the pure philosopher and the pure historian of philosophy. The pure philosopher is interested solely in "doing" philosophy – that is, in discovering the answers to contemporary philosophical questions. She may want to know whether uncaused free action is possible or moral values objective, for example. She may not be particularly interested in the history of earlier attempts to answer these questions. She simply wants to know the answers, and she may not think that a familiarity with the history of her questions will help her find them.

[1] John Herman Randall, *Nature and Historical Experience* (New York: Columbia University Press, 1958), 63.

Indeed, the pure philosopher may suspect that paying too much attention to this history will lead her away from the answers she seeks. After all, if earlier philosophers had succeeded in answering the questions that vex her, then surely these questions would no longer be asked. The work of earlier philosophers may be interesting in its own right, and studying it may be a good exercise for students, but according to the pure philosopher, there is no reason to think that it will help us to solve philosophical problems. To fail to see this is to lapse into antiquarianism.[2]

The pure historian of philosophy, on the other hand, is interested solely in understanding the work of philosophers from the past. He wants to know what their views were, and to understand these views in their own terms – to determine whether Spinoza was a pantheist, what Plato thought about mathematical entities, and so on. Understanding what these philosophers really thought, he claims, is quite different from using their work to advance contemporary philosophical agendas. No doubt a clever reader can make Spinoza say interesting things about our contemporary ecological crisis, or make Plato say interesting things about the state of literary theory. But the pure historian of philosophy is concerned with what Spinoza and Plato really thought, and he doubts whether such appropriations help us to discover this. Whereas the pure philosopher fears antiquarianism, the pure historian of philosophy fears anachronism. To understand the great figures from the history of philosophy, he insists, is to understand them as they understood themselves, not to translate their work into contemporary idioms they would not recognize.

We might provisionally say that those who do philosophy historically take neither the pure philosopher nor the pure historian of philosophy as their ideal. They reject the division between doing philosophy and studying its history, between solving contemporary problems and trying to understand philosophers from the past. They maintain, as Peter Hare puts it, that a philosopher can "at once make a contribution to the solution of current philosophical problems and a contribution to the history of thought."[3] They claim that one can do philosophy *by* studying its history – that an engagement with the history of philosophy can contribute to the solution of contemporary philosophical problems. In the most general terms, then, we might say that to do philosophy historically is to reject the assumptions of

---

[2] The term "antiquarianism" is used by Rorty, Schneewind, and Skinner. See their introduction to *Philosophy in History*, 10. They oppose it to "anachronism," a term I use below.

[3] Hare, "Introduction." *Doing Philosophy Historically*, 12.

the pure philosopher and the pure historian of philosophy, and to pursue both of their agendas at once.

This characterization is useful for fixing ideas. But it faces two problems. First, it is purely negative. It tells us what doing philosophy historically is *not*, but not what it *is*. It has nothing positive to say about this enterprise's goals, methods, or value. Second, and more importantly, the pure philosopher and the pure historian of philosophy are impossibly ideal types, and it is difficult to imagine a living person actually engaging in either enterprise. The problem is not just that most philosophers do both systematic and historical work, at least some of the time – though this is no doubt true. Rather, the problem is that it is not clear that either enterprise is coherent even as an ideal. The pure philosopher, as I have described her, is interested solely in the answers to philosophical questions, not in their history. But it is obviously impossible to try to answer philosophical questions until one has learned "what questions are the genuinely philosophical ones."[4] And this, surely, is something one learns largely through an acquaintance with history – by seeing which questions philosophers have traditionally posed, how these questions differ from those traditionally posed by other enterprises, and so on. Likewise, the pure historian of philosophy, as I have described him, wants to understand past philosophers in their own terms, rather than filtering their work anachronistically through contemporary concerns. But does this goal even make sense? What would it mean to avoid anachronism altogether, and to understand a text purely in its own terms? As Richard Rorty and others have pointed out:

If to be anachronistic is to link a past X to a present Y rather than studying it in isolation, then every historian is always anachronistic… Without some selecting, the historian is reduced to duplicating the texts which constitute the relevant past. But why do that? We turn to the historian because we do not understand the copy of the text we already have. Giving us a second copy will not help. To understand the text just *is* to relate it helpfully to something else. The only question is what that something else will be.[5]

In practice, to accuse someone of anachronism is not to accuse her of relating "a past X to a present Y," but to accuse her of relating a past X to the *wrong* present Y, rather than some other, more fruitful one. It seems, then, that the pure philosopher and the pure historian of philosophy are both impossible ideals. But if that is the case, then it is obviously

---

[4] Rorty *et al.*, "Introduction." *Philosophy in History*, 11.
[5] Rorty *et al.,* "Introduction." *Philosophy in History*, 10–11.

unsatisfactory to say that doing philosophy historically means rejecting these ideals. *Everyone* rejects these ideals, and must, because they are incoherent.

As a result, a number of philosophers have tried to give more precise characterizations of what it means to do philosophy historically. One such account is offered by Peter Hare. As noted above, Hare thinks that to do philosophy historically is to try to contribute to two enterprises at once: the solution of contemporary philosophical problems on the one hand, and the accurate understanding of the history of thought on the other. We all engage in both enterprises to some degree, and must. But those who do philosophy historically, Hare maintains, have a distinctive understanding of the kind of value these activities possess. According to Hare, most of us think these enterprises possess intrinsic value alone. It is good to contribute to the solution of philosophical problems; it is also good to understand past philosophers accurately. But on this view, "the search for philosophical illumination [has] negative, or at least negligible instrumental value as a means to the intrinsic value of historical accuracy."[6] Those who do philosophy historically, by contrast, maintain that each enterprise possesses *instrumental* value as well as intrinsic value, because of the way in which it can assist the other enterprise. Doing philosophy is valuable both for its own sake, and because it helps us to understand the work of historical figures better. Learning about figures in the history of philosophy is valuable both for its own sake, and because it helps us to do philosophy better. Furthermore, Hare claims that we can use the notion of instrumental value to distinguish three different ways of doing philosophy historically:

It appears that among those doing philosophy historically: (1) some consider philosophical illumination valuable primarily as a means to historical accuracy; (2) others consider historical accuracy valuable primarily as a means to philosophical illumination; and (3) still others consider both historical accuracy and philosophical illumination to have much of both intrinsic and instrumental value.[7]

What these approaches share is the conviction that both philosophy and the history of philosophy may be *instruments* of understanding. The accurate understanding of past thought is not just desirable in itself. It is also a means to philosophical illumination.

---

[6] Hare, "Introduction." *Doing Philosophy Historically*, 14.
[7] Hare, "Introduction." *Doing Philosophy Historically*, 14. Hare borrows this scheme from Jonathan Bennett. He also cites Jonathan Rée as an example of the first approach, Bennett as an example of the second, and Daniel Garber as an example of the third.

The difficulty with Hare's account is that it does not explain what this philosophical illumination is. Hare's suggestion that the practice of philosophy and the study of its history possess instrumental value as well as intrinsic value, and that doing one can help us to do the other, are promising starting points. But Hare does not explain *how* they help us to do so, or *why*. Why, exactly, does an accurate understanding of past philosophical thought make us better philosophers? Why does it leave us better able to contribute to the solution of contemporary philosophical problems? Similarly, why does a facility in solving contemporary philosophical problems make us better historians of philosophy? Hare's account does not say. It simply asserts that when we do philosophy historically, the practice of philosophy and the study of its history assist one another. It does not tell us in what this assistance consists. So while Hare's account is a step in the right direction, it is also incomplete. We must look for a different account of what it means to do philosophy historically.

Another such account is offered by Richard Campbell. Campbell claims that there are three major differences between simply studying the history of philosophy and doing philosophy historically. First, doing philosophy historically involves a different *telos* than the study of the history of philosophy:

Whereas historians of philosophy seek as far as possible a correct account of past thinkers, and often "bracket" their own beliefs and values so that they are not "on the line" as they engage in their scholarly work, those who philosophize historically undertake a historically orientated task whose point is precisely to enrich the self-understanding of their own historical situation.[8]

Historians of philosophy seek accuracy – faithful representations of what earlier philosophers believed. Those who do philosophy historically are more interested in identifying and clarifying the "quite particular set of problems" that the past has handed down to them, in the hope of understanding how and why these problems have become important.[9] Second, historians of philosophy and those who do philosophy historically "operate with different conceptions of truth."[10] For the former, truth is correctness. A true history of philosophy is one that accurately represents what Aquinas and Aristotle really thought. For the latter, a piece of work that does philosophy historically is "true" to the extent that it furthers our own self-understanding and illuminates our present condition. Such a philosopher is

---

[8] Campbell, *Truth and Historicity*, 9.   [9] Campbell, *Truth and Historicity*, 9.
[10] Campbell, *Truth and Historicity*, 10.

therefore "operating (perhaps unconsciously) with a conception of truth as a revelatory and transforming event."[11] Finally, Campbell claims that doing philosophy historically involves a different "consciousness" than studying the history of philosophy. The historian of philosophy "remains focused upon the thinkers of the past; *their* thoughts are what the inquiry is about … But whoever philosophizes historically is engaged essentially in a complex act of *self*-consciousness. One enters into the past only to return to one-self."[12] In other words, studying the history of philosophy involves a different type of understanding than doing philosophy historically. Whereas the former is concerned with the views of others, the latter is a meditation on one's own situation.

Campbell's account of doing philosophy historically is clearly an improvement on Hare's. His explanation of this enterprise's goals and methods is instructive and, I think, largely right. But like Hare's account, it does not say enough about the kind of illumination that this enterprise offers. Campbell is surely right to claim that doing philosophy historically is valuable because it promotes self-understanding, an insight into one's present situation. No doubt there is important insight to be gained by identifying and clarifying the philosophical problems that have become decisive for us. But what sort of insight is it? Is it mere historical insight, an understanding of the historical circumstances that have caused these problems to be decisive? If so, then why is this insight *philosophical*, and how does it help us come to terms with these problems philosophically? Moreover, why should this process be characterized as doing *philosophy* historically, as opposed to merely tracing the history of ideas? Or could it perhaps be that identifying and clarifying the roots of our current situation offers philosophical insight in the sense that it shows that certain philo-sophical views are true or false, significant or insignificant? If so, then what is the particular value of acquiring these insights by doing philosophy *histor-ically*? If materialism is untenable, say, or the mind-body problem a pseudo-problem, then what is to be gained by learning this by consulting history? Could we not learn it by reflecting on these positions themselves without tracing their histories? Campbell's account does not, it seems, explain why it is illuminating to do philosophy historically. It labels this illumination a type of "self-understanding," but fails to describe what is valuable about such self-understanding. In short, Campbell does not really avoid the problem in Hare's account. He simply pushes it back a level.

---

[11] Campbell, *Truth and Historicity*, 10.   [12] Campbell, *Truth and Historicity*, 10.

What seems missing from both of these accounts is an explanation of the kind of illumination a study of the history of philosophy offers. We need to understand how knowledge of this history might help one to do philosophy. Perhaps we could determine this if we first asked what kind of illumination the study of history offers in general. How does studying the history of a thing help us to understand that thing? What type of understanding, what type of illumination, is involved here? If we could answer these questions, perhaps we would see how this type of understanding can contribute to the doing of philosophy. In order to do this, I now turn to an account of the goal and the value of historical inquiry: the account of the "genetic method" offered by John Herman Randall.[13]

RANDALL AND THE GENETIC METHOD

In *Nature and Historical Experience*, John Herman Randall poses the following question: "How does a knowledge of the history of anything function as an instrument for comprehending that thing? Just what about that thing does it enable us to explain?"[14] What can we learn about a thing by studying it through a "genetic method"[15] – by understanding "that something is so because it … has come about so,"[16] as Gadamer puts it? Obviously history does not explain everything. If we wish to know why a thing is as it is, it is not enough to discover its historical origins, as though "the mere record of the past somehow explains the present."[17] After all, the historical record, far from explaining everything about the present, is itself a result that has to be explained. More generally, identifying a thing's historical origins does not always, or even often, allow us to understand it

---

[13] In what follows, I restrict myself to Randall's views on the nature of historical inquiry in general. I do not examine his views on the nature of the history of philosophy in particular. Randall does have a great deal to say about the history of philosophy, though. One example is his book *How Philosophy Uses Its Past* (New York: Columbia University Press, 1963). A full discussion of Randall's view of the history of philosophy, however, would take us too far afield.

[14] Randall, *Nature and Historical Experience*, 65.

[15] Randall, *Nature and Historical Experience*, 63. The genetic method, as Randall and I understand it, is any attempt to understand a thing by tracing its temporal development. The "historical method" is one specific version of the genetic method. It traces the temporal development of those things that have histories – that is, those things the development of which is understood with reference to conscious actions and intentions. To anticipate two examples given below, a seed is simply an object in nature, and a study of its temporal development is simply a use of the genetic method. But a human society is a historical entity – since its development is understood in terms of human actions and intentions – and a study of this development is an example of the historical method.

[16] Hans-Georg Gadamer, *Truth and Method*, 2nd edn., trans. Joel Weinsheimer and Donald Marshall (New York: Crossroads, 1992), 5.

[17] Randall, *Nature and Historical Experience*, 64.

adequately. "Historical knowledge may 'reveal,' point to, give the locus of 'origins,'" Randall argues, "but it does not 'explain' them."[18] In short, identifying a thing's origins is no substitute for understanding its nature. The genetic method of learning about a thing through its history is not a general method for understanding all kinds of things.

It is, however, indispensable for understanding *some* things. There are some things the nature of which is to develop. As F. J. E. Woodbridge puts it, "the nature of a thing may be progressive. Time may enter into its substance."[19] Though the study of a thing's genesis is not a general method for understanding all things, it *is* an indispensable method for the study of things the nature of which is to develop. Consider a seed.[20] What is involved in understanding what a seed is and why it is as it is? In one sense, of course, we understand a seed once we have analyzed its chemical makeup – once we have identified its physical structures and determined the materials out of which those structures are composed. After all, there is nothing "more" to the seed than its physical makeup. Everything that will ever happen to the seed is a function of its initial chemical composition. The seed's chemical properties act as a set of "passive powers," "boundaries beyond which the operations of the seed's processes of growth cannot go."[21] And we can analyze this chemical constitution "in isolation,"[22] without knowing what will later happen to the seed as it turns into a plant. In one sense, then, we know what the seed is, and why it is as it is, when we have exhaustively enumerated its chemical properties.

It seems clear, however, that someone who understood the seed solely in this way would be missing something. She would have a complete snapshot of the seed's passive powers. But she would be missing out on the most interesting aspect of the seed: an understanding of what these powers can *do*. She would be able to enumerate the seed's passive powers, but she would not know how they exhibit themselves in the seed's processes of growth. We cannot learn this from an analysis of the passive powers themselves, because these powers manifest themselves only in interaction with other factors. As Randall puts it:

The specific chemical structure is essential …, but it is not the only factor essential. Other factors are needed to set those factors in operation, to serve as stimuli or "active" powers. The soil, moisture, and sunlight interact with the seed as efficient causes or dynamic factors. They are selective of the powers of that constitution, determining which of them shall be realized within the limits set.[23]

---

[18] Randall, *Nature and Historical Experience*, 69.
[19] F. J. E. Woodbridge, *Nature and Mind*, quoted in Randall, *Nature and Historical Experience*, 72.
[20] The example of the seed originally comes from Woodbridge, though Randall discusses it at some length.
[21] Randall, *Nature and Historical Experience*, 74.   [22] Randall, *Nature and Historical Experience*, 74.
[23] Randall, *Nature and Historical Experience*, 73.

This is not to say that the seed has some nature other than its physical properties – a separate entelechy, for example, that is responsible for its growth but that is irreducible to its chemical properties. It is to say, however, that these properties reveal themselves only over time, through the growth of the seed, as they interact with environmental factors. "A complete chemical analysis of the seed," Randall argues, "would not lead us to 'expect' such a growth; but confronted by that growth, we find such a seed to be a necessary factor or condition of its appearance."[24] Someone who could describe a seed's chemical composition but did not know how this composition manifested itself in the seed's growth would fail to understand something crucial about the nature of the seed.

The point is that the seed as we know it is an interaction of two different sorts of properties. The first are the chemical properties that can be determined by analyzing the seed in isolation. Randall calls this collection of properties "the 'material' of [its] career. It is a set of 'passive' powers: but what those powers *can do* is discoverable only when they operate in the career."[25] This operation also requires a set of "active" powers – sunlight, soil, and other "dynamic factors" that cause the potential latent in its chemical properties to become actual. In one sense, of course, it is possible to give an exhaustive account of the seed's passive powers by viewing them "statically" – by describing the seed's chemical makeup without making reference to the role it later plays in the seed's growth. But in another sense, we do not understand the seed's passive powers until we see what they can do. To understand the nature of the seed is not just to recognize that it has certain passive powers, but to see these powers in action, by watching them manifest themselves in the seed's growth. If it is in the nature of the seed to develop, then understanding the seed's passive powers means understanding the role they play in its development.

Now consider a human society. It is obviously far more complex than a seed, and it is unlikely we could ever give an exhaustive list of its "material" properties. But a human society is like a seed in that it is an interaction of active and passive powers. A society's passive powers are its various "patterns of organization, comparable to the chemical constitution of the seed"[26] – patterns of economic, political, and religious organization, for example. These passive powers limit what the society can become. Just as the growth of a seed is constrained by its initial chemical composition, a human society

---

[24] Randall, *Nature and Historical Experience*, 72. Indeed, we often uncover differences in the chemical makeup of seeds – mutations, for example – by observing differences in their patterns of growth.

[25] Randall, *Nature and Historical Experience*, 73.   [26] Randall, *Nature and Historical Experience*, 74.

can develop only within the limits set by its material properties.[27] A society's active powers, by contrast, are specific human actions, or "what men actually do; and such concrete human action is determined not only by social habits, but also by conscious and reflective attempts to deal with the problems forced upon men."[28] As with a seed, we can gain a sort of understanding of the society by looking only at the former – by taking a snapshot of its economic structures or religious institutions, for example. But to do so would be to miss something crucial, namely a recognition of what these powers can do. To understand a human society is not just to identify its passive powers, but to see what those powers can do by observing them in action. It is not just to identify a set of capacities, but to see how these capacities manifest themselves in the development of the society. The way we observe these powers in action is by tracking the society's development over time – by examining its history. In short, "just as in the case of the seed, what these determinations or limits set to the powers of a society by its various organizations – its 'constitution' – actually are, is revealed only in its history."[29]

When we study a society's history, we learn the same sort of thing that we learn by observing the growth of a seed. We learn what the society's structures are capable of – what its passive powers can do – by watching them develop over time. Of course, there is a sense in which we can understand these structures in isolation, just as there is a sense in which we can understand a seed solely by analyzing its chemical makeup. But to do so would be to ignore what is most interesting about a society. We do not really understand a society until we observe its structures in action. We do

---

[27] This is not to say that a society's material properties "determine" its development in the sense of forcing one and only one possible course of development to be actualized. They determine a *range* of possibilities; they set the *limits* within which a society's development must unfold. But as Randall puts it, "though men's materials, the fruits of the past, *determine* or limit what men *can* do, they do not *decide* what men *will* do with them, nor do they decide what new or altered limits will be imposed by what men will do." See Randall, *Nature and Historical Experience*, 90.

[28] Randall, *Nature and Historical Experience*, 82.

[29] Randall, *Nature and Historical Experience*, 79. Like any analogy, the analogy between a seed and a society has limits. One important difference concerns our ways of discovering passive powers. A society is so complex that it is hard to learn what it can do *without* studying what it has done. A seed is different, since we have an independent way of discovering its passive powers: chemical analysis. Thus it is quite easy to distinguish what a seed can do from what it does. It is harder to draw this distinction in the case of a society, since we rely much more heavily on temporal development to learn about its nature. As a result, it sounds almost tautological to say that we have discovered a society's passive powers by studying what it has done. Its passive powers, we want to say, *just are* what it does under certain circumstances. This conclusion is tempting, but I think it is a mistake. It is both possible and desirable to distinguish a society's passive powers from its historical development. But it is true that we typically must learn about the former by studying the latter. I am grateful to an anonymous reader for Cambridge University Press for helping me to clarify this point.

not really know what it can do until we see what sorts of things it *has* done. Tracing a society's historical development is thus an indispensable way of arriving at a full understanding of it.[30]

What this suggests is that the genetic method yields a very specific kind of understanding. It is properly applied to a specific kind of object – namely, something such as a seed or a human society, something whose nature it is to develop. It gives rise to a very specific kind of understanding, one that goes beyond an ability to enumerate a thing's properties. To understand a thing genetically is to know not just what its passive powers are, but what they can do. It is to see what the thing is and is not capable of, by tracking the paths that its development takes and does not take. The type of understanding offered by the genetic method is valuable because there are things whose capacity for development is the most interesting fact about them. For things of this kind, tracing their temporal development yields an indispensable kind of understanding, and a kind of understanding that probably cannot be gained in any other way.

THE EVOLUTION OF PHILOSOPHICAL PICTURES

Let us return to philosophy. To do philosophy historically would be to import the genetic method into philosophy. What would this involve? The short answer, of course, is that it would involve carrying out a genetic study of some object in the philosophical domain. It would be to maintain that this object, like a seed or a human society, is the sort of thing the nature of which is to develop. It would be to claim that the object in question is an interaction of active and passive powers, and that as a result, we cannot understand it without tracing its development. To understand this object, we might say, is to see its powers in action, to see what they can and cannot do by tracing what they do over time. Such an inquiry would have the same goal as the study of the history of a society. It would seek a kind of illumination that consists not just in knowledge of a thing's properties, but in a familiarity with what these properties can do. In short, to do philosophy historically would be to study some object in the philosophical

---

[30] Note that the historical study of a society is a *complement* to the "static" study of its structures, not a substitute for it. To understand a society is to do more than record what happens to it. We must identify its passive powers – its economic and cultural organizations, for example – and *then* see how they manifest themselves in the society's history. In other words, understanding a society has both historical and non-historical moments. Paul Ricoeur has made a similar point about the interpretation of texts. Contra Dilthey, Ricoeur argues that such interpretation always involves both *Verstehen* and *Erklärung*, and that each activity complements the other. See *TA*, 125–143.

domain as we study the growth of a seed or the evolution of a society – to understand that this object "is so because it … has come about so."[31]

But which object? What would be the focus of such a study? What is the philosophical equivalent of the growing seed or the evolving society? One thing seems clear: the object of such an inquiry cannot be the *theories* that philosophers advance, or the *arguments* that they give to support these theories. As we have seen, the genetic method is properly applied only to something the nature of which is to develop. Theories and arguments do not seem to be the sorts of things that develop. A theory is either true or false. We may speak of theories "evolving" over time, but generally what this means is that older theories are supplanted by new, slightly different ones. Theories rise and fall, and their successors are often very similar to them. But a particular theory does not *grow*. The same is true of arguments. An argument is either sound or unsound. Occasionally we may speak of an argument "evolving" – as when we discuss the "evolution" of the onto-logical argument, for example. But in so far as the different versions of the ontological argument contain different premises – and sometimes different conclusions – they are best understood as distinct arguments sharing family resemblances, not stages in the evolution of a single argument.

When philosophers describe what they do, they usually assign a central place to theories and arguments. Consider the following description of philosophy, which Louis Pojman gives in an introductory textbook:

The hallmark of philosophy is centered in the argument. Philosophers clarify concepts, analyze and test propositions and beliefs, but the major task is to analyze and construct arguments … Philosophical reasoning is closely allied to scientific reasoning in that both look for evidence and build hypotheses that are tested with the hope of coming closer to the truth.[32]

Most philosophers, I suspect, would accept Pojman's characterization of what they do. If we accept this characterization, however, then it is difficult to see how there can be any room in philosophy for the genetic method. This method studies things that evolve; philosophers generally take them-selves to be concerned with theories and arguments, things that do *not* evolve. So how can it be possible for philosophers to use the genetic method? How can philosophy be done historically?

The proper response, I think, is that there is another way of under-standing what philosophers do. It is possible to see philosophers as doing

---

[31] Gadamer, *Truth and Method*, 5.
[32] Louis Pojman, *Philosophy: The Quest For Truth*, 4th edn. (Belmont, CA: Wadsworth, 1999), 3.

something other than just articulating theories and supporting them with arguments. As Gary Gutting has argued, "it is very important to distinguish between the *theory* that provides a specific, detailed formulation of a philosophical position such as Platonic realism or Berkeleyan idealism and the general *picture* of reality that such formulations are trying to articulate."[33] An example of a philosophical theory would be the specific version of dualism that Descartes develops in the *Meditations*, or the specific account of moral obligation that Kant gives in the second *Critique*. These theories are specific, detailed answers to specific philosophical questions, and they are supported by equally specific and detailed arguments. Few contemporary philosophers accept these theories just as Descartes and Kant formulate them, and fewer still accept the precise arguments that Descartes and Kant give to support them. Nevertheless, it is relatively common to describe contemporary philosophers and their theories as "Cartesian" or "Kantian." Why?

The answer, it seems, is that in addition to developing detailed theories and arguments, philosophers are simultaneously in the business of articulating pictures of reality. The Cartesian and Kantian pictures of reality are broader and more flexible than the specific theories advanced by Descartes and Kant. They also occupy a different place in our intellectual landscape. Since theories are either true or false, they are the sorts of things that we either accept or reject. Thus it makes sense to speak of theories being "proved" or "refuted." Philosophical pictures are different. As Gutting puts it, "[p]hilosophers are often able to refute a particular theoretical formulation (the dualism of Descartes's *Meditations*, the phenomenalism of Ayer's *Language, Truth, and Logic*). But they seldom if ever refute the general pictures that the theoretical formulations articulate."[34] In a sense, of course, all philosophers develop theories and support them with arguments. Philosophers never advance the Cartesian picture of reality in the abstract; they advance only specific theoretical formulations of this picture. But to say that philosophers develop theories is not the only way of characterizing what they do, and it is far from clear that it is the most illuminating one. It is equally possible to see them as in the business of articulating and refining pictures of reality.[35]

---

[33] Gary Gutting, *Pragmatic Liberalism and the Critique of Modernity* (Cambridge: Cambridge University Press, 1999), 191. Saul Kripke seems to have been the first philosopher to distinguish explicitly between pictures and theories. See his *Naming and Necessity* (Oxford: Blackwell, 1980), 93. For a longer and more detailed discussion of this distinction, see Gary Gutting, "Can Philosophical Beliefs Be Rationally Justified?" *American Philosophical Quarterly* 19:4 (1982), 315–330.

[34] Gutting, *Pragmatic Liberalism and the Critique of Modernity*, 191.

[35] Randall makes a similar point when he says that "while there is in philosophy an accumulated heritage that must be taken into consideration, there is not, as in science, any wholly accepted body of achieved and received ideas. There is rather a plurality of such bodies, grouped in the different philosophical

This point is important because while philosophical theories are not the sorts of things that develop, philosophical pictures are. Pictures change over time by being refined and criticized, by finding different and often increasingly subtle theoretical expressions. This change is not a mere replacement of one picture by another, but a working-out of the picture's possibilities. Tracing the history of a philosophical picture lets us see what this picture can do: what its strengths and weaknesses are, what possibilities and limitations it has. Consider the evolution of what might be called the Cartesian picture of the world. The Cartesian picture has found many different theoretical articulations, from Descartes's own philosophical works, through the work of other early modern philosophers, up to the present. Descartes's own formulation of this picture showed certain promise. It went some way towards explaining how freedom of the will could be reconciled with a mechanistic view of nature, and it illustrated how mathematical methods of reasoning could be fruitfully extended to other areas. But it also had obvious limitations, such as its difficulty explaining the relation of the mind to the body and of finite substances to God. These difficulties were explored by later thinkers working within a broadly Cartesian picture of the world – Malebranche, for example.[36] Malebranche accepted the most central aspects of Descartes's philosophy – for example, the claim that philosophy must proceed by means of clear and distinct ideas – while rejecting other, less central ones, such as the claim that we have a clear and distinct idea of the self. The work of Malebranche and later thinkers probed and refined the Cartesian picture, revealing in more detail what a Cartesian picture of reality can do, and what its advantages and limitations are. This process of criticism and refinement has continued to the present. Even in the middle of the twentieth century, it was not shocking see a philosopher as remote from classical modern philosophy as Edmund Husserl describe himself as a Cartesian.[37] Like the growth of a seed, the

---

traditions." See Randall, *How Philosophy Uses Its Past*, 80. The "bodies of ideas" of which Randall speaks have a great deal in common with what I have called philosophical pictures. Later in the same work, Randall speaks of the "classic visions" and "imaginative perspectives" common to many different philosophers (*How Philosophy Uses Its Past*, 85). These terms also seem quite close in meaning to what I have called philosophical pictures.

[36] I am grateful to David Scott for suggesting the example of Malebranche.

[37] Consider the introduction to the *Cartesian Meditations*, where Husserl calls transcendental phenomenology "a neo-Cartesianism, even though it is obliged – and precisely by its radical development of Cartesian motifs – to reject nearly all the well-known doctrinal content of the Cartesian philosophy." Edmund Husserl, *Cartesian Meditations*, trans. Dorion Cairns (Dordrecht: Kluwer, 1991), 1. Further proof that Husserl distinguishes the Cartesian picture of reality from Descartes's specific version of it comes later in the introduction to this text, where Husserl says that his work "reawakens the impulse of the Cartesian *Meditations*: not to adopt their content but, in *not* doing so, to renew with greater intensity the radicalness of their spirit" (*Cartesian Meditations*, 6).

evolution of the Cartesian picture can be seen as an interaction of passive and active powers. Its passive powers would be the "material" of Cartesianism – its core theses, its internal logic, and what might be called its overall spirit. Its active powers would be the factors that provoke the material's evolution – particular works by particular Cartesian philosophers, their distinctive goals and agendas, the cultural and intellectual milieus in which they worked, and so on. The interaction of these powers is what causes the Cartesian picture of reality to evolve.

One might try to learn about the Cartesian picture by studying Descartes's work alone. But someone familiar only with Descartes's writings – and not with the work of Malebranche, Husserl, and other philosophers who articulate a similar vision of the world – would have a one-sided understanding of the Cartesian picture. Like someone who studies only the chemical composition of a seed, she would have a snapshot of its properties at one stage in its development, but not a full appreciation of what those properties are capable of. This is the sort of appreciation we gain by tracing a picture's historical evolution. By seeing how pictures evolve, we learn what they can do: what their strengths and weaknesses are, what problems they do a good job of addressing, and what stumbling blocks they seem unable to overcome. Just as we do not really understand a seed until we see it in action, we do not really understand a philosophical picture until we have looked at it in light of its history.

What I would like to propose is that doing philosophy historically involves tracing the development of philosophical pictures. It involves studying how one or more of the major pictures of reality – the Cartesian or the Platonic picture, for example – evolve over time. The aim of this activity, however, is not merely to catalogue a series of changes in what people have thought. Rather, it is to see what these changes reveal about what a given picture can do. It is to gain insight into what a picture's strengths and weaknesses are, what it is and is not capable of, by studying this picture in action. This insight is philosophical. When we see what a philosophical picture can do, we learn whether and to what extent it is a live option for us. We learn how powerful and flexible it is, how it compares with competing pictures, and how well it coheres with other things we care about. Moreover, doing philosophy historically yields a kind of philosophical insight that cannot be gained through either pure philosophy or pure history of philosophy. After all, both of these enterprises study philosophical theories, present or past. They may tell us a great deal about specific theoretical expressions of this or that picture. But it is not their job to assess and probe these pictures themselves. This is a task properly left to the enterprise known as doing philosophy historically. When we do philosophy historically, we seek philosophical insight, but philosophical insight of a distinctive kind, and a kind that may be difficult or impossible to gain in other ways.[38]

What reason is there to accept this account of doing philosophy historically? One reason, of course, is that it is consistent with broader reflections on the value of history in general, reflections such as Randall's. A better reason is that it seems to describe accurately what many historically minded philosophers actually do. Those who do philosophy historically – those who seek philosophical illumination by studying the past – rarely have as their object particular theories or arguments. They rarely turn to the past in the hope of solving specific philosophical problems or answering specific philosophical questions. Instead, they tend to be concerned with what I have called philosophical pictures, broad conceptions of the way the world is. Moreover, they typically study these pictures to learn the sorts of things that the genetic method can teach us – an appreciation of what certain pictures can do, and of what their distinctive possibilities and limitations are. Heidegger's historical works, for example, invariably turn to the past in order to show how a certain picture of reality – Platonism, for example, or onto-theology – has both guided Western philosophical theories and blinded them to certain things. The same is true of Derrida's studies of past thinkers. These studies always proceed through close readings of specific texts, but they generally do so to see how these texts embody

---

[38] It should now be clear how far my agreement with Campbell extends, and where I differ with him. Campbell's three claims about the distinctive nature of doing philosophy historically are all true. Those who do philosophy historically have a different *telos* than those who simply study the history of philosophy. While the latter seek accurate reproductions of past thought, the former seek a sort of self-understanding – specifically, a deepened awareness of what the major philosophical pictures that have been handed down to us can and cannot do. Campbell is also right to claim that those who do philosophy historically have a different conception of truth than conventional historians of philosophy. The latter understand truth as correctness, while the former are concerned with things (philosophical pictures) to which the notions of correctness and incorrectness apply very badly. Finally, Campbell is right to claim that doing philosophy historically involves a different sort of consciousness than is found in most history of philosophy. Whereas the latter enterprise focuses on the thought of historical figures, the former looks elsewhere – namely, to the possibilities and limitations of the pictures of reality that earlier figures articulated. Campbell and I differ in that I see doing philosophy historically as distinctive in a fourth way: it has a different *object* than the history of philosophy. Historians of philosophy typically study theories, the specific and detailed answers that earlier philosophers have given to specific, detailed philosophical questions. Those who do philosophy historically, by contrast, take as their object not particular theories, but the broader pictures of reality that these theories articulate. In this respect, the historian of philosophy has more in common with an ahistorical philosopher than with someone who does philosophy historically. The pure philosopher and the pure historian of philosophy both study theories, while someone who does philosophy historically studies a different sort of object altogether.

some broader picture of reality – "logocentrism," for example, or the "metaphysics of presence." Even a work such as Rorty's *Philosophy and the Mirror of Nature*, which poses some very specific theoretical questions in epistemology and philosophy of mind, is largely an exploration of a philosophical picture: the "representational" picture that sees the mind as a mirror that reflects reality.[39] The account of doing philosophy historically that I have given is not only consistent with broader reflections on the value of history. It also sits well with what historically minded philosophers actually do.

MORE ON PICTURES

My discussion so far has relied heavily on the notion of a philosophical picture. To some, this notion will seem unfamiliar and in need of clarification. To others, it will seem problematic and of questionable value. It may appear hopelessly confused, or redundant, or of no practical use. So at this point, it might be helpful to look more closely at the notion of a philosophical picture, in order to clarify its meaning and to justify its use. Perhaps the best way to proceed is by examining a number of difficulties that the notion seems to raise.

One problem is that philosophical pictures may seem too general to be useful, perhaps too general to be intellectually responsible. One might argue that there really *are* no philosophical pictures, only particular philosophers who answer particular questions by advancing particular theories. Philosophers, one might argue, may resemble each other in all sorts of ways, but no two great philosophers share anything as specific or as substantial as philosophical pictures are alleged to be. Any picture we might attribute to them will inevitably turn out to be hopelessly artificial and reified. One might worry that to say that Descartes, Malebranche, and Husserl share the same broad conception of reality – the Cartesian picture of reality – is to impose a vacuous label on these thinkers. It is to view these thinkers in an excessively general way and ignore their subtleties. In short, one might argue that the notion of a philosophical picture is based on a superficial approach to the history of ideas. Rather than imposing common conceptions of

---

[39] Rorty explicitly uses the term "picture" to characterize this view of reality. He writes: "The picture which holds traditional philosophy captive is that of the mind as a great mirror, containing various representations – some accurate, some not – and capable of being studied by pure, nonempirical methods." See Richard Rorty, *Philosophy and the Mirror of Nature* (Princeton: Princeton University Press, 1979), 12.

reality on great thinkers of the past, we ought to pay close attention to what is individual and particular in their work.

This worry is legitimate, up to a point. It is certainly possible to read past philosophers in a superficial way. It is possible to impose labels on them that are too general and that ignore the subtleties of their thought. But it does not follow that all labels do so, or that philosophical pictures must be reifications that fail to do justice to the particularities of a great philosopher's work. A great deal hinges on what pictures are understood to be. If a picture is taken to be a static *thing* – for example, a set of theses accepted by several philosophers – then most pictures will be too general to be helpful. It seems unlikely that there is a list of "Cartesian" theses accepted by Descartes, Malebranche, and Husserl – or at least, it seems unlikely that any such list of theses would be long enough or controversial enough to be very interesting. But philosophical pictures need not be identified with collections of theses. It is more helpful to understand pictures dynamically – not as static sets of principles, but as dispositions to approach philosophical problems in certain characteristic ways. To be a Cartesian, on this view, is to tend to draw on certain strategies and resources while addressing philosophical problems. We might say, for example, that Cartesians are philosophers who attach a great deal of importance to the sorts of evidence that manifest themselves within thinking subjectivity, and who are typically reluctant to draw on other kinds. A general disposition of this sort is, I think, shared by Descartes, Malebranche, and Husserl, even though no single set of theses is. Seen in this light, philosophical pictures are much like what Arthur Danto calls "methodological directives."[40] They are not explanations of phenomena, but *injunctions* to seek explanations of a certain kind. They are not static, but dynamic.

A second problem with the notion of a philosophical picture is that it seems difficult to apply. It can be hard to decide which picture we should use to describe a given figure. Any number of different pictures might seem equally applicable to one and the same philosopher. Consider again the example of Descartes. Which picture, which broad conception of reality, does Descartes's work exemplify? Obviously, we could describe Descartes as an example of the "Cartesian" picture of reality – that is, of the picture that attaches particular importance to the sorts of evidence available to thinking subjectivity. But we could also see Descartes as an example of the picture called "modernity" – roughly, the picture that stresses "the supreme importance of 'reason' in human affairs, contra the claims of tradition, the

---

[40] Arthur Danto, *Narration and Knowledge* (New York: Columbia University Press, 1985), 238.

ancestors, and, especially, the Church"[41] as Robert Pippin has put it. Or we could see Descartes as embodying yet another picture – for example, Rorty's "representational" picture, according to which the mind is a mirror whose job it is to represent reality accurately. Descartes is associated with all of these pictures, and with a great many others as well. Is one of these pictures the right one to apply to Descartes? Do all apply equally? Are some better than others? Matters are complicated further by the complex relations that hold among pictures. The picture called "modernity," for example, presumably contains the Cartesian picture, since Cartesian philosophers are modern philosophers as well. The modern picture, in turn, overlaps significantly with Rorty's representational picture, without being entirely contained by it – many modern philosophers, though not all, are representationalists, and many representationalists, though not all, are also moderns. In short, the complex relations among pictures seem to make them difficult to apply, and perhaps of little value in making sense of past thought.

What should we say about this objection? It is clear that the relations among philosophical pictures are often complicated and messy. But it is not clear that this messiness is a problem. A great many other notions stand in equally complex relations, but are perfectly intelligible, and are often invaluable in making sense of the world. Consider the example of goals.[42] Goals are related to one another in a range of complex and messy ways. Some goals contain other goals, such as when the goal of finishing one's education contains the goal of writing a final exam. Some goals overlap with other goals, as when I read a novel both because it is required by my studies and because I enjoy it. It can be difficult to identify which goal a given action is intended to achieve: there may be several obvious possibilities, or none. Yet it would be absurd to suggest that these complexities make the notion of a goal unintelligible, or that they reduce its value in making sense of the world. A similar example is the notion of a movement or tradition in literature and the arts. It is clear that one and the same figure can belong to several movements at once. Kafka is both an expressionist and a modernist. Stravinsky is both a neoclassicist and an atonalist. It is obviously not a problem that artistic movements are related in these complex and messy ways. On the contrary, the labels associated with these movements are valuable precisely *because* they help us see complexity – that is, because

---

[41] Robert Pippin, *Modernity as a Philosophical Problem* (Cambridge, MA: Blackwell, 1991), 4.

[42] For an interesting discussion of the complex relations among goals, and of the implications of this fact for practical philosophy, see Joseph Raz, *The Morality of Freedom* (Oxford: Clarendon Press, 1986), 340–345.

they draw our attention to the multifaceted character of an artist's work. Philosophical pictures, I suspect, are similar. Viewing a philosopher as a representative of several pictures at once is not only legitimate; it is instructive, because it can help us to notice complexities in his or her work that might otherwise escape our attention. Seen in this light, the diversity of philosophical pictures is not a problem, but a benefit.[43]

How do we decide which picture(s) to apply to a given thinker? How do we individuate pictures, and determine how they are related to each other? The answer, surely, is that we do so in an ad hoc way according to pragmatic concerns. Consider once more the example of artistic and literary traditions. How do we decide whether to call Kafka a modernist or an expressionist? It depends on what we are trying to do with these labels – that is, on which aspects of his work we wish to highlight. Similarly, which picture we associate with a given philosopher depends on what we are trying to point out about that philosopher's work. This, in turn, is a function of our priorities, our goals, and our philosophical agendas. What reason would we have for describing Descartes by means of one picture rather than another? Why, for example, does Rorty see him as embodying the "representational" picture rather than the "Cartesian" or "modern" pictures? Rorty speaks this way because he wants us to see things about the history of ideas that he believes have not been adequately noticed. He wants us to recognize something we may not have seen before – that "[t]he picture which holds traditional philosophy captive is that of the mind as a great mirror, containing various representations."[44] He wants us to see similarities among philosophers that may have escaped our attention – for example, similarities between ancient and modern approaches to knowledge, similarities stemming from a common reliance on the image of the mind as a mirror. Rorty sees these similarities as important because of his background in philosophy of mind, and he speaks of one picture rather than another because he wants us to see their importance too. A different

---

[43] As I will argue in Chapter 2, the fact that philosophical pictures can overlap and be related in other complex ways is closely connected to the nature of narrative, particularly the way in which the elements of one narrative can be construed differently in another. David Carr puts it this way: "Nothing is more common than the retrospective revision whereby the elements of one story become the elements of another: the movements and strokes of my tennis game were supposed to be part of my victory in the tennis match; instead, they are part of the sad story of my developing back problems which forced me out of the match. Similarly, the 'same' elements can be viewed by different persons, at the same time, as parts of very different stories." See David Carr, *Time, Narrative, and History* (Bloomington: Indiana University Press, 1986), 68. We might add that the "same" elements of a philosopher's work can be viewed by different persons, at the same time, as embodying very different philosophical pictures.

[44] Rorty, *Philosophy and the Mirror of Nature*, 12.

philosopher with a different orientation might be struck by other features of the history of thought. She might find the differences between ancient and modern approaches to knowledge more striking than the similarities. She would associate Descartes with a different picture because her goals and agenda are different. In short, the tools we use to understand the history of thought depend to a large extent on what we are trying to do with it.

Does this mean that the study of philosophical pictures is relativistic? No more so than any other enterprise. Any intellectual endeavor must divide up its terrain somehow. It must organize its subject matter by means of some theoretical framework, some body of concepts that make the subject matter intelligible. There is never just one way of doing so. Alternate frameworks are always possible. A historian, for example, might organize her subject matter in terms of classes, or nation states, or any number of other concepts. Clearly, the claims we make in a discipline depend on which theoretical framework we have used to organize its subject matter. A historian who takes the concept of class as fundamental will end up saying very different things about history than one who privileges the concept of the nation state. The study of philosophical pictures is no different in this respect. Two different philosophers might view the history of thought in terms of two very different sets of pictures, perhaps conflicting or incompatible ones. What they say about past philosophy will be a function of – will be relative to – their choice of theoretical framework. But the claims of a historian, or an economist, or a physicist are relative in exactly the same way.

Of course, the term "relativism" is usually taken to mean something stronger – namely, that no way of talking about a subject is better or truer than any other. There is no reason to think that the study of philosophical pictures is relativistic in this sense. Granted, there may be disputes in this enterprise that are difficult or impossible to settle. There may be no fact of the matter about whether Descartes is "really" a modern philosopher or a representationalist. But no matter which set of pictures one uses to make sense of past thought, there will be pictures that clearly do not apply to Descartes. He will clearly never deserve the label "materialist," for example. Moreover, of the pictures that can be applied to Descartes, some might well turn out to be better than others. It may well be that, at the end of the day, it is more instructive, even more true, to call Descartes a modern philosopher than to call him a representationalist, or vice versa. The crucial point, however, is that we should expect to discover this only after the fact. The way to determine whether some pictures are better than others is to try them – to apply them to the history of thought and see how well they work. In all likelihood, some will prove completely unsuccessful, and some will prove more successful than others. But there is no way to know in advance which ones will succeed. It would be foolish to rule out the possibility of right and wrong answers in the study of philosophical pictures. But if we find such answers, we should expect to find them a posteriori. The only way to find them is to look.

One question remains. What is the difference between pictures and theories? It is often easy enough to recognize examples of each when we see them. We have little difficulty, for example, distinguishing the work of Descartes or Malebranche from the Cartesian picture that their work embodies. But what is the basis for such distinctions? Something I have repeatedly mentioned is that pictures are more general than theories. Theories are specific and detailed formulations of pictures; pictures are more flexible and more abstract than the pictures that instantiate them. But generality is not the only difference. After all, some theories are more general than others, and it may well be possible for a theory to be so general that it starts to resemble a picture. So what else distinguishes them? Another difference, as we have seen, is that pictures and theories are different sorts of things. A theory is a set of propositions, or a collection of answers to certain philosophical questions. A picture, by contrast, is a disposition: a tendency to approach philosophical questions in characteristic ways. It is not the answer to any specific question, but an injunction to seek answers of a certain kind. Finally, an important difference between theories and pictures is that they perform different functions. We form theories in order to state what is the case. But as I will argue in Chapter 2, we advance claims about pictures in order to achieve a different goal. That goal is to bring about a change in our audience, and more specifically, a change in our audience's way of seeing the philosophers of the past. But that is a matter for the next chapter.

The role of narrative

In the last chapter, I gave a general account of what is involved in doing philosophy historically. In this chapter, I want to make the account more detailed. The goal of this chapter is to shed further light on *how* one does philosophy historically: how one goes about assessing a picture by tracing its development over time. The concept of *narrative* will play an important role here. I argue that doing philosophy historically involves constructing a distinctive kind of narrative about past thought, narratives that help us to see a position or a figure as an instance of a picture. Thus one of the goals of this chapter is to clarify the role that narrative plays in this enterprise, and to explain how it is able to play this role. The notion of "seeing as," also central to my account, will need to be clarified as well.

Once this has been done, I will turn to a number of further questions about what is involved in doing philosophy historically. I will ask whether the narratives we construct in this enterprise should be considered to be *arguments*; whether the construction of these narratives is a *rational* pursuit; and whether it is a pursuit that aims at *truth*. I will answer all three questions in the affirmative, but I will qualify these answers in important ways.

RORTY, NARRATIVE, AND "SEEING AS"

How does one go about doing philosophy historically? I propose to answer this question by looking at a simple example: Richard Rorty's *Philosophy and the Mirror of Nature*. Rorty's book is clearly an attempt to do philosophy historically. It tries to show that a widely accepted picture is deeply problematic, and it does so by engaging with the historical figures who have accepted this picture. Examining Rorty's project might help us to see this project's essential features – those features that make it an attempt to do philosophy historically, as opposed to a contribution to "pure" philosophy or the history of philosophy. With any luck, we will be able to transfer what we have learned to other cases, and see the distinguishing features of Rorty's project in other attempts to do philosophy historically.

Philosophy and the Mirror of Nature begins with a familiar description of how philosophers see themselves. It points out that most philosophers see their discipline as concerned with "perennial, eternal problems – problems which arise as soon as one reflects … [Philosophy] sees itself as the attempt to underwrite or debunk claims to knowledge made by science, morality, art, or religion."[1] It sees itself as concerned with the foundations of knowledge, or with the question of whether science, morality, and other spheres can legitimate their claims to know. This is not the only possible way of viewing philosophy. In fact, as Rorty tells us elsewhere in the book, it is not his preferred way.[2] But although this view is "optional,"[3] it still holds the vast majority of philosophers under its sway. The reason is not that the philosophers in question share any particular theory. Philosophers of every conceivable theoretical stripe, philosophers with little else in common, all agree in seeing their discipline as foundational. Instead, the reason is the unquestioned acceptance of a certain "picture,"[4] a very general conception of what the mind is. Rorty continues:

Philosophy can be foundational in respect to the rest of culture because culture is the assemblage of claims to knowledge, and it finds these foundations in the study of man-as-knower, of the "mental processes" or the "activity of representation" which makes knowledge possible. To know is to represent accurately what is outside the mind; so to understand the possibility and nature of knowledge is to understand the way in which the mind is able to construct such representations. Philosophy's central concern is to be a general theory of representation, a theory which will divide culture up into the areas which represent reality well, those which represent it less well, and those which do not represent it at all (despite their pretense of doing so).[5]

For obvious reasons, I have called this picture the "representational" one. Rorty claims that it has been accepted by a wide range of philosophers, past and present: Plato and Aristotle, Descartes and Locke, Husserl and Russell.

But Rorty finds this picture deeply problematic. His goal in *Philosophy and the Mirror of Nature* is to "undermine the reader's confidence in 'the

---

[1] Rorty, *Philosophy and the Mirror of Nature*, 3.
[2] Rorty explains that he prefers to see philosophy as "therapeutic" rather than foundational – that is, as based on the conviction that "a 'philosophical problem' was a product of the unquestioned adoption of assumptions built into the vocabulary in which the problem was stated – assumptions which were to be questioned before the problem itself was taken seriously." See Rorty, *Philosophy and the Mirror of Nature*, xiii.
[3] Rorty, *Philosophy and the Mirror of Nature*, 11.   [4] Rorty, *Philosophy and the Mirror of Nature*, 12.
[5] Rorty, *Philosophy and the Mirror of Nature*, 3.

mind' as something about which one should have a 'philosophical' view, in 'knowledge' as something about which there ought to be a 'theory' and which has 'foundations,' and in 'philosophy' as it has been conceived since Kant."[6] Rorty describes this project as "therapeutic rather than constructive,"[7] since its goal is not to advance a new theory of mind, but to help rid us of the desire for such theories. *Philosophy and the Mirror of Nature* proceeds to administer its therapy by drawing on history. It engages critically with a variety of philosophers who have both accepted and shaped the representational picture: Plato, Descartes, Locke, and Kant. But its goal is not to contribute to Plato or Descartes scholarship, at least not as "scholarship" is understood by most historians of philosophy. Rorty's goal is to make a larger philosophical point *by means of* an engagement with history. It is to undermine our confidence in an entire philosophical picture – not just Locke's version of the representational picture, but all versions of it. Rorty engages with the work of individual thinkers, but he draws a conclusion that goes beyond them.

What is Rorty doing here? Clearly, he is making a philosophical point. He wants to convince us that a certain conception of the mind is problematic and needs to be rethought or abandoned. But Rorty makes this point by drawing on history. *Philosophy and the Mirror of Nature* undermines the representational picture by engaging critically with its most famous representatives, and showing that their versions of this picture are incoherent, or based on faulty assumptions, or something of the sort. Indeed, Rorty suggests that he *must* proceed in this way – that the attempt to rid ourselves of the representational picture, or any dubious picture, must trace that picture's history.[8] But how does Rorty use history to make a larger point? There seem to be four distinct parts to his procedure. First, Rorty selects the historical figures with whom he wishes to engage: Locke, Kant, and a number of others. Next, he tries to get us to see these figures as proponents of the representational picture. It is not obvious that Locke and Kant are representationalists; it is not obvious that we should understand these figures in terms of the idea that the mind is a mirror. Rorty's view is a controversial one, and he goes to a great deal of trouble to convince us that his approach to Locke and Kant is appropriate. This involves tracing little-noticed lines of influence among these thinkers, pointing out striking

---

[6] Rorty, *Philosophy and the Mirror of Nature*, 7.   [7] Rorty, *Philosophy and the Mirror of Nature*, 7.
[8] Consider, for example, Rorty's claim that the project of "deconstructing" pictures – which he claims is best exemplified by the later Wittgenstein – "needs to be supplemented by historical awareness." It is not enough to decide that the mind is not a mirror and leave it at that. We must also have an "awareness of the source of all this mirror-imagery." See Rorty, *Philosophy and the Mirror of Nature*, 12.

similarities in their use of certain concepts, and so on. Third, Rorty engages critically with these figures. He not only claims that they embody the representational picture; he argues that their versions of this picture face insuperable difficulties. He tries to show, for example, that Locke's reliance on the representational picture leads to a confusion between the justification of beliefs and the explanation of how they were acquired.[9] Similarly, he argues, Kant's acceptance of this picture causes him to confound synthesis and predication.[10] Finally, having pointed out problems with specific versions of the picture, Rorty uses them as justification to draw a conclusion about the entire picture. He claims that any attempt to see the mind as a mirror that represents reality is misguided. It is not just that there are isolated difficulties with these figures. Their entire conception of the mind is a non-starter.

It seems likely that any attempt to do philosophy historically will involve these four tasks. One must select a number of historical figures with whom one wishes to engage. One must argue for a certain way of viewing these figures, and convince one's audience to see them as representatives of a certain picture, not just isolated thinkers. One must engage critically with these figures, in order to demonstrate something about their version of the picture in question – for example, that Locke's reliance on the representational picture leads to a confused epistemology, or that Husserl's Cartesianism makes it difficult for him to account for social phenomena. Finally, on the basis of these engagements with particular figures, one draws a conclusion about the picture as a whole. It may be the modest conclusion that the picture is strong at some things but weak at others. It may be the stronger conclusion that the picture under consideration is so problematic that it should be abandoned. But some general conclusion about the picture is called for. If we merely examined individual philosophers and their views, we might make important contributions to the history of philosophy. But we would not be doing philosophy historically, since we would not be making a larger philosophical point. Similarly, if we merely assessed a certain conception of reality without tracing how it has evolved over time, we might learn an important philosophical lesson, but we would not be doing so by engaging with history. Again, we would not be doing philosophy historically. For a project to be both philosophical and historical, it must involve each of the above tasks.

---

[9] Rorty, *Philosophy and the Mirror of Nature*, 139–148.
[10] Rorty, *Philosophy and the Mirror of Nature*, 148–155.

Of course, matters are not as neat as this scheme suggests. It is obviously not the case that doing philosophy historically involves following four easily identified steps. Typically, all four of the tasks I have described are done at once, and it may not be easy to tell which parts of a work contribute to one task rather than another. This is clearly the case with *Philosophy and the Mirror of Nature*, which alternates between its historical studies and its larger philosophical agenda, and which draws critical conclusions about the representational picture before beginning any of the other tasks I have outlined. The point is just that when we do philosophy historically, a number of distinct tasks are involved. We may not proceed in a way that makes the differences among these tasks clear, but they can be distinguished all the same.

But there seems to be a problem with this account. When we do philosophy historically, we draw conclusions that are general. We do not just assess the views and arguments of individual thinkers. Rather, we try to learn something about the broader philosophical pictures that these thinkers articulate. The problem is that the evidence offered in support of such a conclusion is inevitably particular. We may want to demonstrate something about the representational picture as a whole, but the way we do this is by examining particular representatives of it, such as Locke and Kant. How can these particular bits of evidence justify a general conclusion? How can we conclude that the representational picture *as such* is misguided, just because there are problems with Locke's and Kant's versions of it? Whenever we do philosophy historically, we draw conclusions that seem to outstrip the evidence available. What gives us the right to draw conclusions of this sort?

One possibility is that the conclusions are justified by induction. Perhaps we defend a general conclusion about a picture by examining as many different representatives of the picture as we can, and showing that each of these cases supports our conclusion. That Locke's version of the representational picture is problematic does not show that the picture as a whole is. But if the versions advanced by Plato, Descartes, and Kant face similar problems, then the general conclusion seems more justified. The more examples we can find, the more justified our conclusion will be. Perhaps, then, the way to defend a sweeping conclusion about a picture is by accumulating cases. Perhaps we make inductive generalizations while doing philosophy historically, and perhaps this enterprise has the same strengths and weaknesses of any sort of induction.

There are two problems with this view. The first is that if induction is to be reliable, it requires large and diverse samples. In order for us to conclude through induction that every S is P, we must have a large number of S's to examine. The fewer we have, the less trustworthy our generalizations will be. But when we study the philosophers of the past, we rarely, if ever, have enough cases to justify our conclusions inductively. Consider *Philosophy and the Mirror of Nature*. How many representationalists would Rorty have to study to show inductively that there are insuperable difficulties with the representational picture as a whole? Ten? Fifty? Even fifty cases are not a lot where induction is concerned. Yet a book that studied fifty philosophers responsibly might take a lifetime to write, and be too unwieldy for all but a handful of readers. In short, there are too many practical constraints for induction to be useful here.

Second, and more importantly, although we do connect general conclusions with particular bits of evidence when we do philosophy historically, the relation between the two is different than in induction. With induction, the relation between general conclusions and particular bits of evidence is *external*:[11] the evidence exists independently of the conclusions that it confirms or disconfirms. When I say "All emeralds are green," it is clear which facts would support or refute my claim. I look for green emeralds, and the more of them I find, the more confident I am in my generalization. I know which things are green emeralds and which are not. The only question is whether I have found enough of them to support my conclusion. When we do philosophy historically, however, matters are different. We cannot assess our general conclusions by counting up cases, because it is typically far from clear whether something should count as a case or not. When Rorty says that the representational picture is flawed, he is not asking us to count up all the representationalists who run into difficulties and see whether the numbers bear him out. It is not yet clear whether there *are* any representationalists – that is, it is not yet clear that this is an appropriate way to understand the philosophers of the past. Rorty's statement is not a generalization about the history of thought. It is an admonition to view the history of thought in a certain way. We cannot evaluate this statement by counting up the number of representationalists who run into difficulties,

---

[11] I am using the term "external" in the sense Alasdair MacIntyre has in mind when he speaks of "external representation." External representation is "the relationship which holds between a passport photograph and its subject: one can inspect the two items independently and inquire as to the degree of resemblance between them." Internal representation, by contrast, is such that "it is by means of the representation that we learn to see what is represented." Rembrandt's paintings, for example, are internal representations of light in that they teach us to see light differently. See Alasdair MacIntyre, "Contexts of Interpretation: Reflections on Hans-Georg Gadamer's *Truth and Method*." *Boston University Journal* 24:1 (1976), 43–44. By extension, we might say that *Philosophy and the Mirror of Nature* offers an internal representation of philosophers such as Locke and Kant. Its aim is not to resemble them in the manner of a passport photograph, but to help us see them in a new way.

because it is only by means of this statement that we learn to recognize a philosopher as a representationalist in the first place. In short, when we do philosophy historically, we are not making generalizations about a given body of facts. We are trying to view the facts in a novel and perhaps controversial way.

So what *does* justify this enterprise's conclusions? Consider the case of Rorty again. Why does he expect us to believe what he says about the representationalist picture? What kind of evidence does he offer in support of his claims? The force of Rorty's conclusion does not come from any of the particular cases he studies – from his reading of Locke or Kant, for example. It results from the way in which these cases fit into a certain kind of story. If we find Rorty's claims convincing, it is because of the context provided by the rest of his book. It is because he tells a compelling story about how the representational picture originated in ancient philosophy and was unwittingly transmitted to later thinkers. It is because this story fits well with what we know about the history of thought, and because it helps answer some of the questions we may have about this history. It is because Rorty's account helps makes sense of a wide range of otherwise puzzling phenomena: Locke's confusion of explanation and justification, Kant's conflation of predication and synthesis, and so on. Above all, it is because of the contrast Rorty draws between the representational picture and other pictures we may find more attractive – his "therapeutic" conception of philosophy, for example. In short, if we find ourselves believing Rorty's claims about the representational picture, it is not because he has airtight arguments against any of its representatives. Rather, it is because of the cumulative force of all the considerations I have listed. If we find Rorty's claims convincing, it is because of the way he shapes all of these considerations into a compelling narrative.

But why does narrative convince us where induction does not? Why do we consider ourselves justified in drawing a general conclusion from particular evidence when that evidence has been shaped into a certain kind of story? Let me return to a point I made earlier: that a narrative such as Rorty's is less a description of the facts than an admonition to view the facts in a certain way. In composing a narrative, I do not relate facts neutrally. I *argue* for a certain way of seeing the facts, and the way I argue is by laying out the facts as they appear to me. In a narrative, *description and justification are inseparable*.[12] I urge others to see the facts as I do by relating how *I* see them.

---

[12] Paul Ricoeur puts this point a little differently: he says that narration is "between" description and prescription. See *OAA*, 152.

Jonathan Dancy has attached a great deal of importance to this feature of narratives. He illustrates it with the example of describing a building. If I wish to describe how a building appears to me, I must do more than enumerate everything I see as my eyes move from left to right. This, Dancy points out, "would not be a description but a list of properties."[13] Any description worth the name also conveys the *shape* of these properties – the way they are organized, the relations in which they stand to one another, and so on. It conveys this shape through "the order they are mentioned," or more generally, through "the narrative structure of the description."[14] The description of how I see the building turns out to be a sort of narrative. Narratives, after all, do not list facts neutrally. They convey the shape of facts by organizing them in a certain way. Thus to describe how I see the building *just is* to explain why I think others should see it in the same way. Describing the building by means of a narrative and arguing that my description is correct are one and the same activity. Or as Dancy puts it:

> To justify one's choice is to give the reasons one sees for making it, and to give those reasons is just to lay out how one sees the situation, starting in the right place and going on to display the various salient features in the right way … In giving those reasons one is … appealing to others to see it (as the building) the way one sees it oneself, and the appeal consists in laying out that way as persuasively as one can. The persuasiveness here is the persuasiveness of narrative: an internal coherence in the account which compels assent. We succeed in our aim when our story sounds right.[15]

The crucial point here is that when narratives sound right, they *compel* assent.[16] If Rorty's story sounds right – if it is internally coherent, if it fits well with other beliefs in which we are confident, and so on – then we simply find ourselves accepting it. We find ourselves viewing the history of thought as Rorty urges. This change in outlook is not like learning a new fact. It is more like undergoing a Gestalt switch. When we look at the history of philosophical thought, we see the same figures and texts, but we see them differently. We now see this history as the evolution of the representational picture, and we see Locke and Kant as embodiments of

---

[13] Jonathan Dancy, *Moral Reasons* (Oxford: Blackwell, 1993), 112.
[14] Dancy, *Moral Reasons*, 112.   [15] Dancy, *Moral Reasons*, 113.
[16] I leave open the question of what *makes* a narrative sound right – that is, what criteria a narrative must meet in order to compel assent. Dancy's criterion of "internal coherence" is surely necessary, but nowhere near sufficient. Plenty of narratives are internally coherent but not compelling. Arthur Danto has identified a number of additional criteria: the narrative must have a single subject; it must thoroughly explain the events it describes; and it must not contain any episodes that are "narratively inert." See Danto, *Narration and Knowledge*, 248–251. But again, while Danto claims that these criteria are necessary in order for a narrative to be "valid," they are clearly not sufficient.

this picture. What we see has not changed. What has changed is what we see it *as*.

It might be helpful at this point to say a little more about the notion of "seeing as." It has long been recognized that seeing an object is not the same as seeing an object *as* something. To see an object as something is to notice an *aspect* of that object, where the "aspect" in question is not identical with any of the object's particular parts or elements. As Stephen Mulhall puts it, seeing an object *as* something involves recognizing it as being a certain kind of thing.[17] This recognition is not forced on us by the object's properties alone, but requires an additional contribution from the viewer. The classic discussion of "seeing as" appears in section II.vi of Wittgenstein's *Philosophical Investigations*. Wittgenstein is fascinated by cases in which my perception of an object suddenly changes, even though I know that the object itself has not changed. He gives the example of a drawing by Jastrow that can be seen as either a rabbit or a duck.[18] The drawing itself does not force me to view it in one way rather than another. This is made clear by the experience that Wittgenstein calls "the dawning of an aspect"[19] – after seeing the drawing as a duck, I suddenly see it as a rabbit, or vice versa. When this happens, I see the drawing differently, while recognizing that it is the same as before. The "air of *paradox*"[20] found in such cases is dispelled only when we realize that "seeing as" is a distinct kind of seeing, one we continually engage in without being aware of it. Another well-known example of "seeing as" appears in Heidegger's discussion of interpretation (*Auslegung*) in *Being and Time*.[21] According to Heidegger, whenever I understand something, be it an everyday object or a scientific theory, my understanding "has the structure of *something as something*" (*BT*, 89). Making sense of things is not a matter of encountering indifferent objects in a neutral way and only later interpreting their significance. We have always already construed things in a certain way, and while these construals can change – as when I say of the drawing, "Now it's a duck!" – these shifts only highlight how natural and spontaneous the perception of aspects is.[22]

---

[17] Stephen Mulhall, *On Being in the World: Wittgenstein and Heidegger on Seeing Aspects* (London: Routledge, 1990), 28.
[18] Ludwig Wittgenstein, *Philosophical Investigations*, trans. G. E. M. Anscombe (Oxford: Blackwell, 1953), 194.
[19] Wittgenstein, *Philosophical Investigations*, 193.   [20] Mulhall, *On Being in the World*, 6.
[21] As the title of his book makes clear, Mulhall is also impressed by the similarities between Wittgenstein's and Heidegger's accounts.
[22] For this reason, Wittgenstein claims that perception involves "continuous aspect perception." See Wittgenstein, *Philosophical Investigations*, 193.

As the discussions of Wittgenstein and Heidegger show, the clearest examples of "seeing as" are visual. But they have obvious implications for understanding considered more broadly. Just as we can see a drawing as a rabbit, we can "see" a painting as a beautiful depiction of a landscape or as a portrait of a friend.[23] More importantly for our purposes, we can and do see philosophers *as* something, as when we see Descartes as a modern philosopher and not just a lone individual. Indeed, this seems to be a pervasive feature of the way we make sense of the history of thought. We rarely, if ever, encounter a philosopher's work *simpliciter*. We have always already construed his work in a certain way. These construals can and do change. As a result of reading Rorty, I may come to see Descartes as a representationalist rather than a rationalist or a modern. But again, the fact that we find such changes startling only shows how natural and instinctive the initial construal was.

When we do philosophy historically, our goal is to bring about a certain kind of "seeing as."[24] It is to trigger the experience that Wittgenstein calls the dawning of an aspect: the experience of seeing a number of philosophers not just as individuals, but as embodiments of a certain picture. As I have argued, we bring about these shifts by constructing narratives. If these narratives are judged by the standards governing induction, they will be found wanting, because their conclusions are more sweeping than the facts warrant. But this is not a problem, because the narratives in question do not claim to describe the facts in a neutral way. Their goal is to bring about a change in the reader, a spontaneous conversion in outlook comparable to a Gestalt switch. When this change occurs – when we find a given narrative convincing – it is not because of any single element of the story. It is because of the way in which the elements have been organized into a whole that sounds right.

An important consequence follows. There is never just one way to tell a story. It is always possible to compose different narratives about the same events. Narratives may share the same subject matter – the same "hyletic,"[25]

---

[23] These examples are Mulhall's. See Mulhall, *On Being in the World*, 27.

[24] In claiming that the point of doing philosophy historically is to trigger a certain kind of "seeing as," I do not mean to suggest that the enterprises opposed to this one – "pure" philosophy and the history of philosophy – do not also involve "seeing as." It seems clear that "seeing as" plays some role in both, since both involve various sorts of interpretation. The "pure" philosopher and the historian of philosophy will both relate to their subject matter "understandingly and interpretatively" (*BT*, 189), as Heidegger puts it. The point is simply that we can describe the *goals* of these enterprises without making reference to "seeing as." In the case of doing philosophy historically, we cannot.

[25] Paul Ricoeur, *Freud and Philosophy: An Essay on Interpretation*, trans. Denis Savage (New Haven: Yale University Press, 1970), 521.

as Paul Ricoeur puts it – while differing in all sorts of ways: the perspectives from which they are told, the emphasis they place on certain elements, the values that inform them, and so on. The narratives we construct while doing philosophy historically are no different in this respect. Two philosophers may look at the same figures and texts and construct very different narratives. A narrative that sees Descartes as a modern philosopher, one who stresses the supreme importance of reason in human affairs, will differ significantly from one that sees him as a representationalist beholden to the image of the mind as a mirror. When doing philosophy historically, we can produce a great many different narratives involving Descartes – perhaps indefinitely many. This seems to be a consequence of the role played by "seeing as" in this enterprise. After all, the goal of this enterprise is to change our way of looking at past thought – to let us see diverse figures and texts as embodiments of a certain picture. As Mulhall points out, to see a thing *as* something is to recognize it as being a particular *kind* of thing.[26] But any given thing can be categorized in indefinitely many different ways, and thus is an example of indefinitely many kinds of things. *Which* kind we see it as will depend on which classification scheme we are using, as well as on what we wish to point out about the thing in question. Just as we should not expect an object to belong to only one category of things, we should not expect there to be only one compelling narrative about the history of thought. This is not to say that anything goes in this enterprise. Some narratives may be totally unconvincing – to use Dancy's phrase, they may not sound right at all. And in the fullness of time, some may prove better than others in all sorts of ways. But we should not be surprised if there is more than one plausible narrative about past thought, and we should not expect there to be an easy way to decide which is best. To this extent, Richard Campbell is surely right: it makes little sense to speak of any one attempt to do philosophy historically as being uniquely correct.[27]

It turns out that doing philosophy historically is a hybrid activity. In some ways, it is a conventional scholarly pursuit. It draws on the same body of evidence used by traditional historians of philosophy. It studies figures and texts closely, and it is discredited when its claims do not cohere with the historical record. Unlike the study of the history of philosophy, however, its goal is not simply to understand past philosophers correctly. Its goal is

---

[26] Mulhall, *On Being in the World*, 28.
[27] Campbell, *Truth and Historicity*, 10. But as Campbell acknowledges, to deny that such narratives can be correct is not the same as denying that they can be *true*. I will return to this point later in the chapter.

creative as well as scholarly: to make us see the philosophers of the past in a new way, or under a different aspect. This is not to say that it glorifies unbridled creation. Nor is it to deny that the work of conventional historians of philosophy is also creative in all sorts of ways. It is merely to say that the enterprises have different aims. Historians of philosophy want to help us understand past thought correctly; those who do philosophy historically want to change our way of seeing it.[28]

ARGUMENT

I have claimed that doing philosophy historically involves constructing narratives. I have also claimed that this activity seeks to demonstrate something about what various pictures can and cannot do. These two claims might seem to be in tension. After all, it is tempting to think that it is one thing to construct a narrative and quite another to argue for a conclusion. Narratives describe what has happened, and how. Arguments show that something is the case by pointing to appropriate evidence. Narratives therefore seem quite different from arguments. One does not defend one's views by telling the story of how one came to accept them. To do so would be to confound a belief's cause with its justification. Similarly, it is natural to think that we cannot justify a conclusion about a philosophical picture by constructing a narrative about how it has evolved. Even Dancy, who defends the use of narrative by philosophers, seems to view matters in

---

[28] I have argued that there is no need to choose between problem-solving philosophy and doing philosophy historically. Both enterprises are legitimate, even complementary; they simply have different goals. One might object, however, that these enterprises are in more tension than I acknowledge. Some narratives that do philosophy historically seem to undermine problem-solving philosophy, by showing that certain philosophical problems captivate us only if we are in the grips of a bad picture. *Philosophy and the Mirror of Nature* is a good example, since it argues that some core questions in epistemology and philosophy of mind are contingent products of the representational picture. If we reject this picture, Rorty suggests, these problems will go away. Furthermore, having read Rorty, we will no doubt wonder whether other parts of the problem-solving enterprise result from bad pictures as well. It seems likely that the more we learn about pictures, the less use we will have for problem-solving. What should we say about this objection? Certainly we cannot rule out the possibility that studying pictures will lead us to take particular problems less seriously. But this is not because doing philosophy historically is essentially in tension with problem-solving philosophy. Here we should distinguish the *nature* of these enterprises from the *results* of carrying them out in specific cases. My goal has been to characterize the nature of these enterprises in general terms. When we do so, we find nothing to suggest that one is essentially in tension with the other. But it is always possible to *discover* something through one of these enterprises that will undermine the other. Rorty's critique of the representational picture is a good example. It is a substantive conclusion that we reach – if we do – as a result of studying a specific picture. It is not a conclusion we must accept while coming to understand what doing philosophy historically is. I am grateful to an anonymous reader for Cambridge University Press for helping me to think through this matter.

this way. He claims, for example, that when one composes a narrative about a situation, "one is not *arguing* for one's way of seeing the situation. One is rather appealing to others to see it … the way one sees it oneself."[29] This way of speaking suggests that asking others to see a situation as one does oneself is quite different from arguing for one's view. Narratives seem different from arguments, and if they are, it is difficult to see how we could engage in both simultaneously when we do philosophy historically.

What should we make of this charge? The first thing to note is that it is based on a view of argumentation that is both quite narrow and relatively recent. On this view, an argument is nothing more and nothing less than it is purported to be in introductory logic classes: an ordered series of statements that establishes the truth of a conclusion by means of certain premises. In assessing an argument, all that matters is whether the conclusion "follows from" the premises. Rhetorical elements – appeals to emotion, eloquent descriptions of one's personal perspective, and so on – are dismissed as extraneous. If one understands argumentation in this way, it is clear that narratives cannot be arguments, since narratives rely heavily on the very rhetorical elements that this view dismisses.

But this is not the only possible way of understanding argument. On the contrary, a growing body of scholarship suggests that this understanding of argument is both implausibly narrow and a product of relatively recent historical developments. Paul Ricoeur, for example, has argued that our insistence on polarizing narrative and argument is a product of the West's recent legal history.[30] It is also a departure from earlier views of argumentation. Properly understood, Ricoeur argues, an argument is "a special case of practical normative discussion in general,"[31] and is thus intimately connected with narration and rhetoric. P. Christopher Smith makes a similar claim. Smith argues that in recent centuries the West's understanding of argument has become unduly truncated. For most of Western history, an argument was taken to be any attempt to make something clear by talking about it – particularly by talking about it in a "narrative-historical mode."[32] But our view of argumentation is now much more narrow. Smith writes:

Whereas argument was originally a community of two or more taking counsel with each other, for us today it has degenerated into a litigious conflict of "rival" interests … What is more, since one side can no longer hear and accept what the other

[29] Dancy, *Moral Reasons*, 113.
[30] Paul Ricoeur, *The Just*, trans. David Pellauer (Chicago: University of Chicago Press, 2000), 116.
[31] Ricouer, *The Just*, 116.
[32] P. Christopher Smith, *The Hermeneutics of Original Argument* (Evanston: Northwestern University Press, 1998), 4.

has to say, each resorts to asserting its own position while demolishing its opponent's, and thus argument has come to mean a dispute in which "claims" are asserted and either successfully defended against a rival's challenges or defeated by them.[33]

If one understands an argument as a litigious conflict between rival interests, it is difficult to see how one could argue for a position by talking about it in narrative-historical mode. In light of the work by Smith and Ricoeur, however, there seems little reason to limit our understanding of argumentation in this way.

If an argument is not just a litigious conflict between rival interests, then what is it? Smith suggests that the process of making something clear by talking about it – a process he calls "original argument"[34] – is primarily practical in its aims. It "seeks not so much to *show* [*deiknunai*] uninvolved observers and onlookers that something is so as it seeks to *move* involved listeners and participants to a decision [*krisis*], the consequences of which will affect themselves in their existence."[35] In other words, the goal of original argument is to change its audience. Accordingly, original argument draws on a wide of factors that an introductory logic class would dismiss as merely rhetorical. It "does not try to eliminate the influence of the feelings or *pathê* we undergo in order that we might 'see' and 'know' something with detached and impassive objectivity."[36] Rather, original argument tries to provoke certain feelings in its audience – namely, feelings that are appropriate to one who sees things as one does oneself, and feelings that will move one to act in the way the situation demands. Consequently, "*how* a rhetorical argument is voiced, the style [*lexis*] and delivery of it, will, in sharp distinction from the purely logical and demonstrative argument, be a crucial consideration."[37] Indeed, one of the most important things an argument can do is convince its audience that the person advancing it is "trustworthy."[38] This is not just a matter of demonstrating the truth of a conclusion. It involves bringing one's audience around to one's way of seeing things, and convincing them that it is the right way. "Here, too," Smith argues, "style and delivery are the communicators, and thus here, too, *how* something is said [is] indissociable from its *logos* or logic."[39]

Are narratives arguments in the broader sense that Smith outlines? Clearly, they perform many of the functions that Smith attributes to

---

[33] Smith, *Hermeneutics of Original Argument*, 5–6.   [34] Smith, *Hermeneutics of Original Argument*, 5.

[35] Smith, *Hermeneutics of Original Argument*, 37.   [36] Smith, *Hermeneutics of Original Argument*, 37.

[37] Smith, *Hermeneutics of Original Argument*, 37.

[38] Smith, *Hermeneutics of Original Argument*, 37. As Smith points out, it is significant that the ancient Greek word for "trustworthy" – *pistos* – is the source of *pistis*, which means "rhetorical proof."

[39] Smith, *Hermeneutics of Original Argument*, 38.

original argument. The aim of a narrative is primarily practical. It seeks to bring about a change in its audience: a change in the audience's way of looking at the subject under discussion. In particular, narratives that do philosophy historically try to persuade their audience to see certain figures and texts as embodiments of a particular philosophical picture. They do this through description – that is, by laying out the facts as they see them, and by urging the audience to see them in the same way. This is quite different from providing a series of ordered statements intended to convince the audience of the truth of a conclusion. But the point is still to persuade an audience of something, and to that extent, constructing narratives is still an exercise in argumentation. Further, like other examples of original argument, narratives attach a great deal of importance to style and delivery. As Dancy puts it, narratives lay out their view of things "as persuasively as [they] can."[40] If they are to convince their audiences, they must "sound right," achieving "an internal coherence … which compels assent."[41] Style and delivery are not extraneous elements that could be purged from a narrative. They play an essential role in making the narrative sound right. This is not to say that a narrative's persuasiveness is a function of its style and delivery alone. Narratives must meet other criteria as well. They must cohere with the full range of evidence available; they should not contradict beliefs in which we have a great deal of confidence; and so on. The point is just that these further criteria do not suffice to make a narrative persuasive. It must also be delivered in the right way. As Smith says, a narrative's style is inseparable from its logic.

It seems, then, that narratives can be arguments – provided that argumentation is understood more broadly than is usual today. Narratives are examples of what Smith calls original argument. They are attempts to bring an audience around to a new way of seeing things, attempts that use rhetoric as well as the elements of deductive, inductive, and abductive reasoning. To some, however, this understanding of argument will seem too loose to be legitimate. Some might object that an argument is not just any attempt to persuade an audience, but one that seeks to persuade an audience *in the right way*. Specifically, an argument tries to persuade its audience on the basis of rational evidence, evidence that compels anyone who accepts it to accept the argument's conclusion as well. One might object that evidence that is "merely rhetorical" – appeals to emotion or authority, for example – does not fall into this category, and that attempts to persuade by means of them should not be considered arguments at all. Since the narratives we construct

---

[40] Dancy, *Moral Reasons*, 113.   [41] Dancy, *Moral Reasons*, 113.

while doing philosophy historically do rely on these elements, one might conclude that they are not arguments in any philosophically interesting sense. They are merely rhetorical. They persuade in any way they can, rather than only in the right ways.

What should we say about this objection? First, we must grant that narratives are arguments in a much looser sense than are instances of deduction, induction, or abduction. Narratives draw on a much wider range of evidence, and they can be used to support a much wider array of conclusions. But it does not follow that narratives can convince anyone of absolutely anything, or that they recognize no distinction between good and bad ways of persuading. It does not follow that when we do philosophy historically, we can view past thought in any way we like or convince others to see it in any way at all. The number of plausible narratives we may construct about past thought may be quite large, but it is not unlimited. Recall a point made by Mulhall: that to see something *as* something is to recognize it as being a certain *kind* of thing. The narratives we construct while doing philosophy historically try to bring about a certain kind of "seeing as." Their goal is to lead us to see certain figures and texts as instances of a philosophical picture – that is, as being a certain kind of thing. As we have noted, a thing may be classified in indefinitely many ways, and thus may be seen as belonging to indefinitely many different kinds of things. But it does not follow that there are no limits on how we classify it, or that we may see it as any kind of thing at all. Think of Wittgenstein's line drawing. It may be seen as either a duck or a rabbit, or perhaps as indefinitely many other things as well. But there is still something that constrains how we see it: the line itself. The line may be seen in many different ways, but it may not be seen in just any way at all. Similarly, we may approach the history of thought with a great many different classificatory schemes. We may divide it into moderns and anti-moderns, materialists and immaterialists, or in indefinitely many other ways. Once we have settled on a scheme, however, certain claims about the history of thought are ruled out as just wrong. Descartes is not a materialist, for example, and any narrative that calls him one is simply wrong. No plausible narrative could convince us to view him as that kind of thing, because he simply is *not* that kind of thing. In other words, the narratives we construct about a given figure are constrained by what kinds of things that figure is. The number of categories to which the figure belongs may be quite large – perhaps indefinitely large – but it is not unlimited. Seen in this light, doing philosophy historically is not an exercise in pure rhetoric or unbridled persuasion. It cannot convince us of absolutely anything. It is constrained by evidence. The evidence about what a thing is constrains what that thing may be seen *as*.

This account might still seem too loose. It implies that there are as many valid narratives about Descartes as there are legitimate ways of categorizing him. The number of ways in which we can view him may not be unlimited, but it is still quite large, and there does not seem to be any obvious way of distinguishing better ways from worse. We could advance indefinitely many different arguments about Descartes's role in the history of thought, and all of them could, in principle, appear equally plausible. There does not seem to be any way around this objection. But we should note that it is not unique to the attempt to do philosophy historically. On the contrary, it arises in every intellectual enterprise, including some – such as natural science – that are paragons of rational argumentation. Every discipline must organize its subject matter by means of some theoretical framework, and the claims it can make are relative to the framework it uses. The claims we can advance about history, economics, or physics depend on how we describe and categorize the subject matter of these disciplines. In principle, it is possible to describe the physical world in indefinitely many different ways, and so in principle, indefinitely many scientific frameworks are possible. This does not mean that there are no right answers to scientific questions. Once we have settled on a framework – and we must always settle on some framework or other – certain answers are forced on us by the nature of things. That these things could, in principle, be described differently does not make our answers wrong. It just means that there is more than one way to divide up an intellectual landscape. It would be absurd to see this as a reason to abandon our best scientific theories. It would be just as absurd to see it as a reason to dismiss narratives that do philosophy historically. This enterprise does not deal in unbridled persuasion. It recognizes a distinction between good and bad ways of persuading, and accordingly, it is an exercise in argumentation.

RATIONALITY

So much for the question of whether the narratives we compose while doing philosophy historically are arguments. Let me now turn to a related question: whether this undertaking is *rational*.[42] This question is a pressing one, for several reasons. As we have seen, doing philosophy historically is a

---

[42] In this section, I ask whether a certain *practice* – doing philosophy historically – is rational. This way of proceeding is somewhat unusual, though not unprecedented. It is more common to predicate rationality of *beliefs*, not practices. For an example of this more common way of proceeding, see Robert Nozick, *The Nature of Rationality* (Princeton: Princeton University Press, 1994).

hybrid activity. It contains elements of conventional studies of the history of philosophy, but is also a creative enterprise more concerned with changing our way of looking at past philosophers than with representing their ideas accurately. Though it seems clear that the study of the history of philosophy is a rational undertaking, and that most creative activities – the creation of literature and music, for example – are rational enterprises as well, it is not clear that a hybrid enterprise containing elements of both is rational. Indeed, some of the best-known practitioners of this enterprise have been accused of doing something irrational. Consider the work of Jacques Derrida. His deconstructive readings of past thinkers are quintessential exercises in doing philosophy historically, in that they seek philosophical insight by returning again and again to earlier figures in the tradition. Yet these readings are sometimes attacked for abandoning rationality altogether – for rejecting "the claims of reason" and the "despised logos," as Calvin Schrag puts it.[43] Similar criticisms are made of Heidegger, Foucault, and even Hegel. All are charged with writing sloppy pseudo-histories that cannot be rationally assessed and that lack any real philosophical interest. If we care about doing philosophy historically, we need to address this charge.

What does it mean to say that an enterprise is rational?[44] This is a difficult question, since the nature of rationality is a matter of considerable philosophical dispute. Moreover, it may be that rationality has different meanings in different enterprises – that scientific theories are rational in a different way than literary theory, for example. However, Ernan McMullin has argued convincingly that at the most general level, the enterprises that we call rational display three features. First, a rational enterprise has identifiable *goals* or *aims*.

---

[43] Calvin O. Schrag, *The Resources of Rationality* (Bloomington: Indiana University Press, 1992), 23. On the same page, Schrag goes on to describe Derrida's position in this way: "we are advised to have done with classical and modernist overarching metaphysical designs and unifying epistemological principles that purport to tell the whole truth and nothing but the truth about our insertion into the world. The question that remains is whether after such a radical overhaul of our traditional philosophical habits of thought there is indeed any truth left to tell."

[44] Note that it is important to distinguish *theories* of rationality from *criteria* of rationality. A theory of rationality is an account of what it means for an enterprise to be rational, or of what the enterprises that we call rational have in common. Criteria of rationality are what we use to identify such enterprises – how we distinguish enterprises that are rational from those that are not. In other words, theories of rationality explain the meaning of a concept; criteria of rationality tell us how to recognize instances of this concept. Just as we can have criteria of truth without a theory of truth – just as we can know how to identify true statements without having an explicit theory of what it means for them to be true – we can give criteria of rationality without formulating an explicit theory of rationality. In asking whether it is rational to do philosophy historically, I will restrict myself to the question of whether this enterprise meets the criteria we use to distinguish rational enterprises from irrational ones. I will not raise the larger question of what it means for an enterprise to be rational.

There are "outcomes that prompt [an] agent to perform the activity,"[45] outcomes whose achievement would make the activity successful. In other words, a rational enterprise has standards of success and failure. It is successful when it accomplishes what it intends; it is unsuccessful otherwise. These goals "may fail to be realized in given cases."[46] They may never be realized. The point is simply that if it is impossible to say what it would take for an enterprise to be successful, or to distinguish a successful instance of it from an unsuccessful one, then it is not rational. Furthermore, it must be possible to say when an enterprise has met its goals or failed to meet them. This explains, at least in part, why astrology is not a rational undertaking: its predictions are so vague that they can never be proved wrong. Whenever they seem to have been disconfirmed by the course of events, an astrologer can say that they were misinterpreted, claiming that what they really forecast was something quite different than was initially thought. An enterprise is not rational if it is impossible to show that it has failed.

Second, a rational enterprise has identifiable *methods*. It does not pursue its goals randomly or by happenstance; it pursues them through systematic procedures. Suppose I ask you to tell me the meaning of life. Having never thought about this question before, you take a wild guess and blurt out, "42!" As it happens, let us suppose, your answer is right. But your search for it does not seem to have been a rational one, since you did not follow any particular method. Such methods are an essential part of any enterprise we call rational. They may take the form of explicit principles, but they need not. More often, "they are learned as a skill of a tacit sort."[47] And they may differ widely. The methods of literary criticism are quite different from the methods of physics. The point is simply that if an activity has no methods at all, we would hesitate to call it rational.

Finally, rational enterprises try to maximize certain *values* in the course of pursuing their aims. Values are "characteristics [regarded] as desirable in the entity that is being assessed."[48] They are not themselves the goals of the enterprise; nor are they instruments used to achieve these goals. They are further conditions to be met by an enterprise's outcomes. Mathematicians often regard it as desirable that their results be as elegant as possible. Natural scientists regard it as desirable that their results be as simple as possible. No

---

[45] Ernan McMullin, "The Shaping of Scientific Rationality: Construction and Constraint," in *Construction and Constraint: The Shaping of Scientific Rationality*, ed. Ernan McMullin (Notre Dame: University of Notre Dame Press, 1988), 23.

[46] McMullin, "The Shaping of Scientific Rationality," 23.

[47] McMullin, "The Shaping of Scientific Rationality," 23.

[48] McMullin, "The Shaping of Scientific Rationality," 23.

doubt we could give many other examples. Different enterprises may seek to maximize very different values, but if these enterprises are rational, they will all have values of one sort or another.[49]

Does the enterprise I have called doing philosophy historically meet these criteria of rationality? It will if we can answer three questions in the affirmative. First, does this enterprise have a goal the achievement of which would make it successful? Second, does it have systematic methods that it uses to pursue this goal? And third, does it have characteristic values, values it tries to maximize in the course of pursuing its goal? First, let us consider goals. It seems clear that those who do philosophy historically have a definite goal. This goal is to assess one or more of the major philosophical pictures. They try to see what a picture can do by studying what it has done – to determine the picture's strengths and weaknesses by studying how it has fared over time. We know what it would take for someone to succeed at this enterprise. Indeed, there seem to be examples of successful attempts to do philosophy historically: namely, books such as *Philosophy and the Mirror of Nature*, books that manage to change our way of looking at the philosophers of the past. So this enterprise not only has clear standards of success; its practitioners meet these standards, at least some of the time.

What about the demand that rational enterprises follow methods? There does seem to be a distinctive method involved in doing philosophy historically. Those who engage in this activity assess a picture's strengths and weaknesses by closely studying a number of its proponents. Like Rorty, they select a number of representatives of a given picture; they engage critically with the work of those representatives; and on the basis of this critical engagement, they advance a conclusion about the picture as a whole. Moreover, they have a characteristic way of doing all these things. They construct narratives, and more specifically, narratives that aim to trigger a certain kind of "seeing as" in their audience. This is not to say that all attempts to do philosophy historically follow a single pattern. There are

---

[49] These criteria leave open the possibility that an enterprise can be rational even when it is spectacularly unsuccessful. Most of us would say that Aristotelian science is not a successful account of the way the world is. It is not consistent with observations in which we have a great deal of confidence; it does not cohere well with practices and values we are unwilling to give up; and it relies on concepts (such as substantial forms and final causes) that many of us find unappealing or unintelligible. But it does not follow that this enterprise is non-rational, or that the people who practiced it in its heyday were stupid. It has goals (a systematic description of the natural world), methods (the explanation of change in terms of concepts such as substantial forms and final causes), and values (simplicity and elegance, if necessary at the expense of observational rigor). Aristotelian science is an eminently rational undertaking. It is simply one to which few of us are drawn.

different ways of engaging critically with a picture's representatives, and there are different ways of constructing narratives about past thought. The point is simply that in doing philosophy historically, we do not proceed by happenstance. We use systematic methods, though these methods leave us some latitude in how we use them.

Finally, let us consider values. It seems clear that those who do philosophy historically seek to maximize certain values in the course of pursuing their goal. It may not be possible to give a complete list of these values, but we can, I think, name a few of the most important ones. One, surely, is historical accuracy. Our narratives about the evolution of philosophical pictures must cohere with the historical record as we understand it, or at least not be wildly inconsistent with it. A study of the development of Cartesianism that makes false claims about Descartes's texts, or that pays no attention at all to these texts and the issues they address, would probably be a bad study. Another such value, I suspect, is relevance. Those who do philosophy historically must discover something philosophically significant if their work is to be successful. They must teach us something about topics we care about (or *should* care about). A history of Cartesianism might be relevant in this way if it explored the picture's strength at addressing certain metaphysical questions and weakness at addressing certain ethical questions. Since most philosophers care (or should care) about metaphysics and ethics, a history of this sort would speak to their concerns. Most philosophers do not care particularly about funny hats, so a history that paid obsessive attention to the tendency of Cartesians to wear funny hats would probably not be a success. One other value that those who do philosophy historically seek to maximize is originality – an ability to make us notice things about the past that might otherwise have escaped our attention. Histories that repeat what we already know are not very interesting. The really successful historically minded philosophers are the Hegels, the Derridas, and the Rortys – the ones who get us to look at the past in startling new ways.

Relevance and originality do not seem to pose any special problems. With historical accuracy, matters are more complicated. As we have seen, doing philosophy historically is a hybrid activity. It is creative as well as scholarly: it does not just engage with what past philosophers actually said, but also constructs narratives that construe these philosophers in new and surprising ways. The creative nature of this enterprise is in some tension with the value of historical accuracy. Those who do philosophy historically are always free to play fast and loose with the historical record, and to offer sweeping reinterpretations of the past that are not supported by the evidence. No doubt the enterprise's critics have this fact in mind when they accuse its practitioners of writing sloppy pseudo-histories devoid of real scholarly interest. A particularly clear example of this temptation can be found in the work of Martin Heidegger. Heidegger's lectures on Parmenides, for instance, come close to dismissing the standards of traditional historical inquiry altogether. For example, while discussing the role of the concept of *aletheia* in Parmenides's thought, Heidegger says:

> It will necessarily appear that we are now more than ever Interpreting back into the essence of the Greek *aletheia* something that does not reside in it. Measured against the barriers of the horizon of historiography [*Historie*], and of what is historiographically ascertainable, and of the "facts," everywhere so cherished, what is said here about *aletheia* is "in fact" an Interpretation read into it.[50]

But Heidegger goes on to explain that this charge is unfounded, since his work "by no means desires, in the self-satisfied zeal of erudition, simply to discover what was once meant or was not meant. That could only be a *preparation* for the essential truth, which is 'more alive' than today's much-invoked 'life' and concerns man's historical destiny."[51] In other words, a good reading of Parmenides is one that does justice to the "essential truth" of which Heidegger speaks – and nothing more. Compared to this "essential truth," values such as historical accuracy seem almost quaint. I find this troubling, and I suspect I am not alone. Of course, Heidegger would never claim that his readings are historically accurate. He says again and again that his goal is more creative. But if his project is to be rational, it cannot simply ignore the value of historical accuracy. It may not have the aim of contributing to the historical record, but it must strive to be consistent with this record. I would certainly not claim that Heidegger never strives for historical accuracy. But playing fast and loose with the record is always a temptation in his work, and this, surely, is a problem.[52]

---

[50] Martin Heidegger, *Parmenides*, trans. André Schuwer and Richard Rojcewicz (Bloomington: Indiana University Press, 1992), 134–135.

[51] Heidegger, *Parmenides*, 135.

[52] The difficult question, of course, is what "historical accuracy" could mean in this context. Most often, historical accuracy is understood as a correspondence to the facts: an accurate history is taken to be one that correctly mirrors the past as it was. But this way of understanding accuracy does not sit well with my discussion. When we do philosophy historically, we construct narratives about the past, and as we have seen, narratives do not passively represent facts that exist independently of them. Narratives *disclose* facts: they seek to make us see the world in new ways, not to copy an established truth about things. Thus we cannot determine which narratives are accurate and which are not by comparing them to the facts, since different narratives will disagree about what the facts are. But perhaps we can understand historical accuracy differently. One promising alternative is suggested by recent developments in virtue epistemology. Virtue epistemologists understand epistemic

Of course, that something can be done badly is no reason to stop doing it altogether. Heidegger may dismiss the value of historical accuracy, but there is no reason to think that everyone who does philosophy historically will do so. Heidegger's case does show, however, that this enterprise faces special pitfalls, and that those who engage in it must be vigilant about avoiding them. Perhaps rationality is less a characteristic of this enterprise than an ideal that it must pursue.

TRUTH

We have seen that the narratives we construct while doing philosophy historically should be considered to be arguments. We have also seen that the construction of these arguments is a rational undertaking. Now we should turn to a final question: can these narratives be true? Is it plausible to say that a given narrative about the development of a philosophical picture is true? What would this mean? As I have argued, there is one thing it cannot mean: these narratives cannot be true in the sense of being uniquely *correct*. To say that an assertion or a theory is correct is, I take it, to say that it is an accurate representation of the facts. As Richard Campbell puts it, it is to accept "the medieval definition of truth as *adequatio intellectus et rei* (conformity of understanding and reality)."[53] This definition is closely connected with the idea that truth is timeless – that a true account of something is one "which once attained will stand for all time."[54] Since there is only one reality to which understanding can conform, there can presumably be only one correct account of the world. Narratives about philosophical pictures obviously do not obtain this sort of truth. There is never just one way to tell a story, and it is possible to construct a great many

---

justification in terms of the exercise of specific character traits. What justifies our beliefs is not whether they stand in the right relation to the facts, but whether they arise from the exercise of the right character traits. Linda Zagzebski, for example, defines knowledge as "a state of true belief arising out of acts of intellectual virtue." See Linda Zagzebski, *Virtues of the Mind* (Cambridge: Cambridge University Press, 1996), 106. For Zagzebski, intellectual virtue includes such traits as "[i]ntellectual care, thoroughness, perseverance, fairness, and courage" (108). Perhaps a concern with historical accuracy amounts to the exercise of a similar list of traits. When we say that a historical narrative is inaccurate, perhaps we mean that it fails to proceed in a thorough or careful way. Perhaps it ignores key documents or reads them in a superficial, ill-informed way, for example. Historical work of this sort is often described as "irresponsible," and while this is not the same as saying that it fails to correspond to the facts, it is no less damning an indictment. For a more detailed discussion of responsibility in historical writing, see Jörn Rüsen, "Responsibility and Irresponsibility in Historical Studies: A Critical Consideration of the Ethical Dimension in the Historian's Work," in *The Ethics of History*, ed. David Carr, Thomas Flynn, and Rudolf Makkreel (Evanston: Northwestern University Press, 2004), 195–213.

[53] Campbell, *Truth and Historicity*, 10. [54] Campbell, *Truth and Historicity*, 10.

narratives about past thought that vary enormously but that are all equally plausible. Indeed, as we have seen, there are as many valid narratives about the philosophy of the past as there are legitimate ways of categorizing it. If there is nothing more to truth than correctness, then there seems to be little room for it in the enterprise known as doing philosophy historically.

But perhaps there is more to truth than correctness. Perhaps there is another way of understanding truth, one that leaves open the possibility that narratives can be true without being uniquely correct. A great many philosophers have thought so. In particular, philosophical hermeneutics has articulated a powerful alternative to the view that truth is identical with correctness. According to this tradition, truth is not merely an epistemic notion, but an ontological one as well. Specifically, truth is a *disclosive event*: a happening or occurrence in which the nature of things reveals itself. No one has contributed more to this understanding of truth than Heidegger.[55] In Heidegger's view, the essence of truth is expressed by the ancient Greek word *aletheia*. *Aletheia* literally means "unconcealment," or perhaps more accurately, "removal from hiddenness." Heidegger uses this term to refer to states of affairs in which things disclose themselves, or present themselves as they are. Fundamentally, truth is a state of things, not a property of our assertions about them. It is not *wrong* to say that an assertion is true when we mean that it is correct. But this use of the term is derivative, since we would be unable to make assertions about things if these things were not first available and intelligible to us.

Hans-Georg Gadamer has applied Heidegger's insights more specifically to the case of history. According to Gadamer, a historical narrative may be true, but not in the sense of being a uniquely correct representation of some set of facts about the past. For Gadamer, there literally are no such facts. "Reconstructing the original circumstances" of the past, he argues, "is a futile undertaking in view of the historicity of our being. What is reconstructed, a life brought back from the lone past, is not the original."[56] The truth uncovered by historians has nothing to do with correctness or with the accurate representation of facts. Rather, it is ontological. It is something that *happens*, an event that takes place in the course of historical inquiry.

---

[55] For presentations of Heidegger's view of truth – particularly of how it differs from correctness – see the following: *BT*, §44; *ET*, §9; and Martin Heidegger, "The Origin of the Work of Art," trans. Albert Hofstadter, in *Basic Writings*, ed. David Farrell Krell (San Francisco: Harper San Francisco, 1971). For an excellent discussion of Heidegger's view of truth, see Miguel de Beistegui, *The New Heidegger* (London: Continuum, 2005), 30–59.

[56] Gadamer, *Truth and Method*, 167. Gadamer's target here is the tradition of romantic hermeneutics, as practiced by Schleiermacher and others. For the proponents of this tradition, understanding the past *is* a matter of reconstructing original circumstances in thought.

Gadamer speaks of this event as an "interplay" or a "relationship,"[57] to convey the idea that the study of history is a dialectical interaction between two poles. One is the "past," but a *past for us* – that is, a past that is inevitably colored by our interpretations of it, and that we cannot hope to know in itself.[58] The other pole is the "present," but a *present affected by the past* – that is, a present that is in turn shaped by historical forces, including the very forces it is trying to interpret. Past and present, interpreted and interpreter, mutually shape one another. Truth is what happens when these poles interact in such a way as to bring about a *fusion of horizons*: an overlap between the range of vision afforded by our historical situation and the range of effects brought about by the past. Truth is "essentially, an historically mediated event."[59]

I am not suggesting that we should accept all the details of Heidegger's and Gadamer's accounts of truth. But they show that it is possible to understand truth as something other than correctness. Thus it is possible that the narratives we construct while doing philosophy historically can be true, even if they cannot claim to be uniquely correct. Perhaps these narratives are true in the sense that they are disclosive. Perhaps, as Campbell puts it, they bring about "a revelatory and transforming event [in which] some phenomenon is unveiled so that it shows how it really is."[60] All that this shows, however, is that there is room for truth in the enterprise known as doing philosophy historically, provided we understand truth as Heidegger and Gadamer do. The larger question is whether we *ought* to understand truth as these philosophers do. What reason do we have to conceive of truth as an ontological notion as well as an epistemic one, and specifically, as a disclosive and transformative event? What evidence is there in support of this view?

There seem to be three main answers to this question. First, the view that truth is nothing more than correctness, far from being self-evident, has a relatively short history. Heidegger's historical and etymological studies make a compelling case that in ancient Greek thought, truth was originally understood as an ontological notion, one connected with the uncovering of things out of hiddenness. A cursory glance at the history of philosophy shows that truth has been seen as primarily ontological in other periods as

---

[57] Gadamer, *Truth and Method*, 299.
[58] As Gadamer puts it, "[i]f we are trying to understand a historical phenomenon from the historical distance that is characteristic of our hermeneutical situation, we are always already affected by history. It determines in advance both what seems to us worth inquiring about and what will appear as an object of investigation." See *Truth and Method*, 300.
[59] Gadamer, *Truth and Method*, 299–300.   [60] Campbell, *Truth and Historicity*, 10.

well, from early medieval discussions of the eternal truths to Hegel's claim that "the true is the whole."[61] The identification of truth with correctness looks like a comparatively recent invention, and one that is at odds with the preponderance of serious reflection on the topic. So there is no reason to see it as forced upon us. Second, equating truth with correctness unduly restricts the sphere in which we may speak of things being "true." We routinely predicate truth of things other than assertions and theories. We often say, for example, that great works of art are a source of truth – not that they make true statements, but that they *reveal* or *present us with* truth in some more primordial way. It is difficult to make sense of such talk if we equate truth with correctness. It is much easier to understand it if we see truth as an ontological notion as well, and more specifically as a disclosive or revelatory event. This is a powerful point in favor of this view.[62] Third, and perhaps most importantly, the claim that truth is identical with correctness does not seem intelligible on its own. This understanding of truth seems to presuppose a deeper one – that is, the epistemic interpretation of truth seems to be derived from, and made intelligible by, an ontological one. As Heidegger puts it, "[t]o say that an assertion 'is true' signifies that it uncovers the entity as it is in itself. Such an assertion asserts, points out, 'lets' the entity 'be seen' in its uncoveredness" (*BT*, 261). We could not make correct assertions about the way things really are if things did not present themselves as being a certain way. The idea that truth is the same thing as correctness, far from being the only possible understanding of truth, seems derivative and secondary.[63]

---

[61] G. W. F. Hegel, *Phenomenology of Spirit*, trans. A. V. Miller (Oxford: Oxford University Press, 1977), 11.

[62] Heidegger makes this point. See, for example, *ET*, 3.

[63] One might object that on my view, it is possible for there to be more than one true story about the history of philosophical thought. Indeed, it is possible that two stories could be quite different, perhaps even incompatible, but both true. I grant this, though it sounds counter-intuitive. But it sounds less counter-intuitive once we recognize two things. First, the idea that different narratives might both be true is troubling only if we identify truth with correctness. If we instead see truth as a disclosive or revelatory event, there is no intuitive problem with the existence of multiple true accounts. After all, we often speak of paintings and novels as being sources of truth, though we would not say that any one work of art is uniquely correct. The claim that two different philosophical narratives could both be true should be no more troubling. Second, and more importantly, philosophers of history have long recognized that there are difficulties in claiming that one and only one story about the past is true. The problem is that historical narratives deal not with events *simpliciter*, but with events *as covered by a certain description*, and there is more than one way to describe any given sequence of events. Two histories might describe the past in very different ways, and thus make very different claims about it. This does not mean that only one of them can be called true. History seeks, and can only seek, truth relative to a description. The suggestion that two historical narratives could both be true is no more problematic than the claim that two historians might describe the past in very different ways. For a more detailed discussion of the relation between truth and description in history, see Danto, *Narration and Knowledge*, 218.

None of this means that truth is *not* an epistemic notion. But it does not seem to be an *exclusively* epistemic notion. Thus it makes perfect sense to claim that our narratives about philosophical pictures are true – provided we understand truth more broadly than we might initially be tempted to do. But there is no reason to reject this broader understanding of truth out of hand, and there is considerable prima facie evidence in its favor. To do philosophy historically is to aim at – and perhaps to obtain – truth.

CHAPTER 3

Defending the historical thesis

In the last chapter, I asked a number of questions about doing philosophy historically. I asked how this enterprise works: how one goes about assessing a philosophical picture by tracing its development through time. I also asked whether this enterprise is concerned with arguments, whether it is rational, and whether it aims at truth. But there is an important question I have not yet asked: *should* we do philosophy historically? Do we have good reasons to engage in this enterprise? Is it, perhaps, one that we *must* engage in? If so, why? These are obviously important questions. If we cannot explain why, or whether, we should do philosophy historically, then it is hard to see why we should care about this enterprise, or read the work of those engaged in it. But these questions are also important for another reason. Since at least the early nineteenth century, some philosophers have argued that philosophy is an essentially historical discipline. Doing philosophy, they claim, is inseparable from studying its history. Charles Taylor calls this view "the historical thesis about philosophy."[1] Despite the prevalence of the historical thesis, however, it is notoriously difficult to explain just what it means, or why one might accept it. As a result, the last two centuries have been marked by what Gary Gutting calls a "tedious and inconclusive debate over whether philosophy is essentially historical."[2]

I want to show that there is a better way of understanding this debate. The historical thesis, I argue, is best seen as a reminder of the importance of doing philosophy historically. It is best understood as the claim that the discipline of philosophy consists of more than just ahistorical problem-solving and conventional research into the history of philosophy. It also involves assessing philosophical pictures by tracing their development through time. If this enterprise is not carried out, we will be deprived of

[1] Taylor, "Philosophy and its History," 18.
[2] Gary Gutting, "Review of Brian Leiter (ed.), *The Future for Philosophy.*" *Notre Dame Philosophical Reviews*, 14 Dec. 2005 (Online). Available: http://ndpr.nd.edu/review.cfm?id=5161

something important. In short, another point in favor of my account is that it sheds new light on some old and puzzling questions about the relation between philosophy and its past.

The rest of this chapter falls into four parts. The first deals with the historical thesis as it has traditionally been understood. I examine what philosophers usually mean when they claim that their discipline is inherently historical. I also look at the arguments typically given in defense of this claim, and I try to show that these arguments are not convincing. In the second section, I argue that the reason most discussions of the historical thesis are unsatisfactory is that they take it to be a claim about the link between traditional work in philosophy and traditional work in the history of philosophy. I propose a different way of understanding the historical thesis, and I examine a number of arguments that might be given to defend this modified claim. The third section describes what I think is the best case that can be made for the revised historical thesis, a case that I see exemplified in the work of Jacques Derrida. I argue that Derrida's approach is more appealing than many of its competitors, but that it forces us to reevaluate some of the conventional wisdom about the current state of philosophy. Finally, in the fourth section, I make some transitional remarks about the rest of this book. The second half of the book presents a series of case studies, close readings of figures who actually do philosophy historically. The end of this chapter outlines how these case studies will be organized, and how the rest of the book will unfold.

My goal in this chapter is to describe what *sort* of argument it would take to defend the historical thesis. I do not actually give such an argument myself. As I point out towards the end of the chapter, the best kind of argument we could give for the historical thesis would be a narrative: a sweeping story that shows that when we do *not* trace the development of the major philosophical pictures, we encounter grave problems. Such a narrative would have to be long and ambitious. I cannot tell it here. What I can do is describe some of its main features, and show that there is good reason to think that it can be told.

THE "HISTORICAL THESIS ABOUT PHILOSOPHY"

No one would deny that it can be helpful for philosophers to be familiar with philosophy's past. The history of philosophy can be a useful tool in a number of ways. It can be a source of inspiration: it can expose us to questions we might not have asked on our own, and methods we might not otherwise have thought to use. Studying the philosophers of the past can also sharpen one's philosophical skills. Reading Kant or Aristotle offers good practice at analyzing arguments and drawing careful distinctions, skills that are essential for doing good philosophical work of our own. And of course, when we study the history of philosophy, we may find what we think are the right answers to our own questions. As Jonathan Bennett puts it, "philosophy's past … may lead us straight to philosophical truths."[3] Some philosophers, however, go further, and argue that a familiarity with the history of philosophy is not just valuable, but necessary. They claim that philosophy is an *essentially* historical enterprise, and that it is *impossible* to do it properly without studying its past. None of the above considerations goes so far. The history of philosophy may be a valuable source of inspiration and training, but it is clearly not the only one. It is not *necessary* that we get our ideas and sharpen our skills in this way. Similarly, philosophy's past *may* lead us straight to philosophical truths, but it is surely not the only way of discovering these truths. If we are clever enough or imaginative enough, we may stumble upon them on our own. So we can distinguish two different ways of thinking about the value of the history of philosophy. According to the first, studying philosophy's past is instrumentally valuable. It helps us do certain things, but we could, at least in principle, do these things in other ways. According to the second, knowledge of the history of philosophy is intrinsically valuable. It is not just an instrument, but offers something we cannot get in any other way. It is this stronger view that Taylor calls the historical thesis about philosophy. It is, in short, the view that "[p]hilosophy and the history of philosophy are one," such that we "cannot do the first without also doing the second."[4]

Philosophers have defended the historical thesis since at least the early nineteenth century.[5] Its best-known proponent is Hegel, who claims that "the study of the history of philosophy is the study of philosophy itself."[6]

---

[3] Jonathan Bennett, "Critical Notice of D. J. O'Connor (ed.), *A Critical History of Western Philosophy*." *Mind* 75 (1966), 437.

[4] Taylor, "Philosophy and its History," 17.

[5] I say "at least" because some philosophers seem to have defended the historical thesis even before the nineteenth century. Interestingly enough, one of them is Kant. In the first *Critique*, Kant argues that once the critical project has determined the proper limits of reason, it will have to construct a *history of pure reason*, a history that discusses earlier philosophies from a critical standpoint. A history of pure reason is required by reason's need for systematicity. Reason seeks to make our knowledge of past philosophy systematic by identifying the ideas in accordance with which its various stages have been articulated, and then combining these ideas into a whole. See *KRV*, A852/B880. While the first *Critique* does not actually construct a history of pure reason, some of Kant's other texts come close to doing so. See, for example, the *Lectures on Metaphysics*, trans. and ed. Karl Ameriks and Steve Naragon (Cambridge: Cambridge University Press, 1997), 121–125.

[6] G. W. F. Hegel, *Lectures on the History of Philosophy*, Volume I, trans. E. S. Haldane (Lincoln: University of Nebraska Press, 1995), 30.

For Hegel, the history of philosophy simply *is* an empirical manifestation of philosophy's conceptual content. To study one, therefore, is to study the other. The historical thesis is also closely associated with twentieth-century continental philosophy. Heidegger, for example, argues that "[w]hatever and however we may try to think, we think within the sphere of tradition" (*ID*, 41). We cannot do philosophy without continually revisiting the history of philosophy, and making a "reciprocal rejoinder" (*BT*, 438) to it. More recent continental philosophy has tended to follow Heidegger in this – so much so that it is sometimes described as dealing not with problems, but with proper names.[7] Derrida argues that even those who would criticize the philosophical tradition have no choice but to revisit this tradition again and again. "There is," Derrida claims, "no sense in doing without the concepts of metaphysics in order to shake metaphysics. We have no language – no syntax and no lexicon – which is foreign to this history."[8] Even Emmanuel Levinas, who is by no means preoccupied with historical matters, describes the history of philosophy as a "drama … in which new interlocutors always enter who have to restate, but in which the former ones take up the floor to answer in the interpretations they arouse."[9] As different as these thinkers are, they all endorse the historical thesis about philosophy.

Why? Why would one think that philosophy and its history are one and the same, and that we cannot do one without also doing the other? On the surface, this claim looks counter-intuitive, even bizarre. Philosophers typically see themselves as being in the business of solving problems. They want to answer questions: what is the best form of government? How is the mind related to the body? And it is far from clear that answering these questions requires one to know about earlier attempts to answer them. Other problem-solving disciplines do not privilege their histories in this way. Mathematicians and physicists do not think they need to study the histories of their disciplines in order to do their own work properly. What matters to them is the state of their disciplines *today*: the history that brought them to that point is no longer relevant. Indeed, it may be dangerous to be too concerned with the histories of mathematics or physics, since these histories presumably contain as much error as they do truth. Those who simply want to answer their own philosophical questions are bound to

---

[7] This way of putting it seems to have been coined by Richard Rorty. See his *Contingency, Irony, and Solidarity* (Cambridge: Cambridge University Press, 1989), 81.

[8] Jacques Derrida, "Structure, Sign and Play in the Discourse of the Human Sciences," in *Writing and Difference*, trans. Alan Bass (Chicago: University of Chicago Press, 1978), 280.

[9] Emmanuel Levinas, *Otherwise Than Being or Beyond Essence*, trans. Alphonso Lingis (Dordrecht: Kluwer, 1991), 20.

have similar concerns about the history of philosophy. At best, it looks dispensable: a source of ideas that the clever and the imaginative can find in other ways. At worst, it looks like a repository for errors. So why have so many great philosophers maintained that the study of the history of philosophy is not just valuable, but indispensable?

Sometimes, the historical thesis is tied to a larger philosophical agenda. It is sometimes supported with some very specific claims about what philosophy is or what sorts of things it studies. Hegel, for one, seems to adopt this approach. Hegel argues that philosophy is inherently historical because of the nature of its subject matter, which he variously calls "spirit," "the True," and "the Absolute." Spirit, Hegel claims, is essentially developmental. It is "purposive activity,"[10] and it "is actual only in so far as it is the movement of positing itself."[11] This means that philosophers cannot simply study what spirit is, once and for all. They must trace its development – that is, study how the nature of spirit is expressed in different ways at different stages in the history of philosophy. Heidegger also ties the historical thesis to a larger philosophical agenda. He takes philosophy to be "the science of Being"[12] – not just the study of some particular type of beings, but a reflection on "the meaning of Being in general" and "the problems arising from that question."[13] The history of philosophy, however, has forgotten the question of Being, and has spread the view that inquiry into the meaning of Being is fruitless, unnecessary, and "an error of method" (*BT*, 21). Philosophy today must actively undo this forgetting by exploring the ways in which past thinkers have forgotten and covered over the question of Being. Our "hardened tradition," Heidegger argues, "must be loosened up, and the concealments which it has brought about must be dissolved. We understand this task as one in which … we are to *destroy* the traditional content of ancient ontology" (*BT*, 45). For Heidegger, as for Hegel, the historical thesis is inseparable from a larger philosophical agenda. And of course, we will have good reason to accept the historical thesis only if we also accept the larger agenda.

Other philosophers defend the historical thesis differently. They give arguments that are more self-contained, arguments that do not require us to share the metaphysical and methodological commitments of a Hegel or a Heidegger. Edwin Curley, for example, argues that the process of posing

---

[10] Hegel, *Phenomenology of Spirit*, 12.   [11] Hegel, *Phenomenology of Spirit*, 10.
[12] Martin Heidegger, *The Basic Problems of Phenomenology*, trans. Albert Hofstadter (Bloomington: Indiana University Press, 1988), 11.
[13] Heidegger, *Basic Problems*, 16.

philosophical questions requires considerable familiarity with the history of philosophy. He claims that "making progress towards solving philosophical problems requires a good grasp of the range of possible solutions to those problems and of the arguments that motivate alternative positions, a grasp we can only have if we understand well philosophy's past."[14] Note that it is not just *solving* philosophical problems that requires a knowledge of philosophy's past; it is *making progress* towards solving these problems. Note as well that it is not enough to be familiar with the history of our own philosophical positions. We must be more broadly knowledgeable about the past, understanding "alternative positions" and the "arguments that motivate" them. Curley gives two reasons for this claim. The first is that philosophers typically argue for their own positions by citing a lack of alternatives. Either explicitly or implicitly, they claim that their solution to a philosophical problem is the only plausible one that has been advanced so far. Consider Bertrand Russell's classic article "On Denoting." This article offers a highly original theory of reference, and defends it by claiming that no rival theory – Meinong's, for example – copes as well with puzzling sentences about the present King of France.[15] Clearly, though, this strategy is only as sound as Russell's grasp of the alternatives. If some other theory of reference actually *is* just as successful in dealing with the hard cases, then Russell's claim to be offering the only plausible theory falls flat. And of course, our contemporaries are not the only source of alternative theories. The history of philosophy is full of them. Thus in order to advance a theory and claim it is the best one available, we must be familiar enough with the history of philosophy to be confident in this claim. If we are not, then we will be supporting our views with bad arguments.

The second reason Curley gives is that early formulations of a position tend to be more perspicuous than later ones. We can, of course, defend a position even if we are ignorant of earlier versions of it. We might be drawn to a Humean account of causation despite never having read Hume. We might even develop a more sophisticated Humean account than the one Hume gives, precisely because we stand on the shoulders of philosophers from the last two hundred years. But according to Curley, if we never read Hume's account of causation, we will miss something crucial. Hume's account is likely to be more informative and more philosophically valuable than that of any of his successors. After all, Hume understands the debate in

---

[14] Edwin Curley, "Dialogues With the Dead." *Synthese* 67 (1986), 33.
[15] Bertrand Russell, "On Denoting," in *Logic and Knowledge*, ed. Robert Charles Marsh (London: Routledge, 1956), 47.

which he is engaged in ways his philosophical heirs might not. He knows what problem he is trying to solve, and what alternative solutions are available to him. As a result, he "just may have a better grasp of the fundamental issues"[16] than a contemporary Humean. The contemporary Humean might not see what is really at stake in Hume's theory of causation. She might be so familiar with this theory, so convinced that she understands it, that she fails to state it "as accurately or fully or suggestively" as Hume does.[17] Hume himself "cannot take so much for granted"[18] as the contemporary Humean, and so is likely to do a better job of stating and defending his position. Lesley Cohen echoes Curley's point, claiming that it is the history of philosophy that "establishes the significance"[19] of the problems we wish to solve. "Not to know the history of philosophy," Cohen argues, "is not to understand *why* the questions we are endeavoring to answer are worth answering – or asking."[20] And understanding the significance of our questions is a crucial step towards answering them. That is why we must study philosophy's past.

Much of this seems right. We are likely to give better arguments for our positions if we are familiar with the full range of historical alternatives. Early formulations of a theory probably do tend to take less for granted than later ones, and so are likely to display a better grasp of the issues at stake. And philosophers who study the history of philosophy are likely to understand the significance of their questions better than those who do not. But does any of this show that philosophy is *essentially* historical, or that it is *necessary* to study its past? I do not think so. The considerations advanced by Curley and Cohen show that it is often helpful to be familiar with philosophy's past. But they fall well short of showing that it is necessary. The problem is that Curley and Cohen rely on generalizations about what might happen, or what often happens. Curley, for example, points out that those who are ignorant of the history of philosophy might overlook plausible alternatives to their own views. That is surely true. But they might not. In principle, there seems to be no reason that a clever, creative philosopher could not imagine all the plausible alternatives to her views on her own, armchair-style. This may be unlikely, but it is possible. And if it is possible, then finding alternatives through historical study cannot be necessary. Similarly, it is no doubt true that a contemporary philosopher might fail to state a

---

[16] Curley, "Dialogues With the Dead," 45.
[17] Curley, "Dialogues With the Dead," 45.   [18] Curley, "Dialogues With the Dead," 45.
[19] Lesley Cohen, "Doing Philosophy is Doing its History." *Synthese* 67 (1986), 53.
[20] Cohen, "Doing Philosophy is Doing its History," 53.

Humean theory of causation as fully or suggestively as Hume does. But she might not. In principle, there is nothing preventing a clever, imaginative philosopher from articulating a version of the Humean theory that is superior to Hume's in every way. And if it is possible for her to do so, then studying Hume cannot be truly necessary. For the same reason, it cannot be necessary to reach an understanding of the significance of our philosophical questions through historical study. It may be the most common way to do so, perhaps even the only way of which most of us are capable. But that is not the same thing as saying that it is necessary.

It seems, then, that the most common ways of defending the historical thesis are not convincing. Why not?

THE HISTORICAL THESIS RECONSIDERED

The arguments we have been considering make an assumption. When they speak of a link between doing philosophy and studying its history, they take both of these terms in their traditional senses. They take "doing philosophy" to be the process of trying to answer our own questions or solve our own problems – questions about the best form of government or the relation between mind and body, for example. Similarly, they take "studying its history" to mean conventional scholarship in the history of philosophy – the attempt to give accurate reconstructions of what past thinkers really thought. In other words, these arguments claim that in order to make progress towards solving our own philosophical problems, we must engage in, or at least be familiar with, scholarly work on the views of earlier philosophers. It is not surprising that it is hard to give a compelling argument for this claim. Solving problems and reconstructing the views of past thinkers are distinct activities. Doing the latter can certainly help us to do the former, by sharpening our skills or exposing us to new ideas. But it is hard to see why doing the former could *require* us to do the latter. It is hard to see why a solution to a philosophical problem would *have* to draw on scholarly work in the history of philosophy. Problems can be solved in all sorts of ways, and it is hard to see why the resources offered by the history of philosophy *necessarily* play a role. If the historical thesis is taken to be a claim about traditional work in philosophy and traditional work in the history of philosophy, then there seems to be little reason to think it is true.

But the historical thesis can be understood differently. Perhaps it should be seen as a claim about doing philosophy historically. Perhaps it should be seen as a claim that the enterprise we call philosophy involves a number of different activities. One, surely, is the process of solving philosophical problems, of trying to answer our questions about the good, the true, and the beautiful. Another activity, important but distinct, is the attempt to understand the views of past philosophers. Yet a third activity is doing philosophy historically, or assessing philosophical pictures by tracing their development. On this view, to say that philosophy is essentially historical is to say that reflecting on pictures is just as much a part of the enterprise we call philosophy as the other two activities. It is to say that one of the functions philosophy performs is to reflect on and evaluate large-scale views of reality, views that cannot be reduced to any particular theory. In other words, it is to say that the activities of solving philosophical problems and reconstructing the positions of earlier thinkers do not exhaust what philosophy is. The reason they do not exhaust it is that there is a sort of object – the philosophical picture – that these activities do not study. Note that this claim concerns philosophy as an institution or a discipline. It does not say that every individual who poses philosophical questions, or who tries to understand the views of earlier thinkers, must also trace the development of philosophical pictures. There is no contradiction in an individual engaging in one of these activities while ignoring the others – though individuals who have a strong interest in one of these activities but none in the other two will probably be rare. Note as well that this claim is not an empirical one. It does not say that wherever we find people doing philosophy or studying its history, we will also find people doing philosophy historically. It is a claim about the meaning of a concept: namely, that the enterprise we call philosophy may be broken into several sub-activities, one of which is the activity of assessing pictures by tracing their development. There might well be times and places in which no one bothers to do philosophy historically, though there is great interest in posing philosophical questions and reconstructing the views of earlier thinkers. But something similar is true of most activities. No doubt there are times and places in which political leaders do not care about the interests of their constituents, even though doing so is almost certainly an essential part of governing. It is one thing to ask what a concept means, and another to ask how common its instantiations are.

When the historical thesis is reinterpreted in the way I have suggested, it seems more plausible. As I have argued, it is hard to see why solving a philosophical problem could require one to draw on scholarly work on earlier thinkers. But it is not hard to imagine that the discipline of philosophy might include, as one of its constituent activities, the assessment of large-scale views of reality. Indeed, this seems to be one of the services we expect philosophy to perform. We expect philosophy to give a general account of what the world is like, and reflecting on our pictures of reality is clearly part of this process. The reinterpreted historical thesis also seems more in keeping with the spirit of the work of those who say that philosophy is essentially historical. It is certainly more consistent with the spirit of Hegel's work. When Hegel says that "the study of the history of philosophy is the study of philosophy itself,"[21] he clearly does not mean that doing philosophy is the same thing as giving accurate reconstructions of the views of earlier thinkers. On the contrary, he mocks those who treat philosophy's past as "a string of bald opinions,"[22] a series of views to be reconstructed. For Hegel, engaging with the history of philosophy is a matter of uncovering the reason in it, and this in turn is a matter of uncovering the principles, the broad views of reality, that past philosophies embody. Studying ancient philosophy, for example, is a matter of uncovering the general metaphysical principles embodied by its major stages. Thus Hegel's own historical studies tell us that Eleatic philosophy "apprehends the Absolute as being,"[23] that Aristotle understands it as "*energeia*,"[24] and so on. This approach has much more in common with the business of assessing philosophical pictures than it does with reproducing "a string of bald opinions." So when the historical thesis is reinterpreted in the way I have proposed, it seems more plausible.

But is it *true*? Is it really the case that we *must* do philosophy historically – that examining philosophical pictures is an essential part of the enterprise we call philosophy? What sort of argument could we give for this reinterpreted claim? One strategy would be to do what Hegel and Heidegger do. We could argue that the business of doing philosophy historically is required by some larger philosophical agenda, perhaps by our metaphysical views. We could, for example, claim that there is something metaphysically significant about the fact that different pictures prevail at different times and develop in certain ways. We could argue that the existence of different pictures shows us something about the nature of reality. Thus if we want to understand reality – and most philosophers do – we need to pay attention to the ways in which pictures develop. Louis Dupré advances an argument of this sort. Dupré claims that there is an important metaphysical lesson to be

---

[21] Hegel, *Lectures on the History of Philosophy*, 30.
[22] Consider the following passage: "If the history of philosophy merely represented various opinions in array, whether they be of God or of natural and spiritual things existent, it would be a most superfluous and tiresome science, no matter what might be brought forward as derived from such thought-activity and learning. What can be more useless than to learn a string of bald opinions, and what more unimportant?" See Hegel, *Lectures on the History of Philosophy*, 12.
[23] G. W. F. Hegel, *Encyclopedia Logic*, trans. T. F. Geraets, W. A. Suchting, and H. S. Harris (Indianapolis: Hackett Publishing Company, 1991), 138.
[24] Hegel, *Encyclopedia Logic*, 215.

learned from the fact that different "world pictures"[25] capture our attention at different times and under different conditions. This lesson is that *novelty* is an important characteristic of reality. We must, Dupré argues, "attribute to the idea of the novel a permanence which historical reality does not possess in itself. Metaphysical novelty discloses hitherto unknown aspects of man's being in the world in such a manner that the disclosure will never again cease to reveal."[26] Dupré's claim is that human beings invariably understand themselves and their world with various conceptual frameworks, or various pictures of reality. As time passes, these frameworks change: new ones are developed, while old ones are altered or discarded. But although pictures are constantly being developed and discarded, they teach lessons of enduring significance. Consider the view of reality articulated by Ptolemy. It is no longer taken seriously as a scientific theory, but it "has led to philosophical reflections of a permanent significance in Aquinas, Dante, and, before Ptolemy himself, Aristotle."[27] Ptolemy's picture therefore helps disclose new aspects of human existence. It "sheds a new and *definitive* light on the meaning of being in the world,"[28] and for that reason, it will never cease to be philosophically significant. The lesson here is that philosophical pictures should not be seen as mere lenses through which we view, with varying degrees of accuracy, an unchanging reality. As our frameworks change, reality changes with them. "Cultural changes," as Dupré puts it, "have a definitive and irreversible impact that transforms the very essence of reality. Not merely our thinking about the real changes: reality itself changes as we think about it differently."[29] When we study the evolution of philosophical pictures, we see reality changing. We see a reality marked by continual novelty, a reality that changes along with our conceptual frameworks. Doing philosophy historically brings us face to face with "metaphysical novelty."[30] It therefore teaches an invaluable lesson about the makeup of reality.

What should we make of Dupré's argument? It has obvious appeal. Dupré defends the historical thesis on metaphysical grounds. He claims that we must do philosophy historically because this enterprise can show us something important about the nature of reality. Most philosophers are

[25] Louis Dupré, "Is the History of Philosophy Philosophy?" *Review of Metaphysics* 42 (1989), 480.
[26] Dupré, "Is the History of Philosophy Philosophy?" 478.
[27] Dupré, "Is the History of Philosophy Philosophy?" 480.
[28] Dupré, "Is the History of Philosophy Philosophy?" 481.
[29] Louis Dupré, *Passage to Modernity* (New Haven: Yale University Press, 1993), 6. Dupré also puts it this way: "The changing symbols of culture determine not only consciousness: they affect the manifestation of Being itself." See Dupré, "Is the History of Philosophy Philosophy?" 469.
[30] Dupré, "Is the History of Philosophy Philosophy?" 478.

interested in the nature of reality, and an enterprise that promises to teach metaphysical lessons is bound to seem worthwhile to them. To be sure, not all philosophers will be drawn to the *type* of metaphysical lesson Dupré expects this enterprise to teach. The conclusions he reaches by studying pictures – that novelty is an important characteristic of the real, that reality changes as our theories about it do – are speculative metaphysics of an especially heady and ambitious type. Still, Dupré's overall strategy is bound to appeal to many, even if his precise conclusions do not. The important question, however, is whether Dupré's argument shows that doing philosophy historically is *necessary*. Suppose we grant that tracing the development of pictures teaches important metaphysical lessons. Is that enough to show that we must engage in this activity, or that it is just as much a part of philosophy as trying to solve our own philosophical problems? I do not think so. At best, Dupré shows that studying philosophical pictures is *one way* of learning certain metaphysical lessons. Nothing in his argument shows that it is the only way. Could we not, in principle, learn these lessons differently? Perhaps we can discover that reality changes along with our conceptual frameworks simply by reflecting on the matter in our armchairs. Perhaps we can learn that novelty is an important feature of the real by reading Whitehead. As far as I can tell, nothing in Dupré's account rules out these possibilities. So while Dupré goes some way towards explaining why it is valuable to do philosophy historically, he stops short of explaining why it is necessary.

There is another problem with Dupré's account. Dupré argues that by tracing the appearance and the disappearance of conceptual frameworks, we discover the importance of metaphysical novelty. We make this discovery because we *see* reality change as our thinking about it does. As we study the rise and fall of the Ptolemaic view of the world, for example, we see the world change too. The problem is that the conclusion Dupré would have us reach from this process is universal: that reality is, always and everywhere, characterized by the prominence of novelty. But the evidence that leads us to this conclusion is inevitably particular: evidence about the rise and fall of this or that particular picture, or some finite number of pictures. And particular bits of historical evidence do not seem capable of supporting universal claims about the nature of reality as such. They can show that novelty played an important role in the shift from one picture to another, or in several such shifts. But they do not seem capable of showing that reality always and everywhere has such and such a character. Of course, it is possible that Dupré intends his claims about novelty to be admonitions to view reality in a certain way, to use an expression I introduced in Chapter 2.

Perhaps they are not descriptions of how the world is, but attempts to trigger a change in what we see the world *as*. If that is the case, however, then the claim that doing philosophy historically teaches us about the nature of reality falls flat. If Dupré's claims are metaphysical propositions, then they are inadequately supported by evidence. If they are not, then they cannot do the job Dupré wants them to do.

Dupré's strategy, then, seems problematic. What other approach could we use? Perhaps we could ground the historical thesis not in a piece of speculative metaphysics, but in an account of human nature. Perhaps there are aspects of human nature that force us to do philosophy historically. Perhaps some side of our being is such that, if we wish to do philosophy at all, we must also study the development of philosophical pictures. Charles Taylor advances a view of this sort. As we have seen, Taylor argues that "[p]hilosophy and the history of philosophy are one," and that we "cannot do the first without also doing the second."[31] Importantly, he understands the historical thesis much as I do. For Taylor, to say that we must study the history of philosophy is to say that we must reflect on the pictures or conceptual frameworks we use to make sense of reality, and that we must do so by tracing their development through time.[32] The reason we must do so is that it is the only way of remedying certain defects in human nature. In Taylor's view, the side of human nature that forces us to do philosophy historically is a specific type of forgetfulness. We tend to organize experience by means of pictures or conceptual frameworks: sets of assumptions about what the world is like and how we fit into it. For example, since the heyday of early modern philosophy, Westerners have tended to filter reality through a framework that Taylor calls the "epistemological model."[33] This framework assumes that "our awareness of the world … is to be understood in terms of our forming representations – be they ideas in the mind, states of the brain, sentences we accept, or whatever – of 'external' reality."[34] The epistemological model has well-documented problems, and, over the last two centuries, philosophers of many different stripes have tried to criticize or reject it. But it is hard to make people see its problems, because it has become so deeply rooted in our thought that we see it as the unquestioned truth about things, rather than as one possible model among many. According to Taylor, reflecting critically on such models is one of the main tasks of philosophy. Philosophy "essentially involves, among other

---

[31] Taylor, "Philosophy and its History," 17.
[32] Taylor explicitly uses the term "picture." See "Philosophy and its History," 21.
[33] Taylor, "Philosophy and its History," 18.   [34] Taylor, "Philosophy and its History," 18.

things, the redescription of what we are doing, thinking, believing, assuming in such a way as to bring our reasons to light more perspicuously, or else make the alternatives more apparent."[35] Redescribing a framework such as the epistemological model involves coming to see it as one possibility among many, rather than as the obvious truth about things. In Taylor's view, the way to do this is to trace its history. We show that the model developed in a contingent way from a contingent starting point, and that as a result, alternatives are possible.

Taylor's claim is not just that those philosophers who have criticized the epistemological model – Hegel, Heidegger, and Merleau-Ponty,[36] for example – have happened to appeal to historical considerations while making their cases. His claim is that historical study is an indispensable remedy for the particular kind of forgetting to which conceptual frameworks are vulnerable. The reason these frameworks resist criticism is that they become embedded in our practices. They become organizing principles for a wide range of important activities, and as a result, we become too close to them to see that they are optional. The epistemological model, for example, "became embedded in our manner of doing natural science, in our technology, in some at least of the dominant ways in which we construe political life (the atomistic ones), later in various of our ways of healing, regimenting, organizing people in society, and in other spheres too numerous to mention."[37] We see this model as the unquestioned truth about things because we live in ways that presuppose it. As long as we adopt the attitude of unreflective practitioners in these ways of life, we will be unable to break the model's grip on us. Historical study plays an indispensable role in helping us adopt a new attitude on these practices. Let me quote Taylor at some length here:

What we need to do is get over the presumption of the unique conceivability of the embedded picture. But to do this, we have to take a new stance towards our practices. Instead of just living in them and taking their implicit construal of things as the way things are, we have to understand how they have come to be, how they came to embed a certain view of things. In other words, in order to undo the forgetting, we have to articulate for ourselves how it happened, to become aware of the way a picture slid from the status of discovery to that of inarticulate assumption, a fact too obvious to mention. But that means a genetic account; and one which retrieves the formulations through which the embedding in practice took place.

---

[35] Taylor, "Philosophy and its History," 18.
[36] These are Taylor's examples. See "Philosophy and its History," 19.
[37] Taylor, "Philosophy and its History," 20.

Freeing ourselves from the presumption of uniqueness requires uncovering the origins. That is why philosophy is inescapably historical.[38]

In other words, to loosen a model's grip on us, we must engage in what Husserl calls a *Rückfrage*, or "return inquiry." We must not only rediscover that the model has alternatives. We must tell the story of how we came to *forget* that it has alternatives.

Taylor's approach is attractive. It seems much easier to ground the historical thesis on facts of human nature than on a theory of the ultimate makeup of reality. Claims about how human beings are seem much easier to justify than the claims of speculative metaphysics, such as the claim that metaphysical novelty is an important characteristic of the real. Human behavior can be observed, and generalizations about it can be confirmed or disconfirmed. Moreover, the particular claims Taylor makes about human beings seem plausible enough. We do tend to forget the foundational assumptions that guide our thinking. We do fail to reflect on the pictures that hold us in their sway. We do find it useful to undo our forgetting by retelling the histories of our practices and institutions. All of these points are well taken. But I doubt that any of them can do the work Taylor wants them to do. Remember that Taylor wants to draw some strong conclusions about doing philosophy historically: that "philosophy is *inescapably* historical,"[39] that he does "not think it is contingent that one has recourse to history,"[40] and that "it is *essential* to an adequate understanding of certain problems, questions, issues, that one understand them genetically."[41] At the same time, Taylor wants to derive these conclusions from some facts about human beings that seem quite contingent: that we forget the origins of conceptual frameworks, that we forget them by embedding them in our practices, that philosophers find this forgetting unacceptable, and that we can overcome the forgetting by telling the story of how it happened. All of these facts seem too contingent to show that doing philosophy historically is truly necessary. What reason is there to think that human beings inevitably forget the origins of their frameworks, and inevitably feel the need to overcome this forgetting? It might be the case that this often happens, or even that it has always happened in our experience. But this is quite different from saying that it *must* happen, that it must always and everywhere be so. It is far from clear that these generalizations

---

[38] Taylor, "Philosophy and its History," 21.
[39] Taylor, "Philosophy and its History," 21. My emphasis.
[40] Taylor, "Philosophy and its History," 19.
[41] Taylor, "Philosophy and its History," 17. My emphasis.

from our experience can justify universal conclusions about how philosophy must "inescapably" be done. As Taylor points out, what seems inescapably true to us is often an assumption we do not question because it is embedded in our practices. How do we know that Taylor's assumptions about forgetting are any different? For that matter, what reason is there to think that philosophers inevitably try to overcome their forgetting, or that they inevitably find historical study an effective way of doing so? Is it not at least as likely that these seeming inevitabilities result from our own contingent frameworks for understanding philosophy and history?

Taylor seems to recognize these problems, and this may be the reason his description of philosophy contains some surprising language. He says, for example, that philosophy "*essentially* involves, among other things, the redescription of what we are doing, thinking, believing, assuming."[42] This claim, if true, would go some way towards explaining why we must do philosophy historically. If redescription is essential to philosophy, then it is easy to see why we cannot stop redescribing the discipline's past. But this claim seems to be in tension with the rest of Taylor's position. If our thinking receives such strong guidance from our conceptual frameworks – frameworks that rise and fall contingently – then it is hard to see how philosophy can *essentially* involve anything. Philosophy might well be understood to be one thing under one framework, but something else under another. Surely the historical record bears this out. Far from being a timelessly identical notion, philosophy has meant different things in different settings, and has studied many different things using many different methods. The claim that it has an unchanging essence, and that this essence involves redescription, just does not seem plausible.

In short, neither of these arguments for the revised historical thesis looks promising. Perhaps there *is* no good argument for it. Perhaps we should stop looking. We might even conclude that the historical thesis is indefensible, and that there is no good reason to accept it. But this conclusion would be too hasty. We should remember a point made by Curley: often, what justifies a philosophical position is a lack of alternatives. We sometimes endorse a position for which we lack sound arguments because all of its alternatives are obviously worse. Can we justify the historical thesis in this way?

A DIFFERENT STRATEGY

Despite the problems with his approach, Taylor puts his finger on an important fact. Philosophers do tend to forget the foundational assumptions

---

[42] Taylor, "Philosophy and its History," 18. My emphasis.

that guide their thinking. This may not be a necessary or universal truth, and it is clearly not enough to show that it is *necessary* to do philosophy historically. But it strongly suggests that when philosophers do not study the histories of their conceptual frameworks, they tend to get into trouble. Perhaps this is how we should think about the need to do philosophy historically. Perhaps we should see this enterprise as one to which we are driven by the barrenness of the alternatives. This view, if we adopted it, would be more inductive than deductive. It would be based on the idea that philosophers have tried to avoid doing philosophy historically, and have run into problems – problems more serious than the lack of a positive argument demonstrating the necessity of this enterprise. What demands it is simply a lack of promising alternatives.

There seems to be an example of this approach in the early work of Jacques Derrida. As I have pointed out, Derrida practices a type of philosophy that insists on revisiting the work of earlier thinkers again and again. He seems to think that what justifies this approach is simply the bankruptcy of its alternatives. An instructive text here is Derrida's commentary on Husserl's *Origin of Geometry*, a text that has long been recognized as playing a crucial role in Derrida's development.[43] Derrida examines Husserl's attempt to trace the origin of geometrical claims – that is, Husserl's search for the meaning-giving acts that put us in contact with geometrical objects. In doing this, Derrida raises the larger question of what is involved in understanding something in light of its origins or first principles. He considers several possible answers to this question. One is that understanding a geometrical proposition involves nothing more than tracing it back to an origin at a particular point in time. On this view, understanding the claim is identical with learning about its discovery: rethinking the process through which "some undiscoverable Thales of geometry"[44] first intuited it. Derrida rejects this view. If we wish to understand a geometrical claim, it is not enough to uncover its origin in time. The reason is that true geometrical propositions are necessarily and universally true, and the fact that one person first intuited them in such and such a way does not prove that all other thinkers must intuit them in the same way. If it did, geometry "would be *absolutely bound to the psychological life of a factual individual*, to that of a factual community, indeed to a particular moment of that life. It would

---

[43] See, for example, Rudolf Bernet, "On Derrida's 'Introduction' to Husserl's *Origin of Geometry*," in *Derrida and Deconstruction*, ed. Hugh Silverman (London: Routledge, 1989), 139–153. See also Joshua Kates, *Essential History: Jacques Derrida and the Development of Deconstruction* (Evanston: Northwestern University Press, 2005), 53–82.

[44] Husserl, *Crisis*, 369.

become neither omnitemporal, nor intelligible for all: it would not be what it is."[45] Factual history is not enough. The origin of geometry must be "*nonempirical.*"[46]

Another possible view is that understanding a geometrical claim has nothing to do with its history. On this view, the only "origin" such a claim can have is a transcendental one: namely, the set of conditions that make it possible to intuit the claim, conditions that hold for all would-be geometrical thinkers in all places at all times. For example, since geometrical objects are spatially extended, any creature that thinks about them must have a cognitive apparatus capable of representing objects in space. On the view being considered, possibility conditions of this sort are the only origin geometrical claims have. The factual history of a claim's discovery is irrelevant. Derrida rejects this view as well. We cannot equate a claim's origin with its discovery in time, but neither can we exclude history altogether. Excluding history rules out the possibility that geometrical entities might be actively constituted by a subject or a community of subjects. And Derrida, like Husserl, insists that geometrical entities *are* constituted in this way, that subjectivity contributes something to them. Geometrical thinking "brings about an essence which did not exist before the ideation. This ideation is therefore more *historical.*"[47] So the origin of geometry must involve more than possibility conditions, as I have described them. It must also involve the actions of what Joshua Kates calls "a community of transcendental inquirers [that] stand over against them."[48] In short, we must understand the origin of geometry as both transcendental and historical, both constituting and constituted. But these notions seem opposed. How can we bring them together?

Derrida's answer is that the origin of geometry must be a peculiar and paradoxical sort of origin. It must be an origin that is presupposed by the existence of geometrical claims, in the same way that any transcendental condition is presupposed by that which it conditions. But it must also be an origin that literally *is not*: an origin that is not a fact or anything else that could ever be present. If it ever did exist, if it ever were made present, then the origin of geometry would be identical with a particular state of affairs or historical event. And as Derrida argues, this would be incompatible with the necessity and universality of geometrical claims. So we must understand the

---

[45] Jacques Derrida, *Edmund Husserl's* Origin of Geometry: *An Introduction*, trans. John P. Leavey (Lincoln: University of Nebraska Press, 1978), 77.
[46] Derrida, *Edmund Husserl's* Origin of Geometry, 38.
[47] Derrida, *Edmund Husserl's* Origin of Geometry, 135.   [48] Kates, *Essential History*, 62.

origin of geometry as an origin that retreats from every attempt to make it present to consciousness, even as it is presupposed by what *is* present. To use Derrida's well-known phrase, we must understand it as an origin that is "present only in being deferred-delayed (*différant*)."[49] This origin is presupposed by our experience, and we must view it as a condition that makes our experience possible. But our search for this origin, though necessary, can never be brought to completion. A "definite arrival"[50] at it is always to come. So how do we relate to this origin? In Derrida's view, we do so precisely by returning to earlier attempts to make it fully present, and showing that they fail to accomplish what they intend. This is Derrida's method of deconstruction: the process of revisiting earlier episodes in the history of philosophical, literary, and scientific thought, and showing that while they imply first principles, they fail to make such principles fully explicit despite their best efforts.

This is a brief discussion of some very complex issues. But it should be clear that the implications of Derrida's discussion go far beyond geometry. What he is discussing is the very attempt to make our practices intelligible by tracing them back to first principles. In other words, he is talking about the kind of thinking we engage in when we do philosophy. And he is claiming that this kind of thinking forces us to adopt an ambivalent attitude towards history. On the one hand, historical thinking has limits and creates problems. We must not think that seeking origins involves *nothing more* than studying history. If we did, we would be embracing a particularly naive type of historicism, one that fails to recognize the difference between a position's genesis and its justification. On the other hand, we must not think that we can understand a position in terms of its first principles *without* studying its history. Doing so would rule out the possibility that a "community of transcendental inquirers" can play a role in constituting the objects of knowledge. In fact, Derrida argues, understanding in terms of origins and first principles requires us to take up the project of deconstruction. It requires us to return again and again to the landmarks in the history of thought, in order to show how a *différant* origin is at work in them. The point is that Derrida nowhere gives a conventional argument for his claim that we must continually deconstruct the history of thought. Unlike Dupré and Taylor, he does not offer a set of premises from which the historical thesis is supposed to follow. On the contrary, he freely acknowledges that the historical thinking at issue here has serious and unavoidable difficulties. But we are justified in engaging in it anyway, because the consequences of *not* doing so are obviously worse. If we

---

[49] Derrida, *Edmund Husserl's* Origin of Geometry, 153.   [50] Kates, *Essential History*, 78.

do not deconstruct the history of philosophy, we will be failing to acknowledge the peculiar and paradoxical nature of the origins of thought. We will lapse into a naive historicism or an equally naive ahistoricism. In other words, we are justified in doing philosophy historically even though we can give no positive argument showing that the historical thesis is true. What justifies this project is simply the bankruptcy of its alternatives.

Perhaps we can use this general line of thinking as a justification for doing philosophy historically – without necessarily accepting Derrida's precise version of it. Perhaps we can say that when philosophy does not continually trace the development of its major pictures, it runs into problems serious enough to discredit it. Perhaps these problems take the form of a Taylor-esque inability to criticize our views because these views are not recognized as contingent developments. Perhaps they take the form of moral, political, or even aesthetic difficulties. Whatever the precise problems, our reasoning will have the same basic form. But how could we make this sort of claim plausible? How would we show that there really are no good alternatives to doing philosophy historically? The answer, it seems, is that we would do so by constructing a sweeping narrative about the history and state of philosophy. We would tell some ambitious story about how philosophers tried to ply their trade without being guided by history, ran into problems, and in doing so, made clear that doing philosophy historically is practically indispensable. Derrida's version of this story is familiar enough. It claims that philosophy since the Greeks has been dominated by the metaphysics of presence: a set of problematic assumptions identifying what is with what can be made fully and unequivocally present to us. Each of Derrida's deconstructive readings adds another chapter to the story, and their cumulative effect is to convince us that a different approach to philosophy is preferable. We need not use this precise story to justify doing philosophy historically. Other stories might have a similar effect. But some such narrative seems required.

In a way, this is fitting. If doing philosophy historically really is necessary, then the attempt to *show* that it is necessary should also proceed historically, and that is just what narratives of this sort do. But the importance of narrative is also surprising. One of the things one hears about philosophers such as Derrida is that they display a postmodern incredulity towards metanarratives.[51] We are told that they are skeptical of sweeping stories

---

[51] The term is Lyotard's, of course. See Jean-François Lyotard, *The Postmodern Condition*, trans. Geoff Bennington and Brian Massumi (Minneapolis: University of Minnesota Press, 1984). For a detailed discussion of this topic, see Gary Browning, *Lyotard and the End of Grand Narratives* (Cardiff: University of Wales Press, 2000).

that legitimate philosophy being done in such and such a way; we are told that they are more inclined to question and disrupt these narratives than to construct them. But we are also told that these figures do philosophy historically, and think they must do so. It is hard to see how they could do this without placing a great deal of faith in the ambitious, legitimating narratives they supposedly scorn. This is not to say that figures such as Derrida use narrative naively or uncritically, or that they stubbornly maintain that their readings of the history of philosophy are the only plausible ones. But however subtle and conflicted their use of narrative is, they are anything but incredulous towards it.

What this suggests is that two of the most common pieces of conventional wisdom about the current state of philosophy are at odds with each other. The idea that philosophers such as Derrida see their discipline as inherently historical does not sit well with the claim that they are postmodern thinkers full of incredulity for metanarratives. This is not surprising, since these pieces of conventional wisdom are prime examples of what Heidegger calls "passing the word along" (*BT*, 212). Nor is it a problem. No reasonable person expects conventional wisdom to be philosophically deep or to stand up to close scrutiny. But it is important to know when our idle talk contradicts itself.

A SIMPLE TAXONOMY

The first three chapters of this book have been largely theoretical. They have described in a general way what is involved in doing philosophy historically. They have explored what this enterprise is, how it works, and what reasons there are to think it is necessary. All of this is important. Without a theoretical account, it is hard to understand how this enterprise differs from closely related ones, or to see what different instances of it have in common. But a theoretical account can take us only so far. To understand this enterprise fully, we must see it in action, by looking at some concrete attempts to *do* philosophy historically. Just as we learn about pictures by seeing what they have done, we learn what it is to do philosophy historically by examining the work of those engaged in the enterprise. That is what the rest of the book will do. It will offer a series of case studies, studies that look closely at a number of figures whose interest in doing philosophy historically is central to their work. With any luck, each of these case studies will be interesting for its own sake, and will shed new light on the figures in question. But more importantly, each will reveal something about doing philosophy historically: how this enterprise works in practice, what special pitfalls it faces, and what instruction it offers.

How should these case studies be organized? Let me answer this question by returning to one of the central claims of this book: that we study philosophical pictures in order to see what they can do. But what *sorts* of things do we learn when we study them? When we examine the work of a number of Cartesian philosophers, for example, what sorts of things are we trying to discover about the Cartesian picture? Moreover, what leads us to be concerned with the picture in the first place? The general answer, it seems, is that we start to reflect on a picture when it troubles us in some way. We become concerned with a picture and what it can do when we notice some sort of problem with the picture or its relation to us. But what sort of problem? What kinds of concerns lead us to start doing philosophy historically?

One concern is that pictures sometimes need to be evaluated or replaced. It may happen that a picture has come to dominate our thinking, serving as the unquestioned starting point for a great deal of philosophical work. But this picture might be flawed or misguided in some way, perhaps in ways we rarely notice. When this happens, it can be immensely valuable to have someone criticize this picture explicitly and expose its difficulties. Conversely, it may happen that a promising picture has become forgotten or unfairly ignored. When this happens, it can be valuable to have someone point out its strengths by showing that the thinkers who have accepted this picture have been remarkably successful in ways that escape most people's attention. Of course, to say that a picture is promising or misguided is not to say that it is correct or incorrect, or that it has been proved or refuted. These are the sorts of claims one makes about philosophical theories, not about pictures. But pictures may be promising or misguided in much the same way as scientific paradigms: in the sense that they promote, or fail to promote, valuable theoretical work that does a good job of answering the questions we care about.[52] The need to assess pictures is one of the most important motives for doing philosophy historically, and is probably the most common. Many of the examples from earlier chapters – Rorty's discussion of representationalism, for instance, or Derrida's engagement with the metaphysics of presence – have been based on it. It is made all the more urgent by the tendency of pictures to slip into the background of our

---

[52] Obviously what I have in mind here is the discussion of scientific paradigms in Thomas Kuhn, *The Structure of Scientific Revolutions*, 2nd edn. (Chicago: University of Chicago Press, 1970). To say that a particular picture is "productive" or "successful" corresponds roughly to saying that a certain paradigm serves as the foundation for a fruitful period of normal science. To say that a picture is "misguided" corresponds roughly to saying that a paradigm is in crisis – that it is no longer "working," because of its incompatibility with certain anomalous observations.

thinking. As Taylor reminds us, we rarely pay much attention to our most basic philosophical assumptions. We tend to forget about them, letting them organize our thinking and our practices unreflectively.[53] Philosophers tend to be more concerned with their specialized theoretical work than with the broader pictures of reality their work articulates, and they rarely ask how plausible these pictures are in comparison with their competitors. For that reason, it is extremely important that pictures be explicitly examined, that their strengths and weaknesses be probed. Work that does so, we might say, takes a *critical* approach to the project of doing philosophy historically.

A second reason to study philosophical pictures is that they can be deceptive. The pictures that shape our thinking are sometimes different from what we take them to be. They may have a meaning or significance that escapes us; they may have far-reaching effects on us that we fail to notice. This fact is particularly important when there is a single picture that dominates our thinking to the exclusion of others. We might be under the sway of the picture known as "modernity," for example, and we might think we know what it means – that it involves a faith in the supreme importance of reason for human affairs, for example. But it might turn out that the real essence of modernity is something quite different. Perhaps modernity is better described as the attitude that all of reality is a resource to be objectified and exploited. Perhaps modernity also involves a certain false consciousness and so is necessarily blind to this fact. If we found ourselves under the sway of a deceptive picture, it would be valuable to have someone point out this fact and uncover the picture's deeper nature. This does not mean that all deceptive pictures should be abandoned. But it does mean that historically minded philosophers can carry out the important function of dragging them into the light. This function has come to appear all the more urgent because of the influence of the thinkers whom Paul Ricoeur calls the "masters of suspicion"[54] – Nietzsche, Marx, and Freud, for example. Since the late nineteenth century, the masters of suspicion have broadened our view of interpretation, teaching us to look for "ruses and falsifications of meaning,"[55] and encouraging us to think that a sign's real significance might be something quite different than it claims. Those who have been influenced by these thinkers will suspect that philosophical pictures, like texts and social institutions, can be shot through with ideology. They may be inclined to trace the development of these pictures as a way of exposing this deceptiveness. We might call this approach to doing philosophy historically

---

[53] Taylor, "Philosophy and its History," 20–21.
[54] Ricoeur, *Freud and Philosophy*, 32.   [55] Ricoeur, *Freud and Philosophy*, 17.

the *diagnostic* approach, and it is an extremely common example of this enterprise.

A third concern we may have with philosophical pictures is that they are multiple. We are rarely, if ever, under the sway of just one picture. It is much more common for us to be influenced by a variety of pictures, sometimes ones that have little in common. When this happens, we naturally find ourselves trying to reconcile the competing pictures. We seek to lessen the tensions between them, to find some way of drawing on the resources of both. The desire to bring together competing pictures is as old as philosophy itself. Augustine and Aquinas, for example, both tried to reconcile a Christian view of the world with their preferred schools of ancient philosophy (Platonism and Aristotelianism, respectively). Plato himself worked hard to bring together the insights of Eleatic thought with the pictures of reality articulated by Pythagoras and Heraclitus. The task of reconciling pictures in this way is made all the more pressing by a fact that we have observed about philosophical pictures: that they are not the sorts of things that can be decisively proved or refuted. As Gary Gutting observes, "[p]hilosophers are often able to refute a particular theoretical formulation …, but they seldom if ever refute the general pictures that the theoretical formulations articulate."[56] As a result, there are indefinitely many pictures vying for our loyalty, and we naturally find ourselves influenced by several at once. Thus a third reason to do philosophy historically is to bring together the resources of pictures that seem to be in tension. We might call this the *synthetic* approach to doing philosophy historically.

These three approaches are not the only ways of doing philosophy historically. But they are a few of the most common and most important. The rest of this book will study an example of each. Chapter 4 will deal with the critical approach to doing philosophy historically, an approach that is illustrated by the work of Alasdair MacIntyre. Chapter 5 will examine the work of Martin Heidegger, and present him as an example of the diagnostic approach. Chapter 6 will discuss the synthetic approach, as it is exemplified by the post-Hegelian Kantianism of Paul Ricoeur.

---

[56] Gutting, *Pragmatic Liberalism and the Critique of Modernity*, 191.

CHAPTER 4

The critical approach: MacIntyre

The last three chapters have advanced a theory of doing philosophy historically. The next three chapters deal more with practice. They present a series
of case studies: close readings of a number of philosophers who do philosophy historically. This chapter contains the first. It deals with the work
of Alasdair MacIntyre, and with the concern for philosophical pictures that
runs through MacIntyre's rich and varied body of work. It traces the ways
in which MacIntyre has tried, at every stage of his career, to learn philosophical lessons by engaging with the history of thought. I want to present
MacIntyre as an example of the *critical* approach to doing philosophy
historically. His work is best seen as an attempt to criticize a prominent
philosophical picture, one that he calls the *enlightenment project*.
MacIntyre's critique of this picture is historical through and through. He
uses historical considerations both to point out this picture's defects, and to
develop an alternative to it.

My study of MacIntyre falls into five parts. First, I will discuss
MacIntyre's early work, which contains important anticipations of the
historical approach he adopts later in his career. I will then turn to his
best-known work, *After Virtue*, and to the critique of the enlightenment
project advanced in this book. The next two sections will examine
MacIntyre's search for an alternative to the enlightenment project in two
later works: *Whose Justice? Which Rationality?* and *Three Rival Versions of
Moral Enquiry.* I will conclude the chapter by asking what MacIntyre's use
of the critical approach teaches us about doing philosophy historically.

HISTORY IN MACINTYRE'S EARLY WORK

MacIntyre's work is so wide-ranging that it is hard to characterize it in a
general way. But one of its recurring themes is a concern with the philosophical significance of history. MacIntyre has always been interested in the
relations between philosophy and larger historical forces. He also has a

longstanding interest in the ways in which historical knowledge can help us to understand philosophical questions better. This is not surprising, given his influences. His sympathy for Marxism is one obvious source of his concern with history; his scholarship on major figures from the history of philosophy, such as Hegel and Hume, is another. So even MacIntyre's earliest publications have a great deal to say about why philosophers should be interested in history.[1] Over the course of his career, however, this interest in history has intensified, becoming a full-fledged resolve to do philosophy historically – a conviction that reflecting on the history of philosophy offers valuable insights that cannot be gained in any other way. There are several examples of this conviction in the work MacIntyre published before *After Virtue*.

One example appears in MacIntyre's work on the history of ethics. In his 1966 book *A Short History of Ethics*, MacIntyre argues that it is crucial for moral philosophers to know a great deal about the history of their enterprise. We find a particularly forceful statement of this view on the book's first page:

Moral philosophy is often written as though the history of the subject were only of secondary and incidental importance. This attitude seems to be the outcome of a belief that moral concepts can be examined and understood apart from their history … In fact, of course, moral concepts change as social life changes … Moral concepts are embodied in and are partially constitutive of forms of social life.[2]

Several pages later, MacIntyre draws some ambitious conclusions from this line of thought. Since moral concepts are "embodied in" and "constitutive of" forms of social life, we cannot understand these concepts properly without knowing how they have evolved historically. MacIntyre writes:

[W]hat I hope will emerge … is the function of history in relation to conceptual analysis, for it is here that Santayana's epigram that he who is ignorant of the history of philosophy is doomed to repeat it finds its point … [W]e can be saved only by an adequate historical view of the varieties of moral and evaluative discourse.[3]

But why? What can we learn about moral concepts by studying their historical development? MacIntyre's thesis is that the concepts studied by

---

[1] A good example is MacIntyre's 1959 article "Notes From the Moral Wilderness I." *New Reasoner* 7 (1958–1959), 90–100. One of MacIntyre's goals in this article is to advance moral criticisms of Stalinism that are not liberal in nature. He suggests that only history can help us here, and that what is needed is "a theory which treats what emerges in history as providing us with a basis for our standards" (100).

[2] Alasdair MacIntyre, *A Short History of Ethics*, 2nd edn. (Notre Dame: University of Notre Dame Press, 1998), 1.

[3] MacIntyre, *A Short History of Ethics*, 3–4.

ethics – "good," "right," and so on – often derive their meanings from social roles. This is particularly the case in the early history of these concepts. To be a good shepherd or a good flautist is to play a certain "socially established role,"[4] and to meet criteria that are publicly accepted and independent of one's will. But societies and their practices evolve, and as they do, the evaluative concepts that emerge from social roles evolve as well. In extreme cases, the social setting that gave rise to a particular evaluative term may cease to exist. The concept "good" may therefore change radically, or perhaps lose its original meaning altogether, because its social context has changed. Philosophers will fail to notice this shift if they do not understand the history of the society that produced this concept. Unless we see these uses "as constituting two successive phases in a historical narrative, we shall miss a large part of the point about the word *good* … The use of the word *good* when it is used only or primarily as an expression of approval or choice is unintelligible except as a survival from a period when criteria of an impersonal, unchosen kind governed its use."[5] As early as 1966, then, MacIntyre insists that historical understanding is indispensable for the moral philosopher. We cannot understand ethical concepts without tracing their development. This view is also an important feature of the enterprise I have called doing philosophy historically.[6]

Another such feature that appears in MacIntyre's early work is a concern with philosophical pictures, or with something very much like them. This concern comes to the fore in MacIntyre's work from the 1970s, especially his work on the nature of rationality. According to MacIntyre, we should not see philosophers as solely in the business of constructing and evaluating specific theories. We should also see them as articulating and refining broader conceptions of reality, the conceptions that I have been calling philosophical pictures – though MacIntyre does not use this term. An important text here is MacIntyre's 1977 article "Epistemological Crises,

---

[4] MacIntyre, *A Short History of Ethics*, 89.   [5] MacIntyre, *A Short History of Ethics*, 91.

[6] It could be argued that MacIntyre's concern with the historical contexts of ethical concepts is part of a larger concern he has with *all* of the contexts in which moral deliberation takes place. MacIntyre's ethical writings from the 1950s, for example, often argue that we cannot understand moral deliberation properly unless we view it against the backdrop of the highly specific contexts in which it occurs. In his 1957 article "What Morality is Not," MacIntyre points out that "[w]here there is real moral perplexity it is often in a highly complex situation … When I am puzzled it is often useful to pick out the morally relevant features of the situation and of my position in it and, having isolated them from the particular situation, I am in a better position to solve my problem." See Alasdair MacIntyre, "What Morality is Not," in *Against the Self-Images of the Age* (Notre Dame: University of Notre Dame Press, 1978), 107. MacIntyre's writings from the 1950s, however, seem not to be terribly concerned with the specifically historical contexts of moral deliberation. In that respect, they are quite different from *A Short History of Ethics*.

Dramatic Narrative and the Philosophy of Science."[7] This article explores the notion of an epistemological crisis: the discovery that one's beliefs have been massively misguided and must be replaced with very different ones. MacIntyre notes that philosophers have been particularly interested in epistemological crises since Kuhn's work on how one scientific paradigm can be supplanted by another. But he points out that these crises are also common occurrences in everyday life ("Someone who has believed that he was highly valued by his employers and colleagues is suddenly fired; some-one proposed for membership of a club whose members were all, so he believed, close friends, is blackballed"[8]), and that they played important roles in the lives of Descartes, Galileo, and other great thinkers. According to MacIntyre, an epistemological crisis is best seen as a breakdown in our *interpretative schemata*. These are the conceptual frameworks we all possess, frameworks that direct us in making sense of experience and in forming expectations about the future. "[T]o share a culture," MacIntyre claims, "is to share schemata which are at one and the same time constitutive of and normative for intelligible action by myself and are also means for my interpretation of the actions of others. My ability to understand what you are doing and my ability to act intelligibly … are one and the same ability."[9] In a crisis, our schemata are exposed as defective because they fail to make accurate predictions. This draws our attention to them – often for the first time[10] – and forces us to reassess them.

When we respond successfully to such a crisis, it is not with the "con-textless doubt"[11] of a Descartes. We do not reject all our old beliefs and search for an indubitable new foundation. Rather, we respond by finding a new schema, one that not only is better at explaining and predicting than the old one, but that helps us understand how we could have been drawn to the defective schema in the first place. This, MacIntyre points out, is how Galileo responded to the breakdown of Ptolemaic astronomy. Galileo

---

[7] For a good discussion of this article, see Christopher Lutz, *Tradition in the Ethics of Alasdair MacIntyre* (Lanham, MD: Lexington Books, 2004), 47–52.

[8] Alasdair MacIntyre, "Epistemological Crises, Dramatic Narrative and the Philosophy of Science." *Monist* 60:4 (1977), 453.

[9] MacIntyre, "Epistemological Crises," 454.

[10] MacIntyre distinguishes two different ways of responding to a breakdown in one's interpretative schema. The first – which he considers a naive response – is to think that one has cast off a deceptive schema and is now seeing the world as it really is. The second, more sophisticated response is to see that one has arrived at "a more adequate interpretation, which itself in turn may one day be transcended" (MacIntyre, "Epistemological Crises," 456). If we respond in the second way, then an epistemological crisis can be valuable, since it draws our attention to the ubiquity of interpretative schemata in our experience.

[11] MacIntyre, "Epistemological Crises," 458.

enables the work of all his predecessors to be evaluated by a common set of standards … For it now became retrospectively possible to identify those anomalies which had been genuine counterexamples to received theories from those anomalies which could justifiably be dealt with by ad hoc explanatory devices or even ignored. It also became retrospectively possible to see how the various elements of various theories had fared in their encounters with other theories and with observations and experiments, and to understand how the form in which they had survived bore the marks of those encounters.[12]

Galileo's new framework was more successful than its competitors because it allowed him to tell the most comprehensive story available so far about them. In MacIntyre's view, this is a perfectly general point. For a new interpretative framework to be successful, it must explain what was wrong with the framework that preceded it. It must also explain why the old framework could have appeared credible to someone who lacked the new framework. A successful interpretative scheme "introduces new standards for evaluating the past," and thereby "recasts the narrative" we construct about the past.[13]

  Though MacIntyre's discussion is primarily concerned with scientific rationality, it is strikingly similar to my account of doing philosophy historically. MacIntyre's interpretative schemata look a great deal like philosophical pictures, and perform many of the same functions. These schemata are extremely general conceptions of how the world is. They are primarily dispositional: their function is to direct us to solve problems in certain ways.[14] They are not themselves theories, but are rather the larger frameworks in which theories are constructed and evaluated. Of course, the notion of an interpretative schema is not identical with that of a philosophical picture. The former notion seems a good deal broader than the latter. Perhaps pictures are best seen as a specific kind of interpretative schema, one directed at those aspects of reality with which philosophers are particularly concerned. In any case, philosophical pictures and MacIntyre's interpretative schemata play much the same role in our thinking, and this is one important similarity between MacIntyre's early work and the project of doing philosophy historically. Another is the connection MacIntyre draws between interpretative schemata and narratives. Assessing a schema involves

---

[12] MacIntyre, "Epistemological Crises," 460.

[13] In keeping with the claim that the best schema is the one that has done the best job so far of accounting for our past mistakes, MacIntyre grants that his account of what *makes* a schema best can claim only to be the best account that we have found so far. See *AV*, 270.

[14] MacIntyre's way of putting this is that interpretative schemata "are not, of course, empirical generalizations; they are prescriptions for interpretation." See MacIntyre, "Epistemological Crises," 454.

constructing a distinctive type of narrative about it. Such a narrative shows that a given schema makes more sense of its competitors than they do of it, and that it is therefore preferable to them. We learn something crucial about a schema – that it is the best one to have emerged so far – by telling the story of how it has fared over time in relation to others. MacIntyre's position here is strikingly similar to my claim that doing philosophy historically involves seeing what a picture can do by seeing what it has done – that is, learning about a picture's nature by constructing a narrative about its historical development. Of course, MacIntyre's account is not an exact fit with mine. He does not, for example, use the term "philosophical picture." But the similarities are more striking than the differences.

In short, even before MacIntyre published the works for which he is best known – *After Virtue* and its sequels – he expressed a good deal of sympathy for the project of doing philosophy historically. His early work recognizes that philosophical pictures play an indispensable role in our thinking. It also recognizes that the most important way of learning about these pictures is to trace their development in historical narratives. It does not, however, tell us which pictures should interest us, or what we discover when we study them. For that – and for the clearest example of MacIntyre's use of the critical approach to doing philosophy historically – we must turn to *After Virtue*.

CRITICISM AS REPUDIATION: *AFTER VIRTUE*

MacIntyre describes *After Virtue* as part of a "single project"[15] in which he has been engaged since 1977. This project – to which *Whose Justice? Which Rationality?* and *Three Rival Versions of Moral Enquiry* are also central[16] – consists in pointing out the fragmentary, incoherent character of contemporary moral life, and in developing an alternative to it. *After Virtue* is the first stage of this project, and as Jean Porter says, it is "essentially a critical book."[17] Its main goal is to document the failings of contemporary moral life. MacIntyre does not present a detailed alternative to contemporary moral life until his later work. According to *After Virtue*, moral life today is "an unharmonious mélange of ill-assorted fragments" (*AV*, 10). It is marked by debates that are shrill and interminable – debates that not only

---

[15] Alasdair MacIntyre, "An Interview with Giovanna Borradori," in *The MacIntyre Reader*, ed. Kevin Knight (Notre Dame: University of Notre Dame Press, 1998), 269. In this passage, MacIntyre suggests that his project might well be called "*An Interminably Long History of Ethics.*"

[16] MacIntyre, "An Interview with Giovanna Borradori," 269.

[17] Jean Porter, "Tradition in the Recent Work of Alasdair MacIntyre," in *Alasdair MacIntyre*, ed. Mark Murphy (Cambridge: Cambridge University Press, 2003), 39.

do not end, but cannot end, because there is no rational way of settling them. Both the defenders and the critics of abortion rights, for example, can construct compelling arguments for their positions.[18] Defenders of these rights can point to the importance of respecting privacy and allowing people to control their own bodies. Their critics can point to the need to protect life, whether actual or potential. Most of us find ourselves drawn to both sets of principles, and it is not at all clear how to choose between them. For MacIntyre, this ambivalence is a general feature of contemporary moral life. To be a moral agent today is to be torn between competing principles and to lack any comprehensive framework in which they might be adjudicated.

According to MacIntyre, the reason for this fragmentation is that what we call morality is just a remnant of something older and larger. In heroic societies, as well as in ancient and medieval Europe, morality was recognized as essentially teleological. These societies had a shared conception of the human good, an understanding of what it is desirable for human beings to become. Moral precepts were therefore seen as instruments – the principles that, when followed, tended to help people achieve their good. In other words, moral norms made sense because of the role they played in a larger teleological structure, a structure in which they bridged human nature as it is and human nature as it ought to be. In such a structure, there is "a threefold scheme in which human-nature-as-it-happens-to-be (human nature in its untutored state) is initially discrepant and discordant with the precepts of ethics and needs to be transformed … into human-nature-as-it-could-be-if-it-realized-its-*telos*" (*AV*, 53). Since the scientific revolution, however, such schemes have fallen out of favor, because the kind of teleology that they presuppose has also fallen out of favor. Ancient and medieval philosophers typically derive their conceptions of the human *telos* from "some account of the essence of man as a rational animal" (*AV*, 52). A good example is what MacIntyre calls the "metaphysical biology" (*AV*, 162) of Aristotle. But such accounts of the human essence are now considered implausible.[19] As a result, few people in the contemporary world accept the idea of a shared good for human beings as such.[20] But without

---

[18] The example of abortion is MacIntyre's own: see *AV*, 6–7. MacIntyre also gives the examples of debates about just war and private education.

[19] It should be remembered that MacIntyre rejects this metaphysical biology as well (*AV*, 162). Interestingly, MacIntyre's recent work is less dismissive of metaphysical biology than in *After Virtue*. *Dependent Rational Animals*, for instance, argues that some important ethical consequences follow from our animal nature, and that philosophers – including himself – have paid insufficient attention to this fact. See Alasdair MacIntyre, *Dependent Rational Animals* (Chicago: Open Court, 1999), 8.

[20] Of course, MacIntyre's hope is that the idea of a human *telos* can be separated from the metaphysical biology on which it was originally based. To simplify dramatically, he will argue that a robust conception of the human good can be derived from our social roles and practices.

a good of this sort, MacIntyre argues, moral norms have no meaning or purpose. They are like the ancient Polynesian *taboos*: rules that, because of their history, exert a powerful grip on us, but whose origin and significance have been forgotten. We find ourselves unable to abandon them, but we can give no good reason to care about them.

This has not stopped philosophers from trying to *find* a reason. Sensing that traditional justifications of morality no longer worked, philosophers of the modern period set themselves the task of finding a purely rational basis for it. They tried to show that any rational human being is obliged to act morally. They tried to identify some feature of human nature as it is that, when properly understood, would compel us to obey traditional moral norms. Of course, modern philosophers have disagreed about what this feature is. For Hume, it is the sentiments, and especially the sympathy we happen to feel for creatures like ourselves. For Kant, it is reason's ability to legislate for itself – that is, its ability to give itself a law that is independent of any particular desire, and to act out of respect for this law. For Kierkegaard, it is a groundless and apparently arbitrary decision to live ethically rather than aesthetically. These theories, and others like them, make up what MacIntyre calls the enlightenment project. He defines this project as

the attempts to find a rational justification for morality in that historical period – say from 1630 to 1850 – when it acquired a sense at once general and specific. In that period "morality" became the name for that particular sphere in which rules of conduct which are neither theological nor legal nor aesthetic are allowed a cultural space of their own. (*AV*, 39)

In other words, the enlightenment project is the attempt to justify the content of traditional Western morality without appealing to a shared *telos*.[21] It is "the project of constructing valid arguments which will move from premises concerning human nature as [we] understand it to be to conclusions about the authority of moral rules" (*AV*, 52). The enlightenment project tries to get by with only two parts of an essentially tripartite structure. It tries to find a reason to act morally in human nature as it is, without the mediation of a vision of human nature as it ought to be. But this project, MacIntyre argues, cannot succeed. "Each of the three elements of the scheme," he claims, "requires reference to the other two if its status and function are to be intelligible" (*AV*, 53). Accordingly, MacIntyre argues that the enlightenment project not only *did* fail, but *had* to fail.

---

[21] According to MacIntyre, one of the most striking facts about the practitioners of the enlightenment project is their conservatism about the content of morality. By and large, they understand us to have the same obligations that Christianity does. They simply seek a different basis for these obligations. See *AV*, 43–44.

This claim serves as the lens through which MacIntyre examines specific examples of the enlightenment project. *After Virtue* tells a highly original story about the philosophers who try to find a rational basis for morality between 1630 and 1850. It depicts these philosophers as making up a continuous and developing movement, one in which each philosopher takes as his starting point the work of an immediate predecessor. More specifically, each takes for granted that his predecessor's attempt to justify morality rationally has failed, and "the vindication of each position," MacIntyre claims, is "made to rest in crucial part upon [this] failure" (*AV*, 49). The narrative begins with what MacIntyre considers the most important recent view of the relation between ethics and reason: emotivism. Emotivism is the view that moral propositions merely express the attitudes of the person uttering them. "Murder is wrong," on this view, is nothing but an expression of my disapproval of murder, or perhaps a plea for you to disapprove of it as well. Emotivism therefore "envisages moral debate in terms of a confrontation between incompatible and incommensurable premises and moral commitment as the expression of a criterionless choice between such premises, a type of choice for which no rational justification can be given" (*AV*, 39). Philosophers tend to think of emotivism exclusively as a philosophical position, one associated with Anglo-American philosophy of the mid twentieth century. Emotivism in this sense was short-lived: it "did not prevail within analytical philosophy" (*AV*, 39), and most philosophers have long recognized that the arguments usually advanced in defense of it are terrible. MacIntyre argues, however, that the position continues to exist in our wider culture. Our society instinctively sees moral debate as a series of interminable squabbles between arbitrary, incompatible premises that cannot be rationally justified. In other words, "what emotivism takes to be universally the case" is "the case by and large about our own culture" (*AV*, 19).

MacIntyre's narrative portrays the emotivist self as the outcome of an earlier stage in the history of moral philosophy. Moral agents, as emotivism understands them, have "suffered a deprivation, a stripping-away of qualities that were once believed to belong to the self" (*AV*, 33). These qualities are aspects of what MacIntyre calls "human-nature-as-it-happens-to-be" (*AV*, 53). They are qualities that earlier philosophers had hoped would compel all rational agents to accept the traditional content of morality, but that proved incapable of doing so. Which qualities are these? One answer is offered by Kierkegaard, the figure who provides the most obvious link between contemporary emotivist culture and the moral philosophy of the classical modern period. Kierkegaard describes moral obligation as grounded in the human capacity for choice, and more specifically in our capacity to choose the ethical way of life over the aesthetic. As Kierkegaard makes clear in *Either/Or*, this choice is not itself a moral one. It is "not the choice between good and evil, it is the choice whether or not to choose in terms of good or evil" (*AV*, 40). It is also a criterionless choice.[22] "I can be offered no *reason* for preferring one to the other" (*AV*, 40), since what counts as a reason for the ethical standpoint will not count as one for the aesthetic standpoint, and vice versa. In basing morality on a criterionless choice, MacIntyre claims, Kierkegaard discovers the ultimate arbitrariness of modern morality. For Kierkegaard, however, this is "a discovery of a disconcerting, even shocking kind" (*AV*, 39). For contemporary culture, it is a commonplace.

But what leads Kierkegaard to ground morality in an arbitrary choice? Quite simply, it is his conviction that none of the philosophers who preceded him had succeeded in justifying morality in any other way. He is particularly struck by what he sees as Kant's failure to ground morality in the structures of pure practical reason. Kant tries to ground morality in reason's autonomy – that is, its ability to have the will determined by a moral law that it gives itself, rather than by empirical causes such as desires. Ethics is therefore a matter of finding "a rational test which will discriminate those maxims which are a genuine expression of the moral law when they determine the will from those maxims which are not" (*AV*, 44). This test, of course, is the categorical imperative, which Kant offers as a way of distinguishing autonomous and therefore permissible maxims from heteronomous and impermissible ones. But Kant's test was widely considered unsuccessful by later philosophers. The problem, as MacIntyre puts it, is that "many immoral and trivial non-moral maxims are vindicated by Kant's test quite as convincingly – in some cases more convincingly – than the moral maxims which Kant aspires to uphold" (*AV*, 45–46). "'Keep all your promises throughout your entire life except one,'" for instance, turns out to pass the test of the categorical imperative, as does "'Always eat mussels on Mondays in March'" (*AV*, 46). The autonomy of reason proves unable to justify morality. Thus "Kant's failure provided Kierkegaard with his starting-point: the act of choice had to be called in to do the work that reason could no longer do" (*AV*, 47).

---

[22] Many Kierkegaard scholars reject MacIntyre's claim that the choice between the ethical and the aesthetic is an arbitrary, non-rational one. See, for example, John Davenport, "The Meaning of Kierkegaard's Choice Between the Aesthetic and the Ethical: A Response to MacIntyre," in *Kierkegaard After MacIntyre*, ed. John Davenport and Anthony Rudd (Chicago: Open Court, 2001), 75–112; and Gordon Marino, "The Place of Reason in Kierkegaard's Ethics," in *Kierkegaard After MacIntyre*, 113–127.

Just as Kierkegaard's work grows out of the shortcomings of Kant's, Kant's work grows out of a still earlier failure: the failure of Diderot, Hume, and other early enlightenment thinkers to derive morality from some empirically observed feature of human nature. Their enterprise is a cruder version of Kant's. Whereas Kant tries to ground morality in a feature of the noumenal self – its ability to give itself a universal law – Diderot and Hume try to ground it in a feature of the phenomenal self. The feature they choose is our affective states: desires, passions, and the like. Diderot argues that desire is the ultimate source of our moral responsibilities. We obey the moral principles recognized by society because we recognize that doing so will help us satisfy our desires in the long run. Hume's strategy is similar, but more sophisticated. He claims that it is the sentiments, and especially the sympathy we spontaneously feel for our fellow creatures, that lead us to accept the principles we do. But this strategy of deriving moral principles from the passions is bound to fail. After all, one of the most important functions of moral principles is to adjudicate among our desires – that is, to determine which desires we should and should not act on. Since desires must be judged by means of moral principles, they "cannot themselves be derived from or justified by reference to the desires among which they have to arbitrate" (*AV*, 48).[23]

MacIntyre's narrative about the enlightenment project is thus a story of decline. Kierkegaard, Kant, Diderot, and Hume all failed to find a justification for morality in "human-nature-as-it-happens-to-be" (*AV*, 53). The implication is that no such justification can be found, and that we should address the shortcomings of contemporary moral life in some other way. But when MacIntyre criticizes the enlightenment project, what sort of thing is he criticizing? His readers generally assume that his target is a philosophical theory – that the enlightenment project is a specific position one might hold on a specific philosophical issue. On this view, when MacIntyre criticizes the enlightenment project, he is criticizing a theory that Kierkegaard, Kant, and Hume all share, a theory that has turned out to be incorrect and that must be rejected. Accordingly, those who reject MacIntyre's conclusions about the enlightenment project typically look for defects in his refutation of this alleged theory. They take him to task for not having proven that a particular theory is incorrect. Some, such as Alan Gewirth, respond to his claim that no rational justification of morality

---

[23] MacIntyre points out that Hume's own writings often condemn certain passions as "deviant," "absurd," and "criminal" (*AV*, 49). These writings therefore rest on "an implicit, unacknowledged view of the state of passions in a normal and what we might call, but for Hume's view of reason, reasonable man" (*AV*, 48).

is possible by giving new justifications of their own. They try to construct new, sound arguments for the conclusion that all rational agents are obliged to act morally in the sense understood by Kant, Hume, *et al.*[24] Others take issue with MacIntyre's historical scholarship, claiming he does not accurately represent the theories held by the figures he discusses. Robert Wokler, for example, criticizes MacIntyre for misrepresenting the Scottish enlightenment and for oversimplifying the views of the thinkers who participated in it.[25] The thinkers of the enlightenment, Wokler maintains, are too numerous and too diverse to have had any one project in common.[26] Clearly, Wokler's criticism assumes that the enlightenment project criticized by MacIntyre is a single philosophical theory or project. Similarly, John Davenport and Gordon Marino take issue with MacIntyre's exposition of Kierkegaard, arguing that Kierkegaard does not really see the choice to live ethically as arbitrary and non-rational, as MacIntyre claims.[27] All of these critics take MacIntyre to be attacking a specific theory supposedly held by a number of historical figures. So they attack him in turn for saying incorrect things about this theory.

But is MacIntyre's critique of the enlightenment project directed at a philosophical theory in this sense? There are good reasons to think it is not. The most obvious reason is that the project MacIntyre is discussing is exceedingly general – as it would have to be, in order to be attributed to Diderot, Hume, Kant, Kierkegaard, and the host of minor figures lumped in with them. It seems unlikely that such a large and diverse group of thinkers could share any theory specific enough to be of much philosophical interest. On the contrary, the theories advanced by these philosophers often seem to respond to significantly different questions. Kant, for example, thinks that the main task of ethics is to find a test that will distinguish maxims that are genuine expressions of the moral law from those that are not. Kierkegaard, on the other hand, understands his task at a much higher level of generality. It is to determine what is involved in accepting the institution of morality in the first place. This is not to say that the theories of Kant and Kierkegaard have nothing in common. But the similarities between them – at least the similarities that interest MacIntyre – cannot be reduced to something as precise as a particular ethical theory.

[24] See Alan Gewirth, "Rights and Virtues." *Review of Metaphysics* 38:4 (1985), 739–762.
[25] Robert Wokler, "Projecting the Enlightenment," in *After MacIntyre*, ed. John Horton and Susan Mendus (London: Polity, 1994), 108–126. Wokler calls MacIntyre's discussion of the Scottish enlightenment "wonderfully confused, both in method and in substance, generally and in detail" (115).
[26] Wokler, "Projecting the Enlightenment," 115–116.
[27] See Davenport, "The Meaning of Kierkegaard's Choice," 101; and Marino, "The Place of Reason in Kierkegaard's Ethics," 116.

A second reason to doubt that the enlightenment project is a particular theory can be found in MacIntyre's descriptions of what he is doing in *After Virtue*. As we have seen, MacIntyre argues that the failings of contemporary moral life can be detected only through historical study. Neither conceptual analysis nor phenomenological description can diagnose the crisis in contemporary morality (*AV*, 2). History is the only tool available to us, which is why MacIntyre's critique of the enlightenment project takes the form of a historical narrative. But *After Virtue* engages in a very specific type of history. The narrative it constructs is not "academic history" (*AV*, 4) as it is usually practiced.[28] Rather, it is "what Hegel called philosophical history and what Collingwood took all successful historical writing to be" (*AV*, 3).[29] Philosophical history, as Hegel and Collingwood understand it, does not merely seek to give an accurate chronicle of past events. By extension, a philosophical history of ethics would not seek to give accurate reconstructions of the theories held by Kant and Kierkegaard. Rather, philosophical history engages in a "*thoughtful consideration*"[30] of the past. For Hegel and Collingwood, this is a matter of uncovering the reason in the past, of showing "that the history of the world … presents us with a rational process."[31] Uncovering this rational process is a difficult business, and involves active, sometimes violent, interpretation. It is quite different from the work of what Hegel calls "the ordinary, the 'impartial' historiographer, who believes and professes that he maintains a simply receptive attitude, surrendering himself only to the data supplied him."[32] To be sure, philosophical historians strive to make their work *consistent* with the historical record, as it is documented by the "ordinary," "'impartial' historiographer."[33] But it is not their goal to contribute to this record. Their goal is to do something more active.[34]

---

[28] MacIntyre notes several differences between his narrative and those of conventional academic history. One of the most important is that academic history tries to adopt "a value-neutral standpoint" (*AV*, 4), while the type of history MacIntyre writes "is informed by standards. It is not an evaluatively neutral chronicle" (*AV*, 3).

[29] Though MacIntyre claims to be doing philosophical history in Hegel's sense, he is also keen to distance himself from certain aspects of Hegel's work. He claims, for example, that his own philosophical history "involves a form of fallibilism: it is a kind of historicism which excludes all claims to absolute knowledge" (*AV*, 270). He also says that he is "irremediably anti-Hegelian in rejecting the notion of an absolute standpoint, independent of the particularity of all traditions." See Alasdair MacIntyre, "A Partial Response to my Critics," in *After MacIntyre*, 295.

[30] Hegel, *Philosophy of History*, 8.   [31] Hegel, *Philosophy of History*, 9.

[32] Hegel, *Philosophy of History*, 9.

[33] MacIntyre seems to consider it quite important that his narrative cohere with conventional scholarly work in the history of philosophy. He says, for example, that he has "a good deal of sympathy" (*AV*, 271) for those who think that *After Virtue* oversimplifies Hume and Kant.

[34] For a more detailed discussion of how the study of past thinkers inevitably involves active reinterpretation, see my "Active Mimesis and the Art of History of Philosophy." *International Philosophical Quarterly* 43:1 (2003), 29–42.

Since *After Virtue* claims to be philosophical history in the mould of Hegel and Collingwood, its aim cannot be to give an accurate chronicle of the views of past thinkers. So the enlightenment project – the centerpiece of the philosophical history MacIntyre constructs here – cannot be a specific philosophical theory. Accordingly, MacIntyre need not be terribly concerned about critics who point out ways in which he has failed to do justice to the subtleties of the Scottish enlightenment, or Kierkegaard, or other figures. He does not claim to be doing them justice. He claims that he is uncovering the reason at work in a larger movement to which these figures belong. In other words, he claims to be bringing to light a conceptual and historical development in the period from 1630 to 1850, a development not recognized by the philosophers in question, or by the conventional historians of philosophy who study this period.[35] One indication of this is that MacIntyre's narrative about the enlightenment project contains elements one would not expect to find in conventional histories of philosophy. It traces developments and lines of influence that would seem bizarre in more traditional scholarship: emotivism growing out of Kierkegaard's *Either/Or*? Kierkegaard responding not to Hegel, but to difficulties in Kant's theory of autonomy? These are not the sorts of claims advanced in dispassionate accounts of what Kant and Kierkegaard really thought. The developments traced by MacIntyre's narrative are conceptual developments visible only to a philosophical historian – someone trying to determine what, from the standpoint of reason, was the *significance* of certain developments in moral philosophy from 1630 to 1850. MacIntyre is trying to *make us see* these developments by fitting them into a distinctive type of narrative. He is trying to trigger a shift in how we view classical modern philosophy, a shift in what we see this period *as*. He is not trying to identify a specific theory held by every modern moral philosopher.

If the enlightenment project is not a theory, then what is it? It is a picture – a general conceptual framework common to a great many thinkers. The enlightenment project is a way of approaching moral questions and understanding moral principles. It is based on the conviction that questions about the justification of moral principles must be answered by appeals to "reason" – where "reason" is understood as the ability to discern present matters of fact. Reason in this sense can see the features of human nature as it currently is, but it is blind to teleological considerations. As is the case with other

---

[35] Indeed, it could be argued that conventional historians of philosophy *cannot* recognize this development, since they strive to understand past thinkers from "a value-neutral standpoint" (*AV*, 4). The development MacIntyre describes cannot be seen from such a standpoint.

pictures, accepting the enlightenment project is a matter of having certain dispositions. It is a resolve to address questions about ethical principles in a distinctive way, and to generate ethical theories of a certain kind. And what does MacIntyre learn about the enlightenment project by studying its historical development? Recall the general description of doing philosophy historically given in Chapter 1. There, I argued that one traces the development of a picture in order to see what it can and cannot do. MacIntyre's engagement with the enlightenment project teaches him that those who share this picture cannot do what they intend. They cannot explain why we should accept traditional moral norms without making reference to teleological considerations. If MacIntyre is right, they should not even try, since these norms require teleological considerations if their "status and function are to be intelligible" (*AV*, 53). So MacIntyre engages with the enlightenment project in order to show that we should reject it, since this picture sets itself a goal that cannot be attained.

We should note that there are several possible explanations of what "cannot" means here. *After Virtue* strongly suggests that trying to justify moral norms without a view of the human *telos* is a conceptual impossibility – that "just too much incoherence and inconsistency is involved in [the enlightenment project] for *any* reasonable person to continue to hold it" (*AV*, 267). MacIntyre claims, for example, that "*any project of this form was bound to fail*, because of an *ineradicable discrepancy* between their shared conceptions of moral rules and … their conception of human nature" (*AV*, 52, my emphasis). MacIntyre's later books, however, tend to describe this failure somewhat differently. They suggest that the enlightenment project is a live option – that it is coherent and consistent, and that it is not simply irrational to subscribe to it – but that some other picture is preferable.[36] That said, MacIntyre clearly thinks that the enlightenment has an unattainable goal, regardless of *why* this goal is unattainable.

To this difficulty, we might add a second one: the enlightenment project does not, and cannot, understand itself. Those who accept this picture take themselves to be addressing ethical questions in the only way possible: by justifying moral norms through appeals to timeless and universal standards of reason. They do not see that what they take to be timeless standards of reason are impoverished remnants of a larger philosophical and social

---

[36] For example, *Whose Justice? Which Rationality?* claims that both liberalism and the Scottish enlightenment are traditions to which one might reasonably be drawn. Other traditions, particularly Aristotelian Thomism, can be shown to be rationally superior to them, but this is not because liberalism or the enlightenment involve too much inconsistency for any rational person to hold them. See *WJ*, Chapter 20.

structure. Indeed, they cannot see this, since these historical and cultural considerations fall outside the scope of reason as they understand it. The enlightenment project necessarily fails to be self-aware. For MacIntyre, this is a serious problem. His debts to Hegel and Collingwood, and his claim to be doing philosophical history in their sense, lead him to attach a great deal of importance to the type of self-consciousness brought about by historical awareness. For this reason too, the enlightenment project is a non-starter, and ought to be abandoned.

MacIntyre's critique leaves us with several questions. Is there a better philosophical picture, one that does not share the shortcomings of the enlightenment project? If so, how can we find it? MacIntyre turns to these questions in his next book.

<h2 style="text-align:center">SEARCH FOR A METHOD: *WHOSE JUSTICE?*
WHICH RATIONALITY?</h2>

As we have seen, MacIntyre is very concerned with epistemological crises: situations in which we learn that our beliefs have been massively mistaken. But an epistemological crisis can involve more than just a loss of faith in our old beliefs. It can also involve a loss of faith in our ability to form new beliefs. Once we have discarded a system of beliefs, it is only natural to wonder whether the new system we subsequently adopt will prove inadequate as well. In "Epistemological Crises," MacIntyre illustrates this point with two examples drawn from literature. The first comes from Jane Austen's novel *Emma*. The plot of *Emma* revolves around the title character's recognition that her way of viewing reality – one drawn from romantic novels – is flawed. Specifically,

> Emma insists on viewing her protégée, Harriet, as a character in an eighteenth-century romance. She endows her, deceiving both herself and Harriet, with the conventional qualities of the heroine of such a romance. Harriet's parentage is not known; Emma converts her into the foundling heroine of aristocratic birth so common in such romances. And she designs for Harriet precisely the happy ending of such a romance, a marriage to a superior being.[37]

Emma's insistence on viewing Harriet through the lens of the romantic novel is misguided, and leads to disastrous consequences for all concerned. Emma's discovery of this fact – her epistemological crisis – leads her to understand

---

[37] MacIntyre, "Epistemological Crises," 456.

what it was in herself that had led her not to perceive the untruthfulness of her interpretation of the world in terms of romance … But Emma, although she experiences moral reversal, has only a minor epistemological crisis, if only because the standpoint which she now, through the agency of Mr. Knightly, has come to adopt, is presented as though it were one from which *the* world as it is can be viewed. False interpretation has been replaced not by a more adequate interpretation, which itself in turn may one day be transcended, but simply by the truth.[38]

A more serious epistemological crisis arises when one *does* entertain the possibility that one's new beliefs "may one day be transcended." This is the situation explored in *Hamlet*. Hamlet experiences such a severe breakdown in his view of the world that he has no idea how to start looking for a new one. Unlike Emma, he does not simply replace a discredited interpretation with the truth, because he does not know how to choose among many different ways of discovering the truth. There are "too many schemata available for interpreting the events at Elsinore of which already he is a part. There is the revenge schema of the Norse sagas; there is the renaissance courtier's schema; there is a Machiavellian schema about competition about power."[39] Nor can Hamlet find the right interpretation by looking at the evidence, since "[u]ntil he has adopted some schema he does not know what to treat as evidence."[40] Not knowing whom to trust, not knowing what the facts are, Hamlet does not just lose faith in his old view of what is going on. He loses faith in his ability to find out what is going on.

A reader who takes *After Virtue* seriously is left not in Emma's position, but in Hamlet's. She will not just wonder whether her inherited ways of thinking about morality are untenable. She will come to doubt her ability to find a better alternative. If I am in the grips of a flawed picture, she will ask, then perhaps I am also in the grips of a flawed picture of how to *choose* among pictures. Thus the question arises: how do we go about finding a replacement for a discredited system of beliefs? More generally, how can we show that one general way of thinking about the world is better than another? These are the concerns of MacIntyre's next book: *Whose Justice? Which Rationality?* This book sets out to find a procedure for adjudicating among rival and incompatible ways of thinking about the world. Its way of doing so is thoroughly historical. It traces the history of conflicts between different ways of thinking about reality, in the hope of discovering what is involved when one triumphs over another. Furthermore, MacIntyre

---

[38] MacIntyre, "Epistemological Crises," 456. MacIntyre goes on to observe that "[w]e of course can see that Jane Austen is merely replacing one interpretation by another, but Jane Austen herself fails to recognize this and so has to deprive Emma of this recognition too" (456).

[39] MacIntyre, "Epistemological Crises," 454.   [40] MacIntyre, "Epistemological Crises," 454.

believes that he *must* proceed in this way. As in *After Virtue*, historical inquiry is the only tool available to him, and it is impossible to find an adjudication procedure in any other way.[41] In emphasizing these aspects of the book, I am giving a somewhat unorthodox reading of *Whose Justice?* The book is often seen primarily as a historical chronicle – as a survey of several well-established ways of thinking about practical rationality.[42] I, on the other hand, see the book as a discussion of philosophical method, albeit a discussion that is historically informed, and necessarily so. It is a search for a method, an inquiry into how to choose among different ways of understanding practical rationality. While it does trace the history of these different views of practical rationality, it does so in order to make a larger philosophical point. In other words, *Whose Justice?* is best seen as an attempt to do philosophy historically. Furthermore, the book does philosophy historically in a way that continues the critical project of *After Virtue*. *After Virtue* uses historical inquiry to discredit the enlightenment project; *Whose Justice?* uses it to discover a way of finding an alternative to this project.

The opening pages of *Whose Justice?* announce that the book is concerned with practical reason. It asks "what makes it rational to act in one way rather than another and what makes it rational to advance and defend one conception of practical rationality rather than another" (*WJ*, ix). These look like familiar metaethical questions: what does it mean to have a reason to do something? What things do we have reasons to do? But according to MacIntyre, these questions take on a new urgency in light of the moral fragmentation of contemporary culture. As MacIntyre argues in *After Virtue*, contemporary culture is torn by interminable debate over what things are good, which actions are right, and what justice requires of us. If we try to settle these debates by consulting some philosophical theory of justice, we immediately encounter the same fragmentation at a higher level. We find "conflicting conceptions of justice, conceptions which are strikingly at odds with each other" (*WJ*, 1). And if we try to settle these debates

---

[41] I have in mind here MacIntyre's claim that we cannot adjudicate among traditions by means of the argumentative strategies found *within* a tradition – say, the types of arguments used by contemporary analytic philosophers. Such strategies may indeed be used to convince members of one tradition that their tradition is superior to its competitors. But they cannot be used to adjudicate among traditions, since other traditions might not accept the legitimacy of these strategies. Using these argumentative strategies would therefore assume the superiority of the first tradition, not demonstrate it, and so beg the question. See, for example, *WJ*, 166.

[42] See, for example, Julia Annas, "MacIntyre on Traditions." *Philosophy and Public Affairs* 18:4 (1989), 388–404; and Robert George, "Moral Particularism, Thomism, and Traditions." *Review of Metaphysics* 42 (1989), 593–605. For an exception to this trend, see J. B. Schneewind, "MacIntyre and the Indispensability of Tradition." *Philosophy and Phenomenological Research* 51:1 (1991), 165–168.

about justice by seeking the *right* theory of justice – the theory that it is most rational to accept – we find still more fragmentation. We discover that "disputes about the nature of rationality in general and about practical rationality in particular are apparently as manifold and as intractable as disputes about justice" (*WJ*, 2). These disputes are most easily seen in historical perspective. At different times and in different places, there have existed different traditions of thought about practical rationality. These traditions have disagreed wildly about what it is to act rationally or justly. Thus it is not enough to investigate our own society's ways of thinking about justice and rationality. We must also investigate our society's histor-ical rivals. For MacIntyre, then, the question of which things we have reasons to do turns into the question of which tradition gives the best account of practical rationality. To ask this question is to ask how we can adjudicate among traditions – that is, how we can show that one tradition is rationally superior to another. MacIntyre's procedure for answering these questions is, and must be, historical. He insists that there are no timeless standards for determining that one tradition is better than another, no "tradition-independent standards of judgment" (*WJ*, 348). What we can do, however, is trace the historical development of several traditions. We can study examples of conflict between traditions, and the resolutions of these conflicts. We can see what has been involved when one tradition has triumphed over another. In this way, and only in this way, we may draw some conclusions about how to adjudicate among traditions.

At this point, it might be helpful to look more closely at MacIntyre's view of tradition. The notion is central to *Whose Justice?* Indeed, MacIntyre describes the book's thesis as follows:

What the enlightenment made us for the most part blind to and what we now need to recover is, so I shall argue, a conception of rational enquiry as embodied in a tradition, a conception according to which the standards of rational justification themselves emerge from and are part of a history. (*WJ*, 7)

As Julia Annas has observed, however, "MacIntyre nowhere fully character-izes tradition in general, preferring to let the idea emerge from the examples that he presents."[43] But his examples do allow us to make some general statements.[44] First, a tradition is a continuous process of inquiry. It is a way

---

[43] Annas, "MacIntyre on Traditions," 389. Jean Porter echoes this point. See Porter, "Tradition in the Recent Work of Alasdair MacIntyre," 38.

[44] MacIntyre grants that his account of tradition, and indeed the concept of tradition itself, are products of one particular tradition. Other traditions might give different accounts of what traditions are and how they work. Some might not use the concept of tradition at all, or even be able to make sense of it. For a more detailed discussion of these matters, see *TRV*, 117.

of thinking about the world that has some identity over time, some "core of shared belief, constitutive of allegiance to the tradition" (*WJ*, 356). Not all traditions are traditions of rational inquiry. But the ones that interest MacIntyre are: they are all traditions constituted by a concern with the nature of practical rationality. A tradition, however, involves dispute and disagreement as well as continuity.[45] MacIntyre goes so far as to characterize a tradition as a type of argument – as

an argument extended through time in which certain fundamental agreements are defined and redefined in terms of two kinds of conflict: those with critics and enemies external to the tradition who reject all or at least key parts of those fundamental agreements, and those internal, interpretative debates through which the meaning and rationale of the fundamental agreements come to be expressed. (*WJ*, 12)

A related point is that a tradition recognizes its fallibility and is willing to revise its principles. It is not an inert body of dogma; it is open to criticisms from within and without. "[A]ttempts to amend or redirect the tradition," MacIntyre claims, "may indeed be as formative and important a relation to a tradition as any other" (*WJ*, 326).[46]

Furthermore, a tradition is self-conscious, at least when certain conditions are met. Its members explicitly identify with it. They recognize themselves as belonging to a continuous process of inquiry, one that is partly constituted by their own contributions to it. Those who belong to a tradition "become aware of it and of its direction and in self-aware fashion attempt to engage in its debates and carry its inquiries forward" (*WJ*, 326). Of course, not all members of a tradition belong to it in such a self-conscious way. Those who start new traditions are typically not aware of belonging to the traditions they found. In fact, MacIntyre grants that the self-awareness he speaks of may be relatively rare. When a tradition is functioning well, we may not bother to reflect on its nature at all. But a tradition displays a tendency to *become* self-aware. As it matures, its members see themselves more and more as constituting an argument extended

---

[45] Stephen Watson also attaches a great deal of importance to this aspect of tradition, though he pushes it considerably further than MacIntyre does. Watson argues that the very idea of tradition is "internally (if not explicitly) differentiated and pluralistic," and is inseparable from "the experience of historical rupture." See Stephen Watson, *Tradition(s) II: Hermeneutics, Ethics, and the Dispensation of the Good* (Bloomington: Indiana University Press, 2001), 3.

[46] One of the most common objections to *Whose Justice?* is that the traditions MacIntyre favors – Aristotelian Thomism, for example – do not meet this test, and are less fallibilist than MacIntyre's account demands. See, for example, George, "Moral Particularism," 594.

through time.[47] The need for self-awareness is thus consistent with MacIntyre's claim that a tradition often "may only be recognized for what it is in retrospect" (*WJ*, 363).

Another important characteristic of traditions is that they are rooted in "the particularities of some specific language and culture" (*WJ*, 371). A tradition is embodied in social institutions. Its principles are not free-floating, but are an "elaboration of a mode of social life" (*WJ*, 349). In other words, a tradition's ways of thinking about the world are both mirrored in and shaped by the organized ways in which its members live and act. This is not to say that its ways of thinking are mere effects of social phenomena; nor is it to say that social phenomena are mere effects of philosophical theories. A tradition's social and philosophical sides go together inseparably, as different aspects of the same thing.[48] Finally, and most importantly, membership in a tradition is a condition of the possibility of rational inquiry. It is impossible to reflect rationally on any topic – such as the nature of practical rationality – from no particular standpoint. There is, MacIntyre claims, "no other way to engage in the formulation, elaboration, rational justification, and criticism of accounts of practical rationality and justice except from within some one particular tradition" (*WJ*, 50). This is an ambitious claim, and MacIntyre does not ask us to accept it without evidence. Appropriately, however, the evidence offered in support of this claim is the long historical narrative that makes up *Whose Justice?* So let us turn to the narrative.

Though traditions could be concerned with nearly any topic, MacIntyre is most interested in those that inquire into practical rationality – those that explore how human beings should act, and what makes it rational for them to act in one way rather than another. He claims that four major traditions of practical rationality have dominated Western philosophy.[49] The first is what he calls the Aristotelian tradition: a way of thinking about practical rationality that originated in Homeric Greece, found definitive expression

---

[47] This seems to be confirmed by MacIntyre's discussion of the three stages of a tradition's development. Typically, it is only at the third stage that those who make up a tradition reflect on their membership in it. See *WJ*, 356. For a detailed discussion of this topic – though one that is more critical of MacIntyre than I have been – see Schneewind, "MacIntyre and the Indispensability of Tradition," 166.

[48] This idea appears in MacIntyre's early work as well as in *Whose Justice?* In *A Short History of Ethics*, for example, MacIntyre writes that "moral concepts change as social life changes. I deliberately do not write 'because social life changes,' for this might suggest that social life is one thing, morality another, and that there is merely an external, contingent causal relationship between them. This is obviously false. Moral concepts are embodied in and partially constitutive of forms of social life" (1).

[49] MacIntyre grants that other traditions have had an important influence on Western practical philosophy, though they are perhaps not as central to it as the traditions he studies. He mentions Jewish and Islamic thought as examples. See *WJ*, 11, 392.

in the work of Aristotle, and was synthesized with Christian thought in thirteenth-century Europe. This tradition originated in an argument about the different goods attainable by human beings, and more specifically, about the relative value of two types of goods. MacIntyre calls the first type "goods of excellence" (*WJ*, 32). These are rewards internal to a practice, rewards that are achieved according to "the standards established within and for some specific form of systematic activity" (*WJ*, 30). In ancient Greece, the list of such activities was originally limited to warfare, rhetoric, and the like, but was later expanded to include "mathematics, philosophy, and theology" (*WJ*, 30). The second type, which MacIntyre calls "goods of effectiveness" (*WJ*, 30), consists of the external rewards one can obtain by defeating others in public competition. They include "riches, power, status, and prestige," goods that human beings can desire "independently of any desire for excellence" (*WJ*, 32).[50] Homeric Greece recognized that these goods are not always found together. In a fair competition, the most excellent competitor will prevail, and thus obtain certain goods of effectiveness. But competition is not always fair. Thus a debate emerged in ancient Greece about which sort of good is more important. This debate has important ethical consequences. If goods of effectiveness are primary, then someone who cheats in a competition, or who otherwise flouts society's rules, hurts only others. If goods of excellence are primary, then the cheater hurts himself (*WJ*, 37). In MacIntyre's view, much of ancient Greek history should be seen as a debate over these goods. Pericles and Thucydides should be seen as defending the primacy of honor, prestige, and other goods of effectiveness (*WJ*, 53), while Sophocles should be seen as warning us of their limitations (*WJ*, 58).

According to MacIntyre, it was the philosophers of ancient Athens who best understood this debate, and who first discovered a way of resolving it. Plato goes part of the way by offering a comprehensive account of human excellence, one that maintains that the goods of excellence always triumph over the goods of effectiveness (*WJ*, 69). Plato systematically dismantles the views of Pericles and Thucydides, arguing that true rationality requires *arête*, and that justice is not simply whatever serves the powerful. The *Republic* plays a particularly important role here. The dialogue not only

---

[50] MacIntyre's distinction between goods of excellence that are internal to a practice and goods of effectiveness that are external to a practice recalls his well-known example of the chess player in *After Virtue*. I might teach a child to play chess by offering him candy for each game he wins. This is a purely external reward. I hope, however, that as the child learns to play, he will come to appreciate the satisfactions internal to the game, and thus acquire a reason to play that does not depend on external rewards. See *AV*, 188.

vindicates the goods of excellence over those of effectiveness; it does so in a way that makes explicit that a debate concerning these goods runs through Greek history. After all, Plato represents this argument as a dialectical debate involving Socrates and Thrasymachus, and in so doing, he "made of the sophists partners in posing these problems" (*WJ*, 84). In other words, Plato discovers that a debate about goods is really a debate involving the different voices of a tradition, and he contributes to this debate by mediating among these different voices. But it is Aristotle who completes Plato's project by explaining how it is *possible* to lead a life devoted to the pursuit of goods of excellence.[51] He shows that such a life is possible only in a *polis* – and not just an ideal *polis* such as the one described by the *Republic*, but an actually existing *polis* (*WJ*, 90). The *polis* integrates and orders the various goods human beings may pursue. It aims "at the achievement of human good as such," and it does so by bringing into systematic relation "all those goods specific to the forms of activity in which post-Homeric Greeks had come to recognize impersonal and objective standards of excellence" (*WJ*, 107). The *polis* ranks goods by making some systematic activities subordinate to others: "excellence at bridlemaking for the sake of excellence at horseriding, excellence at horseriding in part for the sake of military excellence" (*WJ*, 107), and ultimately – according to Book Ten of the *Nicomachean Ethics* – excellence at every other activity for the sake of philosophical contemplation. Further, Aristotle makes both justice and practical rationality dependent on membership in a *polis*. One can distribute goods justly "only within those systematic forms of activity within which goods are unambiguously ordered and within which individuals occupy … well-defined roles" (*WJ*, 141). Similarly, one can deliberate in the ways required by rationality only if one has acquired certain virtues from one's *polis*. The details of Aristotle's view are not important for our purposes. What is important is that we see his view as the outcome of an argument about goods extending over several generations – an argument of the sort MacIntyre calls a tradition. The power of Aristotle's work stems at least partly from the way it articulates this tradition's concerns and responds to them in the most comprehensive way it can.[52]

But other traditions have offered different and incompatible accounts of practical rationality. One is the Augustinian tradition, which combines elements from Jewish and Christian scripture with the philosophical views of early Christians such as Saint Augustine. Members of the Augustinian

---

[51] MacIntyre grants that this reading of Aristotle is somewhat unorthodox. For his defense of it, see *WJ*, 92.
[52] For a fuller discussion of this point, see *WJ*, 143–144.

tradition attach a great deal of importance to the will. In their view, the will's freedom lets individuals choose and rank goods however they see fit. Members of this tradition also see the will – and not, say, a deliberative process such as Aristotle's so-called practical syllogism – as the wellspring of all human action. The Augustinian tradition therefore denies that it is the task of the *polis* to order goods, and it rejects Aristotle's account of deliberation as the origin of action. Above all, it rejects the Aristotelian claim that the pursuit of the good requires membership in a highly specific human community. For an Augustinian, this pursuit is made possible by the universal community of the *civitas dei*, not by any particular *polis*. Another tradition of inquiry into practical rationality emerges with the Scottish enlightenment. Like the Augustinian tradition, the Scottish enlightenment rejects Aristotelianism, but for reasons having to do with the religious conflicts of early modernity. The thinkers of eighteenth-century Scotland took for granted that people would disagree about the good, and they tried to develop a practical philosophy and a social order compatible with this disagreement. Their solution was to give pride of place to the individual – to inquire into which institutions and principles could be accepted by an autonomous individual with her own conception of the good. The Scottish tradition therefore came to be dominated by an argument concerned with "the relationship of principles to passions and to interests" (*WJ*, 214). It asked whether we accept moral principles simply because they serve our interests, or whether some principles are accepted for other reasons. A final tradition – and the dominant one in the contemporary world – is liberalism. Paradoxically, liberalism originates in a desire to escape tradition. It sets out "to construct a morality for tradition-free individuals" (*WJ*, 334). Liberalism is therefore reluctant to recognize itself as a tradition. It seeks to give universal answers to the questions of what is just and how it is rational to act. It tries to give an account of practical rationality that applies not just to members of one tradition, but to anyone from anywhere. MacIntyre argues that this goal has gone unrealized, since liberals disagree wildly about what a morality for tradition-free individuals would look like, and they have found no way to settle these disagreements.[53] But these very

---

[53] MacIntyre goes further, claiming that we have good reason to think they *cannot* settle these disagreements, because what liberalism tries to do – develop a morality for tradition-free individuals – cannot be done. Liberalism has gone much further in separating morality from tradition than any other movement. That it fails to do so gives us the best possible reason to think this separation is impossible. See *WJ*, 346. Interestingly, in *After Virtue*, MacIntyre uses the same style of argument to show that there are no such things as human rights – no "rights attaching to human beings simply *qua* human beings." He argues: "The best reason for asserting so bluntly that there are no such rights is indeed of precisely the same type as the best reason which we possess for asserting that there are no unicorns: every attempt to give good reasons for believing that there *are* such rights has failed" (*AV*, 69).

disagreements have made liberalism what it is. Liberalism "has itself been transformed into a tradition whose continuities are partly defined by the interminability of the debate over such principles" (*WJ*, 335).

In short, the history of philosophy presents us with several competing accounts of practical rationality. According to the Aristotelian tradition, to be practically rational is to engage in certain systematic activities that have been ranked and integrated by a *polis*. For the Augustinian tradition, it is to have one's will oriented correctly – that is, to choose to order one's actions in accordance with the love of God rather than a love of finite goods. For the Scottish enlightenment, it is to assent to the fundamental principles embodied in Scotland's church and legal system, either because these principles will satisfy our own desires and interests (as Hume argues), or because they are immediately intuited by common sense (which is Hutcheson's view). Finally, for liberalism, to be rational is to act in accordance with ethical principles that could be accepted by anyone, anywhere – by self-interested individuals in a hypothetical state of nature, let us say. But which of these traditions should we accept? Which gives the *best* account of practical rationality?[54] Clearly, we cannot expect to show that one tradition is better than another in the same way we would settle a disagreement *within* that tradition. We cannot, for example, show that the Augustinian tradition is superior to the Aristotelian by pointing out that the latter fails to attach sufficient importance to the will, or that it fails to see rational agents as belonging to a universal city of God. An Aristotelian does not accept that a tradition *ought* to do these things. Criticizing Aristotelianism from an Augustinian standpoint begs the question: it assumes the superiority of the Augustinian standpoint rather than demonstrating it. Nor can we show that one tradition is better than another by means of empirical examples – that is, by asking which tradition does a better job of guiding some particular agent through some particular practical dilemma. The two

---

[54] This way of talking is somewhat problematic. *Whose Justice?* argues that we cannot "try on" traditions – that we cannot temporarily adopt the standpoint of a tradition to see whether it suits us and should command our allegiance. MacIntyre insists that "genuinely to adopt the standpoint of a tradition thereby commits one to its view of what is true and false and, in so committing one, prohibits one from adopting any rival standpoint" (*WJ*, 367). This claim might suggest that it is impossible to compare several traditions in order to see which is rationally superior. However, the context of this remark suggests that MacIntyre has something different in mind. He makes this remark while discussing the "perspectivism" he sees in the work of Nietzsche and Deleuze. This perspectivism involves not only a desire to "try on" several different traditions, but a relativistic conviction that no tradition is better than any other. What MacIntyre wishes to deny is that one could investigate traditions from an *entirely* tradition-free standpoint. He does not, I take it, wish to deny that one can compare one's own tradition to others, or raise questions about its adequacy with respect to them. On the contrary, he claims that we *can* do this. See, for example, *WJ*, 393.

traditions, having different accounts of what it is to be rational, might describe the examples differently. As MacIntyre puts it, "each theory of practical reasoning is, among other things, a theory as to how examples are to be described, and how we describe any particular example will depend, therefore, upon which theory we have adopted" (*WJ*, 333). This is not to say that traditions are always incommensurable. Different traditions may well share some standards. But we cannot assume they will always share enough to reach agreement on fundamentals.

History, however, shows that matters are not so grim. As a matter of historical fact, some traditions have proved better than others. Agents faced with a conflict of traditions have found good reasons to choose one over another. What we must do, MacIntyre argues, is look closely at such conflicts, and see what is involved in one tradition proving better than another. The example of Thomas Aquinas is instructive here. Aquinas's work is the site of a conflict between two earlier traditions of inquiry, the Aristotelian and the Augustinian. Aquinas is committed to certain elements of Augustinian Christianity, such as the importance of the will in human action. Yet he is also convinced that Aristotle's philosophy is the pinnacle of what reason can achieve without divine revelation, and that it cannot contradict what Christians believe on faith. His solution is to accept the basic structure of Aristotle's practical philosophy, but to reinterpret some of its elements in Christian terms. For example, Aquinas accepts the Aristotelian claim that practical rationality consists in ranking goods, and in subordinating lower goods to a supreme good. Against Aristotle, however, he argues that this supreme good can only be the supernatural good that is knowledge of God. Similarly, Aquinas accepts the Augustinian claim that human action originates in the will. Against Augustine, however, he argues that the will is always guided by an Aristotelian process of practical deliberation – that it "is always moved to action by intellect" (*WJ*, 190). The structure of Aristotle's practical philosophy remains largely intact in Aquinas's work, but some of its content becomes Augustinian.

According to MacIntyre, what allows Aquinas to preserve what is true in the Augustinian account within an Aristotelian framework is his dialectical method, illustrated in his use of the disputed question. Aquinas begins his consideration of a topic by examining it from every angle he can think of, and by restating the positions one might hold on it as sympathetically as possible. This is a thoroughly Aristotelian way of proceeding. It was Aristotle's achievement to represent his own thought as the outcome of a long debate over goods, and to acknowledge earlier voices in this debate while identifying their limits. The disputed question lets Aquinas place himself in a series of extended historical conversations as well. This method has the effect of convincing his readers that he has "genuinely come to terms" (*WJ*, 204) with the arguments from these conversations. More importantly, it identifies the elements of each that can "withstand dialectical testing from every standpoint so far developed, with the aim of identifying … the limitations of each" (*WJ*, 207). To put it simply, Aquinas mediates between Aristotelianism and Augustinianism by bringing them into conversation, and by developing "a new and richer conceptual and theoretical framework" (*WJ*, 363) in which the resources and critical perspectives of each can come into contact.[55] When Aquinas amends or rejects what one tradition says, it is by showing that the other is more successful in some way that members of the first can understand and accept. He shows that the second tradition can identify and explain the limitations of the first, while the first is unable to identify and explain the limitations of the second. An Aristotelian, for example, acknowledges that the will plays an important role in human action, so he can explain what led the Augustinian to make the will the centerpiece of his practical philosophy. By contrast, an Augustinian does not attach a similar degree of importance to the process of practical deliberation as described by Aristotle. He therefore cannot explain why the Aristotelian tradition could have been drawn to the view that human action originates in a certain type of practical deliberation. On this topic, Aristotelianism can make Augustinianism intelligible to itself, while Augustinianism cannot do the reverse. To that extent, the Aristotelian tradition is preferable to the Augustinian. Of course, this way of proceeding is necessarily tentative, and its conclusions are always revisable. We cannot rule out the possibility that some future position will prove more successful than Aquinas's, according to Aquinas's own standards. But it is Aquinas's achievement to show what it would take for some future standpoint to prove superior to his own. Aquinas "integrate[s] the whole previous history of inquiry, so far as he was aware of it, into his own" (*WJ*, 207). His claim "against any rival out of the past is that the partiality, one-sidedness, and incoherences of that rival's standpoint will have already been overcome in the unfinished system portrayed in the *Summa*, while its strengths and successes will have been incorporated and perhaps reinforced" (*WJ*, 207). Any future rival would have to do the same for Aquinas. She would have to show that she has overcome the limitations of Aquinas's standpoint, while incorporating the successes of this standpoint into her own.

---

[55] As Jean Porter points out, certain conditions must be met before two traditions can be brought into contact in this way. See Porter, "Tradition in the Recent Work of Alasdair MacIntyre," 48–49.

There is a more general lesson here. Aquinas shows that the Aristotelian tradition is superior to the Augustinian by setting up a "dialectical conversation" (*WJ*, 207) between them. He shows that the Aristotelian tradition can recognize and address the limitations of the Augustinian, while the Augustinian tradition is unable to address the limitations of the Aristotelian. More generally, what makes a tradition preferable to its rivals is its ability to make sense of these rivals in ways they cannot make sense of it. The process of showing that a tradition can do this is historical.[56] It involves tracing the history of a rival tradition, identifying why the rival has succeeded in some ways, and explaining why it has failed in others. And it involves developing a vocabulary that members of the rival tradition can understand, a vocabulary that can communicate to them the strengths of the other tradition. Adjudicating traditions in this way is not an everyday occurrence. We do not usually ask whether one tradition is better than another until an epistemological crisis confronts us with dramatic evidence of our tradition's shortcomings. During such a crisis, MacIntyre argues, we naturally look for a different way of thinking, one that meets three criteria:

First, this in some ways radically new and conceptually enriched scheme, if it is to put an end to epistemological crisis, must furnish a solution to the problems which had previously proved intractable in a systematic and coherent way. Second, it must also provide an explanation of just what it was which rendered the tradition, before it had acquired these new resources, sterile or incoherent or both. And third, these first two tasks must be carried out in a way which exhibits some fundamental continuity of the new conceptual and theoretical structures with the shared beliefs in terms of which the tradition of inquiry had been defined up to this point. (*WJ*, 362)

Aquinas's "conceptually enriched" Aristotelianism allows him to do all three of these things for the Augustinian tradition. Aquinas can account for certain features of the will that had long puzzled Augustinians, such as

---

[56] For a more detailed discussion of this point, see *WJ*, 360. "Epistemological Crises" anticipates this claim about the historical character of the process, albeit in the context of a discussion of the philosophy of science. There, MacIntyre argues that the only way to show that one scientific paradigm is preferable to another, and that it is rational to choose one over the other, is to engage in historical study. He claims that "the best account that can be given of why some scientific theories are superior to others presupposes the possibility of constructing an intelligible dramatic narrative which can claim historical truth and in which such theories are the subject of successive episodes. It is because and only because we can construct better and worse histories of this kind, histories which can be rationally compared with each other, that we can compare theories rationally too" (470). MacIntyre goes on to argue that this type of historical awareness is what is missing from the discussions of paradigm shifts by Kuhn and Lakatos: "Without this background, scientific revolutions become unintelligible episodes; indeed Kuhn becomes – what in essence Lakatos accused him of being – the Kafka of the history of science. Small wonder that he in turn felt that Lakatos was not an historian, but an historical novelist" (471).

how it is related to and influenced by reason. With Aristotle's help, he can also explain why the classic Augustinian position is too one-sided to solve this problem on its own. He can identify and explain the Augustinian tradition's failings. Finally, he does all of this while maintaining a "fundamental continuity" between the Augustinian framework and his own. Rather than dismissing the Augustinian tradition, he amends it in ways its members can understand and appreciate.

So *Whose Justice?* learns how to adjudicate among traditions by studying a concrete conflict of traditions in the work of Thomas Aquinas. Moreover, it insists that historical study is the only way of learning how to do this. According to MacIntyre, attempts to give timeless accounts of what it is rational to believe – accounts such as those given by liberalism, for example – invariably fail.[57] History shows that history alone is of any help here. For this reason, however, MacIntyre's account of how one adjudicates among traditions must not be taken for a universal or necessary truth. Like any theory, it emerges from a specific tradition, and this requires us to be tentative about it. We can never rule out the possibility that some future tradition, or some future member of our own tradition, will prove more successful at answering our questions than we have been. All MacIntyre can claim on behalf of his method is that it is the best one to have emerged so far. And this is all he does claim. He insists that his historically informed method of adjudicating among traditions can lay no claim to "the Absolute Knowledge of the Hegelian system" (*WJ*, 361). It can claim to be only "the best theory so far as to what type of theory the best theory so far must be: no more, but no less" (*AV*, 270). But while we must be willing to revise this method, it does not follow that we should have no confidence in it. As long as this method

has successfully transcended the limitations of its predecessors and in so doing provided the best means available for understanding those predecessors to date *and* has then confronted successive challenges from a number of rival points of view, but in each case has been able to modify itself in the ways required to incorporate the strengths of those points of view while avoiding their weaknesses and limitations *and* has provided the best explanation so far of those weaknesses and limitations, then *we have the best possible reason to have confidence that future challenges will also be met successfully.* (*AV*, 270, my emphasis)

To the extent that MacIntyre's method incorporates the strengths of other methods while avoiding their defects – those of a "Hegelian" approach to

---

[57] For more on this matter, see MacIntyre's remarks on liberalism's shortcomings in *WJ*, 346.

traditions, for example (*WJ*, 361) – we have the best possible reason to be confident in it.

What has MacIntyre accomplished in *Whose Justice?* Simply put, he has found a way of adjudicating among different traditions, a method for determining when one tradition is rationally preferable to another. He finds this method through historical study. He finds it by studying the historical development of several different traditions, by tracing their origins, development, and interactions. Throughout all of this, he insists that historical study alone allows us to find such a method. He does not claim to offer a timeless method derived from universal standards of reason. There are, he insists, no such standards, since all inquiry is dependent on the resources of some tradition or other. All we can hope to find is the best method that historical inquiry has justified so far. But it is important to see how relentlessly historical *Whose Justice?* is. At every stage of his argument, MacIntyre appeals to historical considerations, and *only* historical considerations. Historical study establishes the book's premise: that there *are* different traditions of inquiry, traditions that sometimes offer incommensurable accounts of practical rationality. We could not demonstrate the plurality of traditions a priori. Only familiarity with the data of history reveals it to us. Historical study also shows that traditions sometimes prevail over one another. The example of Aquinas shows that agents can overcome a conflict of traditions, that they sometimes find it rational to favor one tradition over another. Historical study also shows *how* agents do so. Again, the example of Aquinas is instructive. It shows that it is rational to endorse one tradition when that tradition shows dialectically that it can make better sense of its rivals than they can of it. Finally, historical study shows MacIntyre how *not* to adjudicate among traditions. The example of liberalism shows that we should not try to settle conflicts between traditions by seeking a rationality that is independent of any particular tradition. We cannot show a priori that there is no tradition-free rationality. Only a knowledge of the history of liberalism can convince us of this.

We should note two further things about MacIntyre's repeated appeals to historical considerations. First, we should note how active these appeals are. MacIntyre does not bolster his argument by appealing to well-known or uncontroversial features of the history of philosophy. He tries to *make us see* certain things in this history, to trigger a change in what we see this history *as*. Like *After Virtue, Whose Justice?* relates a history full of unfamiliar and sometimes startling episodes. It is a history in which Plato's *Republic* is a dialectical conversation involving Pericles, Thucydides, and Sophocles (*WJ*, 72). It is a history in which Aristotle is "Plato's heir" (*WJ*, 88), someone whose disagreements with Plato pale beside his desire to complete Plato's ethical project (*WJ*, 89–96). It is a history in which the Scottish enlightenment is above all a rejection of a certain type of Aristotelianism (*WJ*, 207), as well as a history in which Hume is a subverter of the Scottish philosophical tradition rather than its most distinguished representative (*WJ*, 323–325). This is not to say that MacIntyre's revisionist claims are false or irresponsible. He goes to great lengths to support them with the best evidence available. But it is to say that *Whose Justice?* should not be read as a conventional piece of historical scholarship. Its goal is not to summarize what we know about the history of ethics, but to make us see this history in a surprising new way.

The second thing to note about *Whose Justice?* is the way it uses narrative to bring about a shift in our view of the history of ethics. As I argued in Chapter 2, narratives persuade in a different way than deductive or inductive arguments. Narratives do not neutrally relate facts that would have the same force if communicated in some other way. A successful narrative structures its elements in a way that "sounds right," and in so doing, compels assent. It strives to make its audience see things in a certain way. The elements of a narrative do not stand alone. Their significance derives to a great extent from the way they fit into the larger structure. This dependence on narrative is a crucial feature of *Whose Justice?* No one could fail to notice that the book tells a long, detailed story about the history of inquiry into practical reason. But we might well fail to notice that the particular claims it makes about individual thinkers are inseparable from the larger story. If we assess one of these claims on its own – for example, the claim that Aristotle is Plato's heir to a much greater degree than is usually realized – then we will miss much of its force. This force can be appreciated only when we see the role that this claim plays in the overall story – when we see what this story lets us notice about the history of ethics, how much it explains, and how right it sounds. So *Whose Justice?* does not merely happen to contain a long and immensely detailed narrative. As MacIntyre says in a different context, "its form is dictated by its conclusions."[58] The book's argument is inseparable from its narrative structure.

In short, *Whose Justice?* displays many of the features common to attempts to do philosophy historically. It uses historical considerations to

---

[58] MacIntyre, "Contexts of Interpretation," 41. MacIntyre originally said this about Gadamer's *Truth and Method*. Another remark he makes about *Truth and Method* that applies equally to *Whose Justice?* is that "a good deal that appears early in the argument only becomes fully clear and relevant as one reaches the end" (41).

establish philosophical claims; it tries to bring about a dramatic shift in how its readers see the history of thought; and its argument is heavily dependent on the book's narrative form. But *Whose Justice?* seems to lack one feature that I have argued is crucial to doing philosophy historically: a concern with philosophical pictures. *Whose Justice?* does not seem to trace the development of one or more pictures. Instead, it traces the development of several traditions, and it does so in order to draw philosophical conclusions about what these traditions can and cannot do. But traditions and pictures are not the same thing, and in this respect, *Whose Justice?* does not seem to fit my account of doing philosophy historically.

What should we say here? It is certainly true that *Whose Justice?* is concerned with the development of traditions. But it does not follow that it is unconcerned with pictures. On the contrary, in studying the history of several traditions, *Whose Justice?* is simultaneously tracing the development of a number of pictures, because traditions and pictures are closely related. Traditions, we might say, manifest pictures. Members of a tradition share certain general ways of viewing the world. They share dispositions to approach philosophical questions in characteristic ways. This is not to say that the members of a tradition must share a single picture, one that remains fossilized for the tradition's entire history. A tradition's way of viewing reality evolves. As a tradition develops over time, its members refine, test, and discard the pictures they use to make sense of reality. Surely this is what it means to say that a tradition is an "argument." The members of a tradition do not merely argue about particular theories – say, about "the nature of mathematical truths" (*WJ*, 94), to take one theoretical issue that divided Plato and Aristotle. They also argue about the nature of their tradition, about which questions their tradition should ask and how it should go about answering them. The Aristotelian tradition, for example, passes through a number of stages in which its members try out a number of frameworks for making sense of human action. The early stages of this tradition understand human life by means of a framework that defines and distinguishes two types of goods, goods of excellence and goods of effectiveness. Thanks to Plato and Aristotle, the tradition changes into one concerned with the *polis* and its ability to make possible the pursuit of human good as such. With Aquinas, the tradition changes yet again, in order to make Aristotle's philosophical vocabulary consistent with the view of reality articulated by Christian revelation. In short, the Aristotelian tradition is not an argument about the correct answers to an unchanging set of questions. It is an argument about which questions we should ask about human beings, an argument about which conceptual frameworks we should use to understand them. The history of a tradition is, among other things, a process through which that tradition develops, modifies, and abandons a series of philosophical pictures. And MacIntyre comes close to saying as much. He says that traditions are defined by debate over the large-scale "conceptual and theoretical structures" (*WJ*, 362) they will use to make sense of experience. He also says that traditions involve the development and testing of different "interpretative schemata,"[59] and as we have seen, the notions of interpretative schemata and of philosophical pictures are closely related.[60] So while MacIntyre does not use the term "philosophical picture," he seems to have the notion very much in mind when discussing the evolution of traditions.

There is, however, one important difference between traditions and pictures. Traditions often exclude each other in a way that pictures do not. As I have argued,[61] pictures typically stand in complex relations to one another. One picture can contain another, in the way that the "modern" picture contains the "Cartesian." A picture can overlap with another, as is the case with the "modern" picture and the picture Rorty calls "representationalism." And a single figure, text, or theory can be seen as embodying indefinitely many different pictures. Descartes, for example, may be accurately described as a Cartesian, a modern, a representationalist, and indefinitely many other things as well. Traditions, on the other hand, tend not to overlap with each other in this way. They typically oppose each other, offering rival and often incommensurable ways of viewing the world. To be a liberal is precisely *not* to be an Aristotelian or an Augustinian. True, it is always possible that an Aquinas will come along and fuse two traditions long thought incompatible. But this is an exceptional occurrence, not a common event in the life of a tradition. At any rate, the fact that traditions can oppose and exclude each other does not mean that traditions are *not* arguments about pictures. It just means that they are larger and more complex than any particular picture. Traditions can last for centuries or even millennia, so their lines of questioning have the opportunity to diverge in ways that pictures typically do not. It is their age, their scope, and their complexity that allow them to become incompatible with their rivals, when they do.

We have now considered the first two parts of MacIntyre's critical project. We have seen him use historical study to discredit a flawed picture. We have also seen him use history to develop a method of finding an alternative. We must now see him apply this method. We must see how he

---

[59] MacIntyre, "Epistemological Crises," 454.   [60] See Section 2, above.   [61] See Chapter 1, Section 4.

uses it to argue for his own preferred way of thinking about ethics. That is the task of *Three Rival Versions of Moral Enquiry.*

CRITICISM AS VINDICATION: *THREE RIVAL VERSIONS OF MORAL ENQUIRY*

As we have seen, *Whose Justice?* offers a method for adjudicating among rival traditions. But this method cannot be applied in a tradition-neutral way. According to MacIntyre, all rational inquiry is rooted in the particularities of some tradition, and applying his own method is no exception. So there can be no question of finding the best tradition, once and for all, for anyone, anywhere. We must be content to learn which tradition is rationally superior for a particular agent at a particular moment in history. In MacIntyre's words, what this method reveals "will depend upon who you are and how you understand yourself" (*WJ*, 393). But there is still some room for generalization. MacIntyre expects most of his readers to be in much the same position. They will have been brought up in a certain tradition of thinking about practical rationality, but without reflecting on it, and perhaps without realizing that their tradition *is* a tradition.[62] "Such a person," he claims,

> will characteristically have learned to speak and write some particular language-in-use, the presuppositions of whose use tie that language to a set of beliefs which that person may never have explicitly formulated for him or herself except in partial and occasional ways. He or she will characteristically have found themselves responsive to certain texts, less so or not at all to others, open to certain kinds of argumentative consideration, unpersuaded by others. (*WJ*, 394)

If such a person eventually has a more reflective encounter with her philosophical tradition – if she reads one of its classic texts or meets one of its contemporary defenders – it will be with "a shock of recognition: *this* is not only, such a person may say, what I now take to be true but in some measure what I have always taken to be true" (*WJ*, 394). For someone in this position, seeking the most rational tradition is a matter of confirming or disconfirming this impression over time. It involves learning about "the ongoing arguments within that tradition" (*WJ*, 394), as well as making a good faith effort to understand what rival traditions have to say about these

---

[62] MacIntyre realizes that most people in the contemporary West do not see themselves as belonging to any tradition at all. He argues, however, that this is an illusion, and that most of us acquire implicit and unrecognized ties to some tradition simply by being socialized and learning a language. See *WJ*, 395–396.

arguments. If such a person comes to understand another tradition well enough to be convinced that it is more successful than her own, then it is rational for her to adopt the perspective of the new tradition.

The final pages of *Whose Justice?* offer some hints about how MacIntyre expects this process to go. He suggests that most contemporary agents who think critically about their tradition and who try to understand the resources of others will conclude that Aristotelianism is rationally superior to its rivals. More specifically, he suggests that the version of Aristotelianism articulated by Thomas Aquinas will prove more successful at explaining the strengths and limitations of its competitors than any other tradition. Thomistic Aristotelianism, he argues, has emerged remarkably well from its encounters with other traditions, such as Augustinianism and the anti-Aristotelianism of the Scottish enlightenment. Its adherents have good reason to believe that their tradition is rational. So despite its tentativeness, *Whose Justice?* ends with an "emerging Thomistic conclusion" (*WJ*, 403). It suggests that the Aristotelianism of Thomas Aquinas is rationally preferable to any other tradition available in the contemporary world. But MacIntyre wants to make more than a prima facie case for Thomism. Accordingly, *Three Rival Versions* defends MacIntyre's Thomistic conclusion in a more detailed and more rigorous way.

Three Rival Versions is concerned with what MacIntyre calls three "types of moral inquiry" (*TRV*, 3). Despite the vagueness of this term, it soon becomes clear that the book is concerned with traditions, and specifically with traditions of inquiry into practical rationality. Not only does MacIntyre go on to use the terms "type of moral inquiry" and "tradition" interchangeably; he attributes to these "types" several of the features that *Whose Justice?* attributes to traditions. He describes types of moral inquiry as arguments extended over time, "research programs" (*TRV*, 54) about practical rationality that originate with some seminal figure but evolve in the work of that figure's followers.[63] He also claims that types of moral inquiry are socially embodied. They are not just sets of philosophical theses, but are "something wider than what is conventionally, at least in American universities, understood as moral philosophy," since they include "historical, literary, anthropological, and sociological questions" (*TRV*, 3). Finally, the

---

[63] For example, MacIntyre traces the encyclopedic version of moral inquiry from its origins with the eighteenth-century *encyclopédistes* (*TRV*, 174 *passim*), through its transformations by the contributors to the Ninth Edition of the *Encyclopedia Britannica*, up to its remnants in contemporary academia (*TRV*, 170–171). He also describes the genealogical version of moral inquiry as a research program initiated by Nietzsche but transformed in important ways by Foucault (*TRV*, 49–54), Derrida (*TRV*, 46), and Deleuze (*TRV*, 206–208).

types of moral inquiry that MacIntyre discusses in *Three Rival Versions* overlap significantly with the particular traditions explored in *Whose Justice?* They are, in fact, the same traditions, given different names and studied at different points in their development.[64] The first, which MacIntyre calls the encyclopedic version of moral inquiry, traces its lineage to the Scottish enlightenment (*TRV*, 14–15).[65] It is exemplified by the Ninth Edition of the *Encyclopedia Britannica*, which MacIntyre considers "the canonical expression of the Edinburgh culture of Adam Gifford's day" (*TRV*, 18). The contributors to the Ninth Edition had distinctive views of reason and of morality. They believed in what Christopher Lutz calls "once-and-for-all rationality,"[66] assuming "that there is a single, if perhaps complex, conception of what the standards and the achievement of rationality are, one which every educated person can without too much difficulty be brought to agree in acknowledging" (*TRV*, 14). They believed that there is a single, correct account of how human beings ought to behave, and that anyone not in the grip of prejudice or superstition can discover this account. This view of morality attached a great deal of importance to "rule-following and … ritualized responses to breaches of rules" (*TRV*, 26). It also presupposed a rigid distinction between "*the* moral" and "*the* aesthetic, *the* religious, *the* economic, *the* legal, and *the* scientific" (*TRV*, 26).

MacIntyre's second type of moral inquiry, genealogy, originates in Nietzsche's work, but has more recently found expression in the writings of Foucault and Deleuze. Its "foundation document" (*TRV*, 25), Nietzsche's *Genealogy of Morals*, seeks to discredit the very notions of

[64] As I explain below, "tradition" corresponds to the Thomist version of Aristotelianism; "encyclopedia" corresponds to the Scottish enlightenment, though it incorporates some elements of the liberal tradition as well; and "genealogy" corresponds to one aspect of liberalism (though an aspect that few liberals consciously accept): the conviction that membership in a tradition precludes one from being rational. (Perhaps MacIntyre would say that genealogy is the version of moral inquiry that liberals *would* endorse if they were consistent.) All three of these traditions are studied at a specific point in their development, one unexplored by *Whose Justice?* – the late nineteenth century. Of the four traditions discussed in *Whose Justice?*, only Augustinianism has no equivalent in *Three Rival Versions*. Presumably this is because MacIntyre sees Augustinianism as having been successfully incorporated into the Aristotelian tradition by Aquinas.

[65] Christopher Lutz disagrees with this claim. He sees encyclopedia as corresponding to the liberal tradition studied by *Whose Justice?*, not the Scottish enlightenment. See Lutz, *Tradition in the Ethics of Alasdair MacIntyre*, 52. While I agree that encyclopedia has a great deal in common with liberalism – notably a conception of reason as universal – I am struck by MacIntyre's account of how it emerged out of the social and academic institutions of nineteenth-century Scotland (*TRV*, 14–15). By and large, these are the same institutions described in Chapters 12 and 13 of *Whose Justice?* At any rate, there is no contradiction in claiming that encyclopedia is *both* a descendent of the Scottish enlightenment *and* an embodiment of liberalism, especially since liberalism owes much to the thinkers of the Scottish enlightenment.

[66] Lutz, *Tradition in the Ethics of Alasdair MacIntyre*, 54.

morality and truth by exposing them as disguised manifestations of the will to power. More generally, the genealogical approach to moral inquiry sets out "to write the history of those social and psychological formations in which the will to power is distorted into and concealed by the will to truth" (*TRV*, 39). Where the encyclopedist sees moral duties prescribed by reason, the genealogist sees duplicitous attempts to manipulate others. Genealogy therefore tries "to discredit the whole notion of a canon" (*TRV*, 25) by exposing the secret causes and motives behind other forms of moral inquiry. It is a purely negative enterprise. Genealogy does not seek to construct a new, better morality of its own. It values only the process of critique, the "movement from utterance to utterance in which what is communicated is the movement" (*TRV*, 49). Though genealogy does not look exactly like any of the traditions from *Whose Justice?*, it embodies certain elements of liberalism, as MacIntyre understands it. The liberal, according to MacIntyre, understands rationality as a freedom from all traditions. To the extent that one's beliefs are shaped by one's ties to a particular time and place, one is not being rational. The genealogist shares this assumption. She thinks rationality is incompatible with rootedness, and she seeks to discredit positions that are thought to be rational by exposing their roots.

MacIntyre's third form of moral inquiry – which he calls "tradition" – is clearly Thomism. More specifically, it is the version of Thomism articulated in the 1879 papal letter *Aeterni Patris*. This document "summoned its readers to a renewal of an understanding of intellectual inquiry as the continuation of a specific type of tradition, that which achieved definitive expression in the writings of Aquinas" (*TRV*, 25). As we have seen, Thomism is really a type of Aristotelianism. It traces its origin to ancient Greek debates about the proper ordering of various human goods, and it fuses Aristotle's vocabulary and style of thinking with a broadly Christian view of the world. *Three Rival Versions* emphasizes that for Thomism, practical reasoning is conceived of as a "craft" (*TRV*, 61). It must be taught to new members by more skilled practitioners, and it is "justified by its history so far, which has made it what it is in that specific time, place, and set of historical circumstances" (*TRV*, 65). In opposition to encyclopedia and genealogy, Thomism believes in "historically situated rationality" (*TRV*, 65). It does not try to give a single correct moral code for all agents in all circumstances. Nor does it claim that our failure to find such a code discredits moral inquiry. It is a tradition that recognizes itself as a tradition, and it is therefore willing to engage with and learn from other traditions of moral inquiry.

Which of these traditions is most rational? Which would be most satisfactory to someone who has implicit and perhaps unacknowledged ties to one tradition, but who is making a good faith attempt to understand the resources of others? We know what MacIntyre's method demands: the most rational tradition is the one that is best able to make sense of its rivals in ways they cannot make sense of it. Specifically, the most rational tradition is the one that can best explain why someone might have been drawn to its rivals in the first place. It is also the one that can identify the nagging problems faced by other traditions, explain why these traditions have been unable to solve these problems, and point towards solutions of its own. And it must do all of these things in ways that members of rival traditions can understand and accept. It must develop a vocabulary and a set of concepts that are intelligible to those who belong to other traditions. So what can MacIntyre's three traditions say about each other's strengths and weaknesses? First of all, what can the encyclopedic version of moral inquiry say about the other two versions? The encyclopedist's view of morality forces her to adopt a doctrinaire attitude towards all rival traditions. Encyclopedia insists that there is a single correct moral code for all human beings, and that any educated person not blinded by prejudice or superstition can discover it. Of course, the contributors to the Ninth Edition were aware of the existence of moral disagreement, both among cultures and within their own culture. They explained this disagreement with an elaborate theory of moral progress. From the perspective of this theory,

> the distinctness of morality appeared not as a timeless, but as an emerging, phenomenon. It was through a process in the course of which moral rules were disengaged from a variety of nonrational, superstitious entanglements both with rules concerning pollution and contagion and with rules prescribing ritual observances that moral progress was taken to have occurred, a progress towards just such an apprehension of moral truths as the eighteenth century had envisaged but one exhibited in full clarity only by the civilized rather than the primitive or savage mind. (*TRV*, 176)

For the encyclopedist, it is an article of faith that her own, allegedly "civilized" standpoint, is rationally superior to all others. When faced with other cultures who understand morality differently than she does, she can only dismiss these cultures as "primitive" or "savage." Note, however, that in asserting that all other cultures are inferior to her own, the encyclopedist cuts herself off from the possibility of *explaining* to these cultures why they are inferior. She cannot explain their alleged inferiority in terms they would accept and understand, because these cultures are supposed to be insufficiently advanced to engage in rational debate about morality. It is not that the encyclopedist cannot identify any problems in other traditions. She can, after all, criticize these traditions for their alleged savagery. But in doing so, she is invoking her own standards and vocabulary, not those of the other traditions. And MacIntyre's method demands more. It requires that the encyclopedist explain "the limitations and failures of that rival tradition as judged by that rival tradition's own standards, limitations and failures which the rival tradition itself lacks the resources to explain or understand" (*TRV*, 181). In short, the encyclopedic tradition cannot demonstrate its superiority to other traditions, because it refuses to engage in genuine dialogue with them. "The authors of the great canonical encyclopedias," MacIntyre claims, "just because they insisted on seeing and judging everything from their own point of view turned out to have no way of making themselves visible to themselves" (*TRV*, 185).[67]

What about genealogy? What can it say about rival traditions? Genealogy is quite skilled at pointing out the failings of other traditions. Its mission is to debunk the claims of other traditions, to expose other forms of moral inquiry as disguised manifestations of the will to power. So it is easy to imagine the sorts of criticisms that this tradition might direct at an encyclopedist, for example. It would attack what it saw as "the false claims to objectivity," the spurious "value-neutrality" (*TRV*, 40), and the naive faith in progress embodied in the Ninth Edition of the *Encyclopedia Britannica*. But while genealogy has a great deal to say *about* other traditions, it is not clear what it has to say *to* them. It is not clear that genealogy has the conceptual resources needed to conduct a genuine dialogue with other traditions – which, as we have seen, is what MacIntyre's method demands. The reason is that genealogy seems to reject the presuppositions of a dialogue between traditions. A dialogue between traditions is an argument extended over time, and in order to engage in such an argument, one's own standpoint must possess a degree of temporal identity and continuity. It need not remain totally static, of course. Traditions constantly evolve. But in order for genealogy to enter into an extended argument with other traditions, we must be able to recognize it as the same form of inquiry at

---

[67] A related problem is that a tradition's claim to superiority must be based on "a rationally justifiable rejection of the strongest claim to be made out from the opposing point of view" (*TRV*, 181). In other words, a tradition cannot claim to be better than another unless it has "rendered itself maximally vulnerable to the strongest arguments which that other and rival view can bring to bear against it" (*TRV*, 181). Aquinas's use of the disputed question is a classic example of this procedure. But in dismissing all other traditions as "primitive," the contributors to the Ninth Edition cut themselves off from the possibility of doing this. It "never even occurred to [them]," MacIntyre writes, "to enter imaginatively into the standpoint of those allegedly primitive and savage peoples whom they were studying, let alone to inquire how they and their moral and religious theory might be understood from the point of view of those alien cultures" (*TRV*, 182).

different points in the argument. Moreover, we must be able to attribute a certain identity over time to its members: "because I within my community undertake projects extended through time," MacIntyre writes, "it must be possible throughout this bodily life to impute continuing accountability for agency" (*TRV*, 197). But genealogists are famously skeptical about this sort of identity. Nietzsche is well known for rejecting "any notion of *the* truth and correspondingly any conception of *what is* as such and timelessly as contrasted with what seems to be the case from a variety of different perspectives" (*TRV*, 205). More recent genealogists such as Foucault echo this rejection with their talk of the death of the author. But if genealogy denies that persons and traditions have identity over time, then how can it coherently see itself as *a* form of inquiry at all? That would require temporal continuity, and the genealogist must be "as suspicious of his or her own ascriptions of selfhood as anyone else's" (*TRV*, 206). More importantly, how can genealogy enter into dialogue with other traditions, as MacIntyre's method demands? That would require that it co-exist with them and share something with them – namely, enough of a common vocabulary and a common stock of concepts to allow it to identify their strengths and weaknesses. In rejecting temporal identity, the genealogical project deprives itself of any "adequately shared way of characterizing such common ground as there is" (*TRV*, 209). Clearly, however, the genealogist *wants* to talk about other traditions. At the very least, she wants to point out their failings and suggest that her own approach is superior to theirs. But she lacks the conceptual resources to do so.

Finally, let us turn to tradition – to Aristotelian thought, as embodied in Thomism generally, and in *Aeterni Patris* in particular. MacIntyre argues that it is the most successful of the three traditions, because it is the only one capable of doing what his method demands. It is the only one capable of conducting a successful dialogue with the encyclopedic and the genealogical approaches, which makes it the only one capable of demonstrating its superiority to its rivals. Unlike these approaches, Thomism does not deprive itself of the conceptual resources required for genuine dialogue. It does not dismiss other traditions as irrational; on the contrary, it strives to make itself vulnerable to the strongest objections its rivals have to offer. Nor does it deny the temporal identity of persons and traditions; on the contrary, it sees both as possessing "the continuity and unity of a quest, a quest whose object is to discover the truth about my life as a whole" (*TRV*, 197). More importantly, Thomism does not merely assert that its rivals fail to accomplish what they intend. It can explain *why* they fail, and why one might nevertheless have been drawn to those approaches in the first place. The encyclopedist, as we have seen, is hard pressed to explain moral disagreement within her own culture. She can only assert that those who disagree with her are at a primitive stage in their moral development, though in principle she cannot convince her rivals of this with evidence. The Thomist, on the other hand, can explain this disagreement by telling the very story MacIntyre tells in *After Virtue*. She can explain that there is "a history of moral thought in and through which moral apprehensions are articulated and moral practice provided with its theory, a history initially generated by Socrates" (*TRV*, 191). This history, however, "was interrupted in the most radical way" (*TRV*, 191). The Thomist can explain moral disagreement by describing it as the outcome of the disappearance of teleological conceptions of human nature after the scientific revolution. She can explain that without the notion of a human good, enlightenment moralists were unable to give compelling reasons to accept the content of traditional Christian morality. She can also explain why the philosophers who lived through this development might have been drawn to the enlightenment project, even though this project was bound to fail. Since these philosophers possessed only the remnants of a "predecessor culture" (*AV*, 36), they lacked the social setting necessary to develop a more coherent conception of morality. The enlightenment project seemed like the only option available to them. In a similar way, the Thomist can explain the appeal of the genealogical enterprise. In the wake of the enlightenment project, the remnants of morality look much as Nietzsche says they do. They are part of an emotivist culture in which moral claims appear to be nothing more than arbitrary assertions of one's own will. But while the genealogist sees this state of affairs as the true nature of all moral discourse – something she can only assert – the Thomist can explain it. She can tell a story much like the one MacIntyre tells in *After Virtue*, a story in which our emotivist culture results from the steady decline in Western morality since the scientific revolution. The Thomist can also solve certain problems that genealogists have proved unable to solve. Genealogy cannot explain how selves and traditions can possess any identity over time, even though its own discourse presupposes that they do. The Thomist, however, understands human life as a "quest" (*TRV*, 197), a "teleologically ordered" (*TRV*, 199) search for the good. She therefore sees human life as possessing the unity of a narrative. Thomism has the conceptual resources to explain what genealogy cannot. "The Thomist," in short, can "render intelligible the history of both modern morality and modern moral philosophy in a way which is not available to those who themselves inhabit the conceptual frameworks peculiar to modernity" (*TRV*, 194). This is the source of its appeal for modern agents.

Three Rival Versions is a defense of Thomism. It is a historical defense, as it claims it must be. In MacIntyre's view, the only way to vindicate Thomism is to do philosophy historically, and *Three Rival Versions* bears all the marks of this enterprise. It understands Thomism not as a specific theory, but as something broader. MacIntyre refers to it as a "type of moral inquiry" (*TRV*, 3), a "research program" (*TRV*, 54) concerned with the nature of practical rationality. He also understands Thomism as a tradition, albeit a tradition that *Three Rival Versions* examines at one specific moment in its development. And as we have seen, traditions manifest philosophical pictures. They express very general ways of looking at the world, and they are extended arguments about which ways of looking at the world we ought to adopt. In defending Thomism, MacIntyre is arguing that a certain cluster of pictures is superior to its rivals. Furthermore, MacIntyre argues for the superiority of Thomism by examining what it has done. He claims that Thomism has the best resources available for making sense of human action and for solving the nagging philosophical questions we have inherited. These resources, however, are not mere abstract potential. MacIntyre shows what Thomism can do by tracing what it *has* done over time. He shows that Thomism's dialectical method, and its willingness to adopt resources from other traditions, have given it a unique ability to make sense of its rivals in ways they cannot make sense of it, and to do so in ways that its rivals can accept and understand. Note as well MacIntyre's insistence on examining Thomism and its rivals at a single, relatively recent point in their history: the late nineteenth century. Asking what these traditions can do is not a matter of speculating about what they might do at some indeterminate point in the future. It is a matter of asking which tradition comes to us with the most impressive history, and which tradition is best able to speak to our current situation. To defend Thomism is therefore to say something about *us*. It is to say that we have a certain set of philosophical needs, and that Thomism has proved better able to address these needs than any other option available to us. Finally, none of the claims MacIntyre makes on Thomism's behalf could stand alone. They are inseparable from the narrative he constructs about the history of moral inquiry. Thomism is superior to its rivals because it can explain what they cannot, and it explains these things – encyclopedia's bafflement in the face of moral disagreement, genealogy's appeal in an emotivist culture – through its own historical narrative. MacIntyre does not defend Thomism by giving deductive or inductive arguments for its theses. He defends Thomism by highlighting its resources in a story that sounds right.[68]

THE BIGGER PICTURE

MacIntyre obviously has a great deal to teach us about the enlightenment project. But what does he teach us about doing philosophy historically? The simplest answer is that he shows that historical inquiry may function as a form of criticism. We can use historical considerations to repudiate a picture, as when we conclude from a picture's development that it is incapable of doing something crucial, and should therefore be abandoned. Beyond that, MacIntyre's work offers several more specific lessons.

The first is an enriched understanding of what criticism is. MacIntyre's critique of the enlightenment project is complex and multifaceted. It involves several distinct steps, each of which is defended with historical evidence. It has a purely negative moment: its discovery that the project of finding a purely rational basis for morality is bound to fail. But it also has a more positive side. *Whose Justice?* uses history to find a method for determining whether one tradition is rationally superior to another. *Three Rival Versions* applies this method, using it to argue that Thomism is preferable to its competitors. MacIntyre shows that criticizing a picture can involve more than just rejecting it. Historical study can also vindicate a picture, and can even be used to justify methodologies and metaphilosophical stances. In a similar vein, MacIntyre shows that criticism is closely related to narrative. Successful criticisms of a picture do not simply claim that it violates universal standards of rationality. Since different pictures can have different conceptions of what rationality is, that sort of criticism would raise "insoluble incommensurability problems" (*AV*, 268). Successful criticisms take the form of a narrative, a narrative that explains how a picture encountered certain difficulties it could not solve, and how a rival picture does a better

---

[68] The defense of Thomism in *Three Rival Versions* echoes the one advanced in another major work MacIntyre published in the same year: *First Principles, Final Ends and Contemporary Philosophical Issues. First Principles* argues that Thomism's rational superiority to other traditions consists in its ability to show that "an Aristotelian and Thomistic conception of inquiry, in terms of first principles and final ends, can provide us with an understanding and explanation of types of philosophy which themselves reject root and branch the possibility of providing a rational justification for any such conception." See Alasdair MacIntyre, *First Principles, Final Ends and Contemporary Philosophical Issues* (Milwaukee: Marquette University Press, 1990), 67. For an excellent summary of this book, and of its importance for MacIntyre's defense of Thomism, see Kent Reames, "Metaphysics, History, and Moral Philosophy: The Centrality of the 1990 Aquinas Lecture to MacIntyre's Argument for Thomism." *Thomist* 62 (1998), 419–443.

job of addressing those difficulties. "It is," MacIntyre claims, "only because we can construct better and worse histories of this kind" that we can criticize pictures without begging the question.[69] Pictures may be criticized, but not as though they were stand-alone arguments. Asking which picture is most rational is inseparable from asking which story sounds right.

MacIntyre's second contribution is closely connected. He shows that although criticizing pictures is not the same thing as criticizing theories, the two activities are related. Their relation, however, is different than we might expect. It is tempting to think that philosophizing starts with theories: that the most basic part of inquiry is to ask which theories have the strongest evidence in their favor. Having determined which theories are most likely to be true, we then ask which traditions of inquiry, or which general pictures of reality, are compatible with them. But if MacIntyre's account of rationality is right, matters are the other way around. We do not choose our theories before choosing our traditions, because traditions give us the standards of rationality needed to assess theories in the first place. Rather, the most basic part of inquiry is to determine whether a given tradition deserves our loyalty. This is a matter of assessing the story it tells about itself and its rivals, of determining whether its narrative sounds right. If it does sound right – if the tradition proves better at making itself intelligible to its rivals than they are at making themselves intelligible to it – then the tradition deserves our loyalty. This in turn means that it is rational for us to assent to its theories. We do not accept a tradition because it has the best theories about metaphysics and epistemology; we accept the metaphysical and epistemological theories that we do because they are entailed by the tradition we have judged to be best. So it is not the case that criticizing traditions has nothing to do with criticizing theories. When we criticize a tradition, we thereby criticize its theories, though in an indirect, second-order way.

What does this have to do with philosophical pictures? As I have argued, traditions manifest pictures. They are, among other things, expressions of our most general ways of looking at reality. Accordingly, what MacIntyre says about the criticism of traditions applies to the criticism of pictures as well. Criticizing a picture is not the same thing as criticizing a theory. We do not reject Platonism or Cartesianism because it is logically untenable, or because one of its theories is demonstrably false. We reject these pictures, when we do, on the basis of more global considerations – because they fail to make sense of their rivals in ways that their rivals can make sense of them. This does not mean that we are indifferent to the truth or falsity of the

---

[69] MacIntyre, "Epistemological Crises," 470.

theories associated with a given picture. If a picture proves more successful than its rivals in the ways MacIntyre describes, then that fact gives us the best possible reason to accept the theories associated with it. When we do philosophy historically, theories are not our main concern. But we are nevertheless engaged in learning about them and making judgments about them. We simply do so indirectly.

Finally, MacIntyre makes a third contribution to our understanding of doing philosophy historically: he highlights the social dimension of this enterprise. A tradition, as MacIntyre understands it, is not just a philosophical outlook. It is a philosophical outlook embodied in and inseparable from the practices of a specific community. We do not merely find a tradition in the theoretical pronouncements of its members. We find it in its language, its institutions, and its way of orienting itself towards the good. When we study a tradition, we are studying more than a collection of philosophical views. We are studying a mode of social life, a set of institutions and practices. And when we accept or reject a tradition, we are accepting or rejecting a mode of social life, expressing our preference for one form of life over another. Since traditions manifest philosophical pictures, all of this applies, *mutatis mutandis*, to pictures as well. A philosophical picture is a social phenomenon. It is a general conception of how the world is, one that finds expression in practices and institutions as well as in philosophical pronouncements. If we want to understand a picture well, we should expect to study more than the writings of philosophers. We should expect to study the ways that picture is embodied in the rest of a culture: in science, literature, and political practice, for example. This is a daunting task, and few philosophers may be up to it.[70] But it has the advantage of helping to dismantle the sharp divide between philosophy and practice, between the way we think and the way we live.

---

[70] MacIntyre has little hope that philosophers will study all the social phenomena required to understand traditions properly. "Contexts of Interpretation" addresses precisely this point. It insists that such study is necessary, since "we cannot develop even a minimally adequate view of the particulars … until we have drawn on materials – philosophical, literary, linguistic – which are now allocated to what are now taken to be different disciplines. There is *no* enquiry which ought not be comparative from the outset" (46). But MacIntyre doubts that many philosophers will "spare the time" for this study "from such arduous cultural tasks as reading *The New York Times Book Review* section or *The New York Review of Books*" (41).

CHAPTER 5

The diagnostic approach: Heidegger

This chapter deals with the second approach to doing philosophy historically, which I have called the *diagnostic* approach. This approach is rooted in the fact that philosophical pictures can be deceptive. A picture may be widely accepted: it may serve as the unquestioned starting point for a great deal of our thinking, and we may take for granted that we understand it. But it may have a hidden significance that escapes us. It may have far-reaching effects on our thinking, perhaps negative ones, that we fail to notice. When this happens, we frequently find it necessary to diagnose the picture. We inspect it with a suspicious eye, in the hopes of discovering its true nature and unearthing the ways in which it distorts our thinking. Typically, this involves tracing the picture's origin: examining how it came into existence, how it came to govern our thinking, and what it led us to neglect in the course of doing so. In returning to the picture's origin, we learn how and why it began to deceive us. We may also discover alternatives to it, competing pictures that it supplanted and that have long been overlooked. Diagnosis of this sort often serves as a form of therapy. Pictures deceive us when we fail to understand their true nature or recognize their effects. In other words, pictures deceive us when we fail to reflect on them. Reflecting on how a picture came to deceive us helps to lessen its hold on us. By using the term "diagnostic," I mean to invoke certain parallels with psychoanalysis. A psychoanalyst treats a present dysfunction by tracing it back to its origin in some past trauma. This process both explains why the dysfunction exists and helps free the patient from its influence. Similarly, when we trace a deceptive picture back to its origin, we simultaneously learn about the limits on our thinking and are helped to overcome them.

The diagnostic approach is therefore different from the critical. Both engage in "criticism," in a very loose sense of the term. Both study philosophical pictures in order to show that there is something wrong with them. But they take aim at different sorts of pictures, and point out different sorts of problems. The diagnostic approach is directed at pictures that are essentially deceptive. As our engagement with Heidegger will show, there can exist pictures whose failure to understand themselves is constitutive of what they are. Adherents of these pictures are *in principle* incapable of understanding their thought properly. This is quite a different problem than the ones typically unearthed by the critical approach. When MacIntyre criticizes the enlightenment project, for example, it is to show that this picture is unpromising – that its proponents are wasting their time trying to do things that cannot be done. If they fail to see this, it is not because the enlightenment project is essentially deceptive. It is simply because they have not acquired enough information about it. In short, the critical and diagnostic approaches differ in their objects and their goals. It may not always be easy to distinguish the two in practice. Some narratives may contain elements of both. But the existence of hard cases does not make the distinction unimportant.

The practitioner of the diagnostic approach with whom I will be concerned is Martin Heidegger. I will explore how Heidegger engages with the history of philosophy in order to learn something about the pictures that govern our thinking: how they distort our understanding of what it means to be. I will argue that Heidegger's approach to past philosophy is diagnostic, in that it seeks to uncover the true nature of ways of thinking that are widely accepted but deceptive. I will also try to show that for Heidegger this engagement with the past acts as a form of therapy. The way to address our flawed understanding of Being is to tell the story of how we came to misunderstand Being in the first place.[1] My discussion of Heidegger falls into five parts. In the first, I explain how Heidegger's project – a reflection on the question of Being – leads him to be concerned with the large-scale pictures that govern our thinking. I also describe the method of investigating philosophical pictures that emerges in Heidegger's work of the 1930s. Heidegger characterizes this method as an attempt to think the unthought in past philosophy and, as I will argue, it is best seen as an instance of the diagnostic approach to doing philosophy historically. The next three sections examine several examples of Heidegger's diagnostic approach. They deal, respectively, with his reading of Plato in *The Essence of Truth*; with his engagement with Nietzsche in his lecture courses of the same name; and finally, with his reading of Hegel in *Identity and Difference*. The final section draws some general conclusions about Heidegger's use of the diagnostic approach, and asks what it teaches us about doing philosophy historically.

---

[1] In keeping with the standard practice for translating Heidegger into English, I render *Sein* as "Being" (with a capital "B"). I do this to distinguish *Sein* from *Seiende*, which I render as "being" or "entity." It should be remembered, of course, that *Sein* is a verb, and that Being is not a thing. The *Seinsfrage* is the question of what it means *to be*.

Finally, some caveats are in order. The first is that this chapter deals primarily with the so-called later Heidegger – that is, with his work from the 1930s and after. This work differs in important respects from his equally influential work of the 1920s, especially *Being and Time*. Though I focus on Heidegger's attempt to do philosophy historically in his later work, I do not mean to suggest that this enterprise is absent from his early writings. On the contrary, his early work insists that raising the question of Being requires us to revisit past philosophy again and again.[2] To this extent, even the early Heidegger does philosophy historically. That said, it is Heidegger's later work that most forcefully articulates his concern with philosophical pictures. It is his later work that grapples most clearly with the ways in which our large-scale views of reality can be deceptive and in need of diagnosis. For that reason, the later Heidegger will be my main concern.

I should also note that Heidegger would surely disapprove of the way I describe him in this chapter. I present Heidegger as someone concerned with philosophical pictures, someone who studies the development of these pictures in order to learn how they deceive us. But Heidegger is suspicious of the very idea of a philosophical picture – or "world picture" (*Weldbild*), as he usually puts it. He sees this idea as the product of some questionable and uniquely modern positions in metaphysics and epistemology. In his essay "The Age of the World Picture," Heidegger describes his objections to this idea as follows:

Where the world becomes picture, beings as a whole are set in place as that for which man is prepared; that which, therefore, he correspondingly intends to bring before him, have before him, and, thereby, in a decisive sense, place before him. Understood in an essential way, "world picture" does not mean "picture of the world" but, rather, the world grasped as picture. Beings as a whole are now taken in such a way that a being is first and only in being insofar as it is set in place by representing-producing [*vorstellend-herstellenden*] humanity. Whenever we have a world picture, an essential decision occurs concerning beings as a whole. The being of beings is sought and found in the representedness of beings.[3]

---

[2] The clearest example is Heidegger's insistence that the project of *Being and Time* requires us to "destroy" the history of ontology – that is, to engage in an active dismantling of traditional ways of thinking about Being. On this view, fundamental ontology is not a simple break with the past, but a repetition (*Wiederholung*) of it. See *BT*, 41. Heidegger revisits this theme in his discussion of historicality later in the book. There, he characterizes Dasein's relation to tradition as a "reciprocative rejoinder" (*BT*, 438). It is not a mere reproduction of the past as it was, but involves "*handing down explicitly* – that is to say, going back into the possibilities of the Dasein that has-been-there" (*BT*, 437).

[3] Martin Heidegger, "The Age of the World Picture," in *Off the Beaten Track*, trans. and ed. Julian Young and Kenneth Haynes (Cambridge: Cambridge University Press, 2002), 67–68. Heidegger's critique of world pictures has a great deal in common with the rejection of "worldview" philosophy in his early work. See, for example, Martin Heidegger, *Towards the Definition of Philosophy*, trans. Ted Sadler (London: Athlone, 2000), 187–188.

In other words, Heidegger thinks that the idea of a philosophical picture makes sense only if we identify beings as a whole with that which is opposed to, and represented by, the modern subject. Since this identification is suspect, in Heidegger's view, the notion of a picture is suspect as well.[4] Whatever one makes of this criticism, it need not render my description of Heidegger illegitimate. All that my description assumes is that we *do* sometimes find ourselves under the sway of philosophical pictures – not that we *ought* to do so. In claiming that Heidegger seeks to diagnose the pictures that govern our thinking, I do not mean to suggest that he endorses these pictures, or indeed, that he endorses any pictures at all. He might well prefer that we do without pictures altogether. But this does not show that we should stop identifying and scrutinizing the pictures that are currently accepted. On the contrary, it may make it all the more urgent that we do so. Before we can reject a picture, we must know what we are rejecting.

HEIDEGGER'S PROJECT AND THE FORGETFULNESS OF BEING

Anyone familiar with Heidegger knows that his main concern is the *Seinsfrage*: the question of Being. This question motivates all his major works, and it preoccupies him for his entire career. The *Seinsfrage* concerns the difference between beings and Being, between things that are and what it means for them to be. Heidegger claims to have stumbled upon this question after reading Franz Brentano's dissertation on Aristotle's *Metaphysics*. In the essay "My Way to Phenomenology," Heidegger describes the *Seinsfrage* in this way: "If being is predicated in manifold meanings, then what is its leading fundamental meaning? What does Being mean?"[5] He presents it in a similar way in *Being and Time*, the first pages of which announce that "[o]ur aim in the following treatise is to work out the question of the meaning of *Being* and to do so concretely" (*BT*, 19). According to Heidegger, the question of Being is the most fundamental one we can possibly raise, and it is presupposed by every other type of thinking. Other types of thinking – physics and history, for example – are regional ontologies that study a specific type of being. Though regional

---

[4] Furthermore, on this view, much of its use is anachronistic. It is properly applied only to those thinkers who share its uniquely modern metaphysical and epistemological presuppositions. Thus "a 'medieval world view' was an impossibility, and a 'Catholic world view' is an absurdity." See Heidegger, "The Age of the World Picture," 71.

[5] Martin Heidegger, "My Way to Phenomenology," in *On Time and Being*, trans. Joan Stambaugh (New York: Harper and Row, 1972), 74.

ontologies presuppose some answer to the more general question of what it means to be, they do not and cannot pose this question explicitly. But while the question of Being is the most fundamental one imaginable, it is also a question on which philosophy has turned its back. We not only fail to ask this question; we are not even "perplexed at our inability to understand the expression 'Being'" (*BT*, 19). Above all, Heidegger's project is to reawaken our perplexity about Being.

But if Heidegger's project is to have any force, he must answer another question: *why* has philosophy turned its back on the *Seinsfrage*? Why do we not pose this most fundamental of questions, and why are we not perplexed at our failure to raise it? The introduction to *Being and Time* gives a topical answer, blaming our lack of interest in Being on contingent features of the philosophy of Heidegger's day. It tells us that "[t]his question *has today* been forgotten" (*BT*, 21, my emphasis), and it attributes this forgetting to certain orthodoxies in contemporary philosophy – for example, the assumption that Being is the "'most universal' concept" (*BT*, 22) and is therefore "indefinable" (*BT*, 23). The opening pages of *Being and Time* therefore seem almost optimistic. Replace the old orthodoxies with some new ones, they suggest, and our concern with the *Seinsfrage* might be reawakened. As the book progresses, however, a deeper explanation emerges. It turns out to be no accident that we have neglected the question of Being. It is not just a mistake made by the philosophers of the recent past. Rather, our tendency to forget the *Seinsfrage* is deeply rooted in the kind of beings that we are. These beings – which Heidegger famously labels Dasein – display a characteristic called "*falling*" (*BT*, 219). Falling refers to Dasein's "absorption in Being-with-one-another" (*BT*, 220), or its tendency to accept the ways in which things have been publicly interpreted. We tend to believe what "the others" believe. We assume that we understand what they claim to understand. As a result, "everything that is primordial gets glossed over as something that has long been well understood. Everything gained by a struggle becomes just something to be manipulated. Every secret loses its force" (*BT*, 165). Seen in this light, our forgetting of the *Seinsfrage* is not a chance mistake that might have been avoided. As "an essential tendency of Dasein" (*BT*, 165), it is rooted in the structure of our Being.[6] Accordingly, we should not expect this tendency to go away. "We would," Heidegger says,

---

[6] Division Two of *Being and Time* sheds further light on this matter, explaining that Dasein's falling is rooted in the nature of temporality. "Temporality," Heidegger claims, "is essentially falling, and it loses itself in making present … [F]rom those spatial relationships which making-present is constantly meeting in the ready-to-hand as having presence, it takes its clues for Articulating that which has been understood and can be interpreted in the understanding in general" (*BT*, 421).

"misunderstand the ontologico-existential structure of falling if we were to ascribe to it the sense of a bad and deplorable property of which, perhaps, more advanced stages of human culture might be able to rid themselves" (*BT*, 220). There is no hope of escaping our tendency to fall.[7] In short, for the Heidegger of *Being and Time*, it is the nature of Dasein that explains why we forget the question of Being, and therefore, why fundamental ontology is necessary. What justifies Heidegger's project is an account of the kinds of beings that we are.

But as Heidegger's thought develops, this strategy is no longer available to him. The key development here is the so-called "turn" (*Kehre*) in Heidegger's work that occurs in the early 1930s. The turn is Heidegger's attempt to distance himself from certain elements of *Being and Time*. He remains preoccupied with the question of Being, and he still strives to awaken our perplexity in the face of it. But he becomes convinced that *Being and Time*'s approach to this question depends too heavily on a problematic vocabulary, and is tainted by several questionable assumptions. Specifically, Heidegger comes to suspect that the standpoint of the early book is too subjectivistic. *Being and Time* approaches the question of Being through a phenomenological description of Dasein. It claims that the way to clarify the meaning of Being is to perform a phenomenological description of the entity that we ourselves are. Dasein, Heidegger tells us, is that being whose Being is an issue for it. Dasein wrestles with the meaning of Being, and it does so by existing. So if we observe how Dasein exists, we will gain privileged insight into what Being means. Of course, even in *Being and Time*, Heidegger insists that the term "Dasein" is not simply a synonym for "human being" or "subject."[8] Heidegger's insistence on using this term at all, as well as his practice of describing Dasein with novel categories such as *Vorhandenheit* and *Zuhandenheit*, show that he takes himself to be describing something quite different than a traditional subject. But the established vocabulary of Western philosophy makes it difficult for Heidegger to

---

[7] Granted, *Being and Time*'s discussion of authenticity does hold out the hope that we can gain "mastery" over our tendency to fall, even if "just 'for that moment'" (*BT*, 422). But this discussion also makes clear that such moments of authenticity are limit situations, and rare ones at that. We may temporarily suspend our tendency to fall, but we "can never extinguish it" (*BT*, 422).

[8] For a good discussion of this topic, see Jeffrey Barash, *Heidegger and the Problem of Historical Meaning* (New York: Fordham University Press, 2003), 205. Barash points out that the early Heidegger frequently speaks of "the Dasein *in* humanity" (205, my emphasis), thus showing that Dasein and humanity are not identical. According to Barash, the Dasein in humanity is a certain "openness to Being underlying the temporal and historical structures of human existence," an openness that "is more fundamental than human experience itself, and is irreducible to human modes of objectification" (205).

prevent his readers from identifying Dasein with human beings.[9] Hence the tendency to read Division One of *Being and Time* as a philosophical anthropology, a reading Heidegger decries as shallow and incompatible with fundamental ontology.[10] To combat this tendency, Heidegger no longer approaches the *Seinsfrage* by way of a phenomenological description of Dasein. After the turn, he pursues his project in a different way. But this means that he must explain our forgetting of the *Seinsfrage* in a different way. Attributing this forgetting to the nature of Dasein is no longer an option.

How does Heidegger explain our forgetfulness of Being after the turn? The short answer is that the forgetting once attributed to Dasein is now attributed to Being itself. This is not to say that the later Heidegger conceives of Being as an agency, or indeed as any type of entity at all. But it is to say that he increasingly speaks of the forgetting of Being as something that *happens*, rather than as something Dasein *does*. Forgetting, as Werner Marx puts it, is now "thought 'historically,' but in such a way that any given change would not depend on the power of man."[11] One of Heidegger's favorite ways of doing this is to speak of the "sending" of Being. In "Nietzsche's Word: God is Dead," for example, he claims that humanity invariably finds itself on a certain "path," understanding the meaning of Being in a particular way. "The destiny of Being," he says, "makes its way over beings in abrupt epochs of truth; in each phase of metaphysics, a particular piece of that way becomes apparent."[12] "Destiny" here translates *Geschick*, which derives from the verb *schicken* or "to send." It is also closely related to the word *Geschichte*, or "history."[13] Thus Heidegger's claim could

---

[9] Heidegger sometimes speaks in ways that encourage this interpretation. When he introduces the term "Dasein" in *Being and Time*, for example, he defines it as "this entity – man himself" (*BT*, 32). In the light of such passages, it is not surprising that some of Heidegger's readers take "Dasein" to be just another name for "human being."

[10] In the "Letter on 'Humanism,'" for example, Heidegger tries to distance his work from the statements about "man" advanced by Sartrean existentialism. See Martin Heidegger, "Letter on 'Humanism,'" trans. Frank Capuzzi, in *Pathmarks*, ed. William McNeill (Cambridge: Cambridge University Press, 1998), 239–276. As Jeffrey Barash points out, the turn is also closely connected to a number of concerns Heidegger has regarding what he sees as the "anthropological" character of most Western philosophy. See Barash, *Heidegger and the Problem of Historical Meaning*, 201.

[11] Werner Marx, *Heidegger and the Tradition*, trans. Theodore Kisiel and Murray Greene (Evanston: Northwestern University Press, 1971), 163. In Marx's view, Heidegger does not entirely de-anthropomorphize the forgetting of Being. He says, for example, that "a certain role in the occurrence seems to be due to man" (163).

[12] Martin Heidegger, "Nietzsche's Word: God is Dead," in *Off the Beaten Track*, 157–158. In keeping with my other translations of Heidegger, I have rendered *Sein* as "Being" in this passage, though Young and Haynes translate it as "being."

[13] On these points I am indebted to de Beistegui, *The New Heidegger*, 114.

be rephrased as follows: we always find ourselves inhabiting a particular historical period, and as a result, we always find ourselves understanding Being in a certain way. That we understand Being in this way is not entirely within our control, and to that extent, it may be thought of as our "destiny," or as the way Being "sends" itself in our epoch. In "The Question Concerning Technology," Heidegger cites modern technology as an example of such sending. He writes:

The essence of modern technology starts man upon the way of that revealing through which the real everywhere, more or less distinctly, becomes standing-reserve. "To start upon a way" means "to send" in our ordinary language. We shall call that sending-that-gathers [*versammelde Schicken*] which first starts man upon a way of revealing, *destiny* [*Geschick*]. It is from out of this destiny that the essence of all history [*Geschichte*] is determined.[14]

Heidegger is quick to add that this destiny, this sending, "is never a fate that compels," and that humanity is not "simply constrained to obey" it.[15] Still, that we understand Being as we do, rather than in some other way, is not wholly up to us. If this understanding is defective – if, for example, we fail to pose the *Seinsfrage* explicitly – it is because of how Being sends itself in our epoch.

But what, concretely, does this amount to? If the forgetting of Being is a path on which we are sent, then what form does it take? The answer seems to be that this forgetting manifests itself in the dominance of certain types of thinking and acting. As inhabitants of a particular epoch, we invariably find ourselves under the sway of certain ways of viewing reality and of responding to it in our behavior. We find our thinking and acting shaped by general conceptions of what the world is like and how we fit into it. These ways of thinking and acting reveal certain things, making it possible for us to notice certain aspects of reality. But they also conceal. They prevent us from seeing other things, and from asking certain questions. One might even say that they reveal *by* concealing, since by leading us to see reality in one way, they invariably lead us to ignore others. Modern technology is an example. To belong to the technological era is to be led to see reality as "standing-reserve," or as material to be opposed to and manipulated by a thinking, willing subject. It is therefore to overlook, or "forget," non-technological ways of relating to reality. Epochs other than our own are defined by different ways of thinking and acting, ones that also reveal at the same time they conceal. Together, these

[14] Martin Heidegger, "The Question Concerning Technology," in *The Question Concerning Technology and Other Essays*, trans. William Lovitt (New York: Harper and Row, 1977), 24. In this passage, I render *Geschick* as "destiny." Lovitt translates it as "destining."

[15] Heidegger, "The Question Concerning Technology," 25.

ways of thinking and acting make up what Heidegger calls the history of Being (*Seinsgeschichte*) – a process through which the "basic traits"[16] of Being are again and again "concealed and thus 'forgotten' by thought."[17] An epoch's way of thinking and acting is not simply identical with the philosophical theories that flourish in it. The technological world view is not reducible to the works of any specific philosopher. But these conceptions of reality have an important philosophical dimension. They are both articulated and, in some sense, made possible by the works of great philosophers. As Jeffrey Barash puts it, the great philosophers of the past "were anything but isolated exponents of an age or culture and its determinate productive modes. They inaugurated a historically constitutive language, demarcating the domain of inclusion within which the approach to the truth of beings as a totality could legitimately operate."[18] Thus in "The Age of the World Picture," Heidegger speaks of "the interpretation of the being and of truth opened up by Descartes," an interpretation in which "[t]he whole of modern metaphysics, Nietzsche included, maintains itself."[19] Similarly, in "Nietzsche's Word: God is Dead," Heidegger cites Plato[20] and Leibniz[21] as examples of philosophers who both embody and make possible the conception of reality that he calls nihilism. So when Heidegger speaks of Being "sending itself" in a specific way in a particular epoch, he means that we invariably find ourselves under the sway of some deceptive way of thinking, one that conceals as much as it reveals. A particularly important part of these ways of thinking is the philosophical work that articulates them.

How should we respond to these ways of thinking? How should we come to terms with the deceptive views of reality that we inherit from our epoch? Heidegger claims that we must actively reappropriate them. We must investigate these ways of thinking by tracing their histories and revisiting the decisive moments in their evolution. Heidegger describes this process as a *repetition* (*Wiederholung*) of the history of philosophy.[22] Again, there are obvious parallels to psychoanalysis. An analyst asks a

---

[16] Marx, *Heidegger and the Tradition*, 164.

[17] Marx, *Heidegger and the Tradition*, 165. Or as Barash puts it, Heidegger now thinks of the forgetting of Being as "a predisposition running through the long history of Western ideas of truth since Greek antiquity, one that favored the advent of the *Seinsvergessenheit* he now conceived as the historical movement of Western metaphysics toward the unrestrained anthropomorphism of modernity." See Barash, *Martin Heidegger and the Problem of Historical Meaning*, 204.

[18] Barash, *Martin Heidegger and the Problem of Historical Meaning*, 207.

[19] Heidegger, "The Age of the World Picture," 66.

[20] Heidegger, "Nietzsche's Word: God is Dead," 162.

[21] Heidegger, "Nietzsche's Word: God is Dead," 172.

[22] Of course, as we have seen, the term "repetition" also appears in *Being and Time*'s discussion of history. See, for example, *BT*, 437 *passim*. Heidegger continues to use this term in his later work, apparently in much the same way.

patient to repeat or work through certain elements of her psychological past. Typically, this involves revisiting decisive moments in that past, moments that helped give rise to a present trauma. Similarly, Heidegger asks us to respond to the forgetfulness of our present ways of thinking by repeating the decisive moments in their evolution. This involves revisiting the work of those philosophers who helped give rise to these ways of thinking. To address the forgetfulness of the technological era, for example, we must repeat the work of Descartes, Bacon, and other great philosophers who made it possible for us to see the world as standing-reserve in the first place. But what does this repetition achieve? What is its goal? Let us recall a point considered in Chapter 2.[23] Heidegger understands truth as *aletheia*, an ancient Greek word that literally means "unconcealment" or "removal from hiddenness." Heidegger's intention in using this term is to show that truth is fundamentally a property not of assertions, but of things. Truth is a disclosive event in which something presents itself as it is. But in order for something to be revealed in this way, it must first be hidden. Only something concealed can be unconcealed. In that sense, truth depends on untruth; unconcealedness requires concealedness and is made possible by it. Something similar obtains in the history of thought. Great thinkers reveal: they make it possible for us to see reality in a certain way. But in doing so, they also conceal, leading us to overlook, or "forget," other possible ways of relating to things. Accordingly, a great philosopher's work involves not just what he explicitly thinks, but what he leaves *unthought*.[24] It involves possibilities for thinking that the philosopher opened up but did not actualize, paths that he cleared but did not himself take. According to Heidegger, we repeat the work of past philosophers in order to think what was unthought by them, to uncover possibilities for thinking that

---

[23] See the discussion of Heidegger in Chapter 2, Section 4.

[24] The notion of the unthought runs throughout Heidegger's career. In his early work, he uses this term to refer to anything "not thematically apprehended for deliberate thinking." See Heidegger, *Basic Problems*, 163. *Basic Problems* gives as an example of the unthought the contexts in which physical objects are encountered. When I enter a room through a door, for instance, the doorknob and the rest of the room are given along with the door, but I do not actively investigate them, and to that extent they remain "unthought." For a discussion of the role of the unthought in Heidegger's early work, see Carol White, "Ontology, the Ontological Difference, and the Unthought." *Tulane Studies in Philosophy* 32 (1984), 95–102. After the turn, Heidegger increasingly uses the term "unthought" to refer to unexploited possibilities for thinking in the works of past philosophers. See, for example, Martin Heidegger, "The End of Philosophy and the Task of Thinking," in *On Time and Being*, 64. For a discussion of this later usage, see Michel Haar, "The Doubleness of the Unthought of the Overman: Ambiguities of Heideggerian Political Thought." *Research in Phenomenology* 20 (1990), 87–111.

they did not exploit.[25] We revisit possibilities that the tradition pointed towards but covered over, or more accurately, pointed towards *by* covering over. In doing so, we not only learn how our own deceptive ways of thinking came to be. We also explore the extent to which the history of thought offers a way around them.[26]

What does all of this amount to? Simply put, Heidegger is arguing that the *Seinsfrage* requires us to do philosophy historically. For Heidegger, doing philosophy means posing and grappling with the question of Being. An important part of this project consists in explaining why the question of Being has been forgotten, why we do not explicitly ask what it means to be. After the turn, Heidegger insists that we explain this forgetting with reference to the large-scale conceptions of reality we inherit from our historical epoch. He calls these the ways in which Being "sends itself," but they might equally be described as philosophical pictures – extremely general understandings of what reality is like and how we fit into it. Philosophy demands that we trace the historical development of these pictures. We study how they were articulated and shaped by the great philosophers of the past. But our goal in doing so is philosophical and not merely antiquarian. In tracing the development of the technological picture, for example, we do not merely seek to determine what Descartes and Bacon actually believed. Our goal is to see whether a different understanding of Being is possible, an understanding of Being that does not overlook what those thinkers did. In other words, our intentions are diagnostic. We revisit the philosophy of the past in the hopes of finding what was left unthought by it. We seek to discover its real significance, a significance quite different from the ways in which this past is usually understood. For Heidegger, we must trace the history of our pictures because these pictures are deceptive. They lead us to forget something essential, and the only way to respond to this forgetting is to tell the story of how it happened. By returning to the decisive moments in the development of our pictures, we see how they have led us to forget Being, and how we might go about remedying this forgetting. History is the only therapy available to us.

We now have a general account of how Heidegger does philosophy historically. Let us turn to some examples.

---

[25] *Being and Time* also insists that repetition deals with possibilities, not actualities. When we repeat the past – as we do while "destroying the history of ontology" (*BT*, 41), for example – we are not concerned with "what is 'past,' just in order that this, as something which was formerly actual, may recur" (*BT*, 437–438). Rather, our goal is to respond to past *possibilities*.

[26] In *Identity and Difference*, Heidegger puts the point this way: "Only when we turn thoughtfully toward what has already been thought, will we be turned to use for what must still be thought" (*ID*, 41).

The first text I will consider is *The Essence of Truth*. This is a lecture course from 1931–32,[27] and as such, it stands at a pivotal moment in Heidegger's development.[28] It is one of the first texts after the turn, one of the first texts to describe the forgetting of Being as something that happens rather than as something Dasein does. *The Essence of Truth* finds Heidegger diagnosing this forgetfulness, trying to identify the moment at which a misguided understanding of Being came to dominate Western thought. He locates this moment in ancient Greek thought, in a shift that took place around the time of Plato. This shift concerns our way of understanding truth. It is a shift from a pre-Socratic view of truth, which sees truth as a feature of things, to a later view, which sees it exclusively as a property of judgments and assertions. As momentous as this shift is, Heidegger argues, it is not enough to note that it has taken place. We must understand its origin, its true nature, and its consequences, because until now, none of these have been properly understood. *The Essence of Truth* offers a reading of key texts by Plato, since Heidegger believes they play a crucial role in the shift in our understanding of truth. In these Platonic texts, we can see the shift taking place: we can see an earlier and more fundamental view of truth being replaced by a newer, derivative one. We can see a problematic picture of reality emerge and begin to take us in. And if we are perceptive, Heidegger suggests, we may see a way not taken, a possibility for thinking that Plato overlooked but that might be open to us today.

　None of this is apparent from the book's first sentences. They simply ask us to think about the *essence* of truth – about what makes something an instance of truth and not something else. This looks like a perfectly ordinary philosophical question. We all think we know what essences are. We can all define the essence of a table as "what applies to *everything* that is a table," or "[w]hat all actual and possible tables have in common" (*ET*, 1). So it is tempting to say that the essence of truth is whatever truth is "in general," or whatever all cases of truth have in common. Once we start down this road, however, peculiar difficulties arise, suggesting that we do not understand

---

[27] *The Essence of Truth* should not be confused with Heidegger's 1930 essay "On the Essence of Truth." These texts do cover some of the same ground: both deal with the ancient Greek understanding of truth, and both relate truth to the topic of freedom. Understandably, though, the lecture course is much more detailed than the essay, and it approaches the topic of truth in a somewhat different way. See Heidegger, "On the Essence of Truth," trans. John Sallis, in *Pathmarks*, 136–154.

[28] Mark Wrathall has also argued that *The Essence of Truth* plays a particularly important role in Heidegger's development. See Mark Wrathall, "Heidegger on Plato, Truth, and Unconcealment: The 1931–32 Lecture on *The Essence of Truth*." *Inquiry* 47 (2004), 443–463.

the essence of truth as well as we think we do. One problem is that the word
"true" is predicated of a wide range of things that have little in common. We
speak of judgments, friends, and gold all being "true," and it is hard to see
what ties these different usages together.[29] Even if we apply the term only to
judgments, it is not easy to explain what it could *mean* to say that a
judgment is true. Instinctively, we want to say that a true judgment is one
that "corresponds with the facts" (*ET*, 2). But when asked what these facts
are, we can only say: the facts are what we know to be true. Truth therefore
turns out to be "correspondence with a correspondence," while "the latter
itself corresponds with a correspondence, and so forth" (*ET*, 2). An infinite
regress looms, suggesting that correspondence cannot illuminate the notion
of truth. So we face an aporia. We think we know what truth is, and we
speak of it as though its meaning were self-evident. But this self-evidence
masks a lack of understanding. If we want to understand the essence of
truth, we cannot rely on common sense alone. We must find an approach
that will "distance ourselves from this self-evidence" (*ET*, 5). But what sort
of approach?

Heidegger proposes that history can help where common sense cannot.
The way to understand the essence of truth is to go back to the origin of our
current way of thinking about it. We must go "back to the way in which
truth was *earlier* conceived; therefore by looking around in the *history* of the
concept of truth" (*ET*, 5). But a very specific sort of historical study is called
for. A mere "historical recording of earlier concepts and names" (*ET*, 6) will
not help. It is not enough to survey what earlier thinkers explicitly said
about the topic of truth. What matters are the decisive moments in the
history of the concept of truth: those moments that led to its being conceived
as it is now. Our way of thinking about truth is confused, and if we are to find
a way out of it, we must see where the confusion set in. For the same reason, a
history of the concept of truth must be prepared to look in unexpected places.
What Aristotle and Aquinas say about truth may be widely read, but according
to Heidegger, their work comes after the important developments in the
history of truth, and presupposes them. Aristotle and Aquinas already understand truth as we do, so they cannot show us where this way of thinking
comes from. We need to go back further – "back to what *happened* at
the beginning of Western philosophy" (*ET*, 6), when a certain way of understanding truth was first put in place. This event is not widely recognized
as the origin of our current conception of truth. Its significance has

---

[29] For a more detailed discussion of this topic, see W. B. Macomber, *The Anatomy of Disillusion: Martin
Heidegger's Notion of Truth* (Evanston: Northwestern University Press, 1967), 10–12.

not been noticed by the tradition, and perhaps could not be noticed by the tradition. What we must seek is the *hidden significance* of an early episode in the history of philosophy. But our goal in doing so is not antiquarian, or concerned with the past for its own sake. Heidegger hopes that a grasp of this episode will help us understand "what is actually happening *today*" (*ET*, 7).

So what is this decisive moment? According to Heidegger, it is the moment at which the West's original understanding of truth – one articulated in pre-Socratic thought – was abandoned. The pre-Socratic view seeks to describe "those primordial experiences in which we achieved our first ways of determining the nature of Being – the ways which have guided us ever since" (*BT*, 45). The pre-Socratics understand truth as "*privative*" (*ET*, 7). They see it as an *absence* of something, a *lack* of something. Heidegger makes much of the fact that the ancient Greek word for truth, *aletheia*, is a privative term, one that might be translated as "unhiddenness" or "unconcealedness." The true is therefore "what is *without* hiddenness," or "what has been torn away from hiddenness [*Verborgenheit*] and, as it were, been robbed of its hiddenness" (*ET*, 7). The experience of truth is bound up with the experience of hiddenness. One must know what it is for something to be hidden in order to make sense of its no longer being hidden. A related point is that for the pre-Socratics, truth has to do with *things*. It is not only, and not primarily, a property of judgments or propositions. What is true in the first instance are beings – beings that have been removed from hiddenness, beings that show themselves as they are. The claims we make about things may be called true in the derivative sense that they point us towards entities that are unhidden. But truth must not be *defined* as a property of judgments; "true" is not simply a synonym for "correct." Clearly, the pre-Socratic view clashes with contemporary intuitions about truth. We tend to identify truth with the correctness of propositions, and we find it hard to understand truth in any other way. But according to Heidegger, "[t]ruth as unhiddenness and truth as correctness are quite different things; they arise from quite different fundamental experiences and cannot be equated" (*ET*, 8).

At a certain point in Greek history, however, the pre-Socratic view of truth gave way to one much closer to our own. This new view is what Heidegger calls "truth as correctness": the view that truth may be predicated only of judgments, not of things, and that a true judgment is one that correctly represents the facts. It would be misleading to describe this as a shift within the history of philosophy, since it takes place near the beginning of this history. Plato and Aristotle are already under its sway, despite being among the first systematic philosophers. Heidegger claims that "in Aristotle and Plato we can see how the indicated fundamental experience has already begun to be ineffective" (*ET*, 11). But for Plato, at least, the shift is a recent event, and an event that is still playing itself out in his texts. Heidegger therefore proposes that if we read his dialogues carefully, we can see him vacillating between truth as unhiddenness and truth as correctness, and tentatively privileging the latter over the former. The *Republic* is especially significant here. Its cave allegory offers an unusually clear look at Plato's shifting view of truth. The allegory's general features are well known. It describes the experience of education, or the process of coming to know the truth. It compares the human condition to that of prisoners in a subterranean cave, and it compares enlightenment to the difficult journey out of this cave and into the outer world. The allegory does not explicitly discuss the essence of truth. But for that reason, Heidegger claims, it offers special insight into Plato's *assumptions* about truth, and it is these assumptions that really concern us.

   Heidegger sees the allegory as consisting of four stages. The first describes the condition of prisoners in the cave before being liberated. Shackled in place, the prisoners can only look straight ahead at the shadows cast by objects behind them. They take these shadows to be what truly is, since they know nothing else. They do not even think of them as shadows, since they are unaware of any other sort of object. The prisoners clearly represent human beings in their untutored state. Before learning the truth about things, we assume that what is immediately before us is what is real – that physical objects, for example, are fully real, and not, say, copies of intelligible forms. As Heidegger reads it, however, the allegory describes a natural but naive way of thinking about truth. A human being "straight-forwardly takes whatever presents itself before him as un-hidden, to be beings" (*ET*, 21). Truth is "what is immediately before him, without any doing on his part, as it gives itself" (*ET*, 20). A second way of understanding truth emerges at the next stage, when the prisoner is freed (*ET*, 23). Once his shackles are removed, the prisoner can turn around and walk towards the source of the shadows. He can now see the shadows *as* shadows, and he can recognize that they are less real than the objects that cast them. So he starts to think of truth as something that exists in degrees. "The unhidden," he realizes, "can therefore be *more* or *less* unhidden" (*ET*, 25). There are "gradations and levels" (*ET*, 25) of truth, and depending on where one looks, one will see more or less "*correctly*" (*ET*, 26). This is a crucial shift. Since the cave allegory describes some beings as "more beingful" (*ET*, 26) than others, it allows us to conceive of truth as something predicated of our way of *looking* at things, not just the things themselves. It lets us think of truth as correctness, as a correspondence between our way of looking and the way things really are. Granted, the allegory still sees unhiddenness as a more fundamental sense of truth. Beings must disclose themselves in order for us to see them more or less correctly. But at the second stage, the notion of truth becomes ambiguous. It refers to both the unhiddenness of things, and the correctness of our claims about them.[30]

This ambiguity becomes more serious at the third stage, when the prisoner leaves the cave and emerges into the world outside. He "now sees through the shadowy character of his whole cave-existence" (*ET*, 33), recognizing that what he previously thought of as reality was a dimly lit fragment of it. He encounters a wider range of entities than he has known before: natural objects, the heavens, and above them all, the sun. He also encounters more degrees of correctness. To see a mountain at night is to see it less accurately than in bright sunlight, and to see it reflected in a pond is to see it less correctly than to see the thing itself. More importantly, the prisoner now discovers a standard for distinguishing more and less correct ways of looking at things. This standard is the sun, source of the visibility and existence of everything else. The closer things are to the sun, the more illuminated they are, and the more correctly we may see them. The lesson of this analogy is clear. The sun represents the Good, "the most beingful" (*ET*, 51) of beings. The Good is responsible for the intelligibility of everything else. It is "the most unhidden, the primordially unhidden, because the unhiddenness of beings *originates* in [it]" (*ET*, 49). Above all, the Good acts as a standard of truth, enabling us to distinguish more correct accounts of reality from less correct ones. So the third stage of the allegory identifies truth with a specific type of correctness: a correctness made possible by a transcendent principle. Our claims about things are true to the extent that they reflect, or correspond to, a reality structured by a super-sensible ground.[31]

The fourth stage consists in the prisoner's return to the cave. Having seen the outside world, the prisoner "understands the *Being* of beings … He can therefore decide whether something, e.g. the sun, is a being, or whether it is only a reflection in water; he can decide whether something is shadow or a real thing" (*ET*, 65). The prisoner now sees the cave properly for the first

---

[30] Heidegger echoes this claim in "Plato's Doctrine of Truth," where he says the following: "With this transformation of the essence of truth there takes place at the same time a change of the locus of truth. As unhiddenness, truth is still a fundamental trait of beings themselves. But as the correctness of the 'gaze,' it becomes a characteristic of the human comportment toward beings." See Martin Heidegger, "Plato's Doctrine of Truth," trans. Thomas Sheehan, in *Pathmarks*, 177.

[31] For a different view, and a criticism of Heidegger's interpretation, see David White, "Truth and Being: A Critique of Heidegger on Plato." *Man and World* 7 (1974), 127.

time. He recognizes that it is darker than the world outside, thanks to his familiarity with the sun. He has seen the source and the standard of all visibility, and his previous surroundings look like a world of deception and illusion. Thus Heidegger calls the freed prisoner "the bearer of a *differentiation.* Since he can distinguish between beings and Being, he insists on a *divorce* between beings and what appears to be, between the unhidden and what (like the shadows) conceals itself in its self-showing" (*ET,* 66). That which he previously took to be real – that which immediately confronted him – he now dismisses as mere appearance. By extension, Plato suggests, seeing the Good changes the way we see the world of immediate experience. It leads us to see this world as lacking in something, as a defective copy of a super-sensible principle. It leads us to understand truth in terms of "a confrontation involving beings and illusion, what is manifest and what is covered up" (*ET,* 65). Finding the truth means escaping illusion, leaving behind the shadows of the cave. To grasp the truth is to look away from the shadows and fix our gaze on a permanent, super-sensible standard. According to Heidegger, this is a major shift from the pre-Socratic view of truth. In pre-Socratic thought, truth is bound up with untruth. Only if we have experienced things as hidden can we make sense of their being unhidden. But from the standpoint of the cave allegory, untruth is simply "the *opposite* of truth" (*ET,* 67). "What already happens in Plato," Heidegger concludes, "is the waning of the fundamental experience, i.e. of a specific fundamental *stance* [*Grundstellung*] of man towards beings, and the weakening of the word *aletheia* in its basic meaning" (*ET,* 87).

But the story does not end there. Plato's move away from the pre-Socratic view of truth is not simply a mistake, much less a mistake he just happens to make. It has a deeper source: namely, a certain way of understanding the relation between Being and time. As we have seen, the *Republic* ultimately identifies truth with correspondence to something super-sensible, claiming that an assertion is true if it mirrors reality as structured by the Good. This standard is static and unchanging. The *Republic* characterizes the Good as that which "is not itself coming to be," and opposes it to "what comes to be and passes away."[32] The Good *must* be unchanging in order to play the role that the *Republic* assigns to it. Only something that is always and everywhere the same can act as a standard for assessing the reality of all other beings. The "most beingful" (*ET,* 51) of beings must be something that does not change. According to Heidegger, this way of thinking about truth ultimately stems from an assumption about time: the assumption that only

---

[32] Plato, *Republic,* trans. G. M. A. Grube (Indianapolis: Hackett, 1992), 182, 509b and 508d.

what occupies an unchanging present truly *is*. Plato tacitly thinks of "the being of beings as presence. The most serious and therefore most dangerous thing that can happen to beings is their becoming absent: the emergence of *absence*, the being-gone, the gone-ness of beings" (*ET*, 101). Heidegger argues that this equation of what is with what is present runs through Plato's view of truth. The untrue, the "not-unhidden," is "what is *not yet* unhidden," or "what is *no longer* unhidden" (*ET*, 92). If one identifies Being with presence, then only what is permanently present can be true, and only an unchanging principle such as the Good meets this criterion. As is well known, though, Heidegger rejects the identification of Being with presence, insisting that the link between Being and time is far more complex. We must, Heidegger argues, understand Being in terms of an ecstatic temporality in which the future, and not the present, is fundamental. *Being and Time* describes this as a process through which "temporality temporalizes itself in terms of the authentic future and in such a way that having been futurally, it first of all awakens the Present. *The primary phenomenon of primordial and authentic temporality is the future*" (*BT*, 378). Even after the turn, Heidegger continues to see the future as fundamental, and to reject the equation of Being with presence.[33] That Plato understands Being as presence explains why "*aletheia* (unhiddenness) withers away to mere being present (not-gone)" (*ET*, 103) in his work. The continued dominance of this way of thinking about Being explains why we still equate truth with correctness today. And in Heidegger's view, the most significant feature of this way of thinking is what it conceals. It "prevents the incipient fundamental experience of the *hiddenness* of beings from unfolding" (*ET*, 103).

The Essence of Truth, then, consists largely of a reading of Plato. It offers a lengthy and detailed interpretation of the most famous parts of the *Republic*. That said, *The Essence of Truth* is clearly not a piece of Plato scholarship, in any traditional sense of the term. It does not seek to explain what the *Republic* really means. It does not try to give a correct interpretation of the dialogue, or to determine what the cave allegory actually says. It offers a *reinterpretation* of the dialogue, one that is unapologetically creative, even violent.[34] And

---

[33] For a few of the many examples, see Martin Heidegger, "Anaximander's Saying," in *Off the Beaten Track*, 262–263; Martin Heidegger, "Kant's Thesis About Being," trans. Ted Klein and William Pohl, in *Pathmarks*, 360–363; and Martin Heidegger, "The End of Philosophy and the Task of Thinking," 66–70.

[34] Wrathall echoes this point. See Wrathall, "Heidegger on Plato, Truth, and Unconcealment," 445. Wrathall goes on to say that Heidegger's reading might be *so* creative that it is "historically invalid" (445). This phrase suggests that Heidegger's reading of the *Republic* ought to be judged by the standards of traditional Plato scholarship – that we should expect Heidegger to give a correct description of what *The Republic* "really says." As I argue below, however, Heidegger is engaged in a very different enterprise than traditional Plato scholarship, so he should not be held to its standards.

Heidegger admits as much. He grants that his reading of the cave allegory "goes beyond Plato" (*ET*, 52), in that it seeks to identify features of the allegory that Plato did not recognize, and to draw conclusions that Plato did not intend. Accordingly, Heidegger's methods are not those of a conventional Plato scholar. He ignores the longstanding practice of viewing particular passages from a dialogue in the context of the dialogue as a whole – for example, of interpreting particular arguments against the backdrop of a dialogue's dramatic structure and rhetorical devices. Near the start of his exegesis of the cave allegory, Heidegger writes:

> In the following interpretation, we deliberately leave unconsidered the precise placement of the allegory within the dialogue. To begin with we leave aside all discussion concerning the dialogue as a whole. What is crucial about this allegory is that it can stand entirely on its own, so we can consider it by itself without in any way minimizing its content or meaning. (*ET*, 12)

Heidegger realizes, of course, that Plato scholars will be suspicious of his approach to the *Republic*. But this does not trouble him. Anticipating their objections, he says the following:

> It is *we* who, subsequently in our interpretation, have gathered together all these considerations about light, freedom, idea, beings, in order from the unity of these to assess what can be learned about the essential determinations of unhiddenness itself. When we say that *aletheia* is deconcealment, this is an *interpretation* which analyzes the ground of unhiddenness itself. (*ET*, 90)

The last sentence of this passage is telling. Heidegger claims that his goal is not to understand Plato's text correctly, but to "analyze the ground of unhiddenness *itself*" (*ET*, 90, my emphasis). He is interested in the phenomena that Plato allows us to see, and he considers the *Republic* useful only to the extent that it helps us see these phenomena for ourselves. This may mean seeing them differently than Plato did; using Plato as a stimulus to thought may involve thinking something that Plato leaves unthought. Yet another sign that *The Essence of Truth* is not a traditional piece of Plato scholarship is the way it treats the cave allegory as a symptom of something. Heidegger repeatedly says that the allegory is interesting because it crystallizes a way of thinking about truth found not just in Plato's work, but in the entire Western tradition. As a result, Heidegger describes his reading of the allegory as a "debate with Plato himself *and thus with the whole Western tradition*" (*ET*, 35, my emphasis). Heidegger is not just concerned with the views of a single thinker. He wants to use one thinker's views as a way of bringing into focus a more general type of thinking. He wants to draw our attention to a philosophical picture: a general understanding of how the world is, one that is first articulated in Plato's dialogues but that endures long after. Heidegger uses the *Republic* to examine a picture that we might call Platonism.

What is Platonism, as Heidegger understands it? It is a way of approaching philosophical questions, one that involves making things intelligible by referring them back to a super-sensible ground. It is the tendency to understand reality in terms of "ideas" – that is, to see the entities encountered in immediate experience as imperfect copies of an unchanging standard. It is the tendency to think that grasping the truth involves turning one's mind away from the world of becoming and towards something that does not change, something that occupies an eternal present. For the Platonist, one knows the truth to the extent that one's judgments mirror a transcendent standard – Plato's Good, or Augustine's divine ideas, or something of the sort. Of course, Heidegger is not the first to be suspicious of this type of thinking. Philosophers from Aristotle to Nietzsche have criticized the tendency to turn our attention towards the heavens and away from the world of immediate experience. But few thinkers see Platonism as an all-pervasive threat in the way Heidegger does. For Heidegger, it seems, nearly all of humanity's problems derive "from a decision about the essence of truth that was taken long ago."[35] In "Plato's Doctrine of Truth," Heidegger describes the problem in this way:

> The story recounted in the "allegory of the cave" provides a glimpse at what is really happening in the history of Western humanity, both now and in the future: Taking the essence of truth as the correctness of the representation, one thinks of all beings according to "ideas" and evaluates all reality according to "values." That which alone and first of all is decisive is not which ideas and values are posited, but rather the fact that the real is interpreted according to "ideas" at all, that the "world" is weighed according to "values" at all.[36]

This criticism is strikingly similar to ones that Heidegger advances in other texts from his later period. In the "Letter on 'Humanism,'" for example, Heidegger attacks the tendency to understand reality in terms of values, claiming that "through the characterization of something as a value what is so valued is robbed of its worth. That is to say, by the assessment of something as a value what is valued is admitted only as an object for human estimation."[37] Similarly, in "The Question Concerning Technology," Heidegger rails against the tendency to see "the real everywhere, more or less distinctly,

[35] Heidegger, "Plato's Doctrine of Truth," 182.   [36] Heidegger, "Plato's Doctrine of Truth," 182.
[37] Heidegger, "Letter on 'Humanism,'" 264.

[as] standing-reserve"[38] – that is, as nothing but material to be represented and manipulated through human activity. Both of these criticisms are ultimately attacks on Platonism. If we view beings "only as an object for human estimation," or as "standing-reserve," then we have decided that beings *are* only to the extent that they correspond to the super-sensible standard of our ideas. Humanist values and modern technology turn out to be versions of Platonism, and Platonism turns out to be the West's dominant way of coping with reality.

But to leave it at that would be to miss the full force of Heidegger's discussion. Heidegger is not simply criticizing Platonism. He is not just attacking the tendency to interpret reality in terms of ideas. His real concern is that Platonism has not been understood: that its consequences have not been noticed, and its nature has not been grasped. It is one thing to see that philosophers like to make sense of things by referring them back to super-sensible principles. It is another to learn that this tendency is the source of phenomena as diverse as humanism and modern technology. More importantly, it is one thing to notice that philosophers since Plato have tended to equate truth with correspondence to super-sensible standards, and another to explain why they have done so. The reason Platonism appeals to philosophers is that it articulates a widespread but rarely stated assumption about time: that only what is present truly *is.* In Heidegger's view, we will not understand Platonism until we see it as a thesis about the link between Being and time. But we have failed to see it in this way, because we have failed to investigate time in a sufficiently radical fashion. The tradition has been blind to ecstatic temporality, and as a result, it has not noticed the questionable assumptions about time and presence that are crystallized in Platonism. In short, Heidegger is not simply criticizing a philosophical picture. He does criticize Platonism, to be sure, but he also argues that criticizing it properly requires that we grasp its true nature. We must *diagnose* Platonism: look beneath its surface, see what it really is, and learn what effects it really has. This is something we do through historical study. We investigate the origin of Platonism, that moment at which a set of assumptions about Being and time became an orthodoxy. It is not necessary to trace the development of Platonism right up to the present. It is the origin, a single decisive moment, that is the key to understanding it. And in keeping with Heidegger's reflections on destiny and sending, we should see the emergence of Platonism as an *event*: not something we do, but

---

[38] See Heidegger, "The Question Concerning Technology," 24.

something that happens. Plato does play a crucial role in its appearance, but that appearance "is never up to humans alone."[39]

FORGETFULNESS AS METAPHYSICS: THE NIETZSCHE LECTURES

Let us now turn to a second Heideggerian text that does philosophy historically: the lectures on Nietzsche, from the years 1936 to 1940. These lectures have the same general goal as *The Essence of Truth*. They investigate a philosophical picture, a picture that dominates our thinking and that explains our failure to pose the question of Being. But while *The Essence of Truth* examines Platonism, the Nietzsche lectures study an even broader picture called *metaphysics*.[40] These lectures present Nietzsche as "the *last metaphysician* of the West" (*N3*, 8) – a thinker who both embodies a certain picture and exhausts its possibilities. Once again, Heidegger's real concern is with what this thinker leaves unthought. For Heidegger, the important question to ask about Nietzsche is whether the end of metaphysics that he ushers in might be "the counterpart to another beginning" (*N3*, 8).

What does Heidegger mean by "metaphysics"? He obviously does not use this term in the way most philosophers do. He does not take metaphysics to be the branch of philosophy that investigates the nature of reality. Metaphysics in that sense poses many questions: whether non-physical entities exist, whether every event has a cause, and so on. For Heidegger, on the other hand, metaphysics asks "one single question" (*N1*, 187): what is "the basic character of all beings" (*N1*, 3)? To think metaphysically is to ask about "the truth of beings as such and as a whole" (*Seinde im Ganzen*) (*N3*, 187). It is to advance some view about the characteristics all beings have, the characteristics they have simply because they are beings. Christianity thinks metaphysically when it conceives of all entities as effects of God's creative activity. Enlightenment *philosophes* do the same in their idea of "a government of all beings under cosmic reason" (*N3*, 7). And Plato does likewise when he maintains that "beings have their essence in the 'Ideas,' according to which they must be estimated" (*N2*, 6). These thinkers

---

[39] Heidegger, "Plato's Doctrine of Truth," 182.

[40] That said, Platonism still plays an important role in Heidegger's *Nietzsche*. Heidegger describes Plato as the first metaphysical thinker, and he argues that later metaphysical thinking – including Nietzsche's – bears the stamp of Plato's innovations. He occasionally goes so far as to claim that "[t]he collective history of Western philosophy is interpreted as Platonism" (*N2*, 171). Still, in his lectures on Nietzsche, Heidegger presents Platonism as *one version* of the problem he wishes to diagnose – not the problem in its entirety.

make different claims about the nature of beings as beings. But they all try to characterize beings as a whole, and they all believe that it is possible and desirable to grasp beings in this way. When Heidegger speaks of metaphysics, then, he has in mind a picture rather than a theory. He is "not thinking of a doctrine or only of a specialized discipline of philosophy but of the fundamental structure of beings in their entirety."[41] Nor is he thinking of a picture that is always adopted self-consciously. Typically, we think metaphysically without being fully aware that we are doing so. Metaphysics is less a matter of explicit theorizing than of the unarticulated assumptions we make about reality. These assumptions manifest themselves in our actions as well as our thoughts. The metaphysical picture is "a *stance* toward being as a whole" (*N2*, 184, my emphasis), one that can be discerned in the ways we lead our lives and organize our societies.

But why study metaphysics? Heidegger's answer is that the dominance of this picture helps explain our failure to pose the question of Being. "The whole of Western thinking from the Greeks through Nietzsche," Heidegger argues, "is metaphysical thinking" (*N3*, 7). Metaphysical thinking is concerned with *beings*. It asks whether real beings are supersensible ideals, or effects of divine creation, or something else. But to ask about the nature of beings as such is precisely not to ask the more fundamental question of what it means to be at all. When we think metaphysically, we flatter ourselves that we have posed the most important question philosophy can ask: what are the general features of reality as a whole? In Heidegger's view, however, "this *as a whole* is actually a locution that tends more to veil than to pose and to explicate an *essential question*" (*N1*, 171). "Veil" is a crucial word here. The problem is not just that metaphysical thinkers fail to ask the essential question about the meaning of Being. Rather, their thinking covers up this question, making it seem unimportant and sanctioning its neglect. To a metaphysical thinker, someone concerned with the character of beings as a whole, "Being" can name only a property possessed by every entity. Once we have conceived of "Being" as a property, we are bound to see it as the most general of properties, one that is wholly indeterminate and therefore uninteresting. This is why Heidegger claims that metaphysics "thinks beings as a whole according to their *priority* over Being" (*N3*, 7, my emphasis). A preoccupation with beings as a whole leads us to ignore the question of what it means to be. Seen in this light, the history of metaphysics is the history of how the *Seinsfrage* not only *was not* asked, but *could*

---

[41] Heidegger, "Nietzsche's Word: God is Dead," 165.

not be asked. The West fails to pose this question "not just incidentally, but in accord with metaphysics' own inquiry" (*N4*, 207).[42]

What does all of this have to do with Nietzsche? For one thing, Heidegger claims that Nietzsche is himself a metaphysical thinker, and one who illustrates particularly well what this type of thinking involves. Studying Nietzsche's claims about beings as a whole can help us understand what metaphysics is and how it works. More importantly, Nietzsche occupies a special place in the history of metaphysics. Nietzsche consummates the history of metaphysics: he brings the metaphysical era to a close by exhausting its possibilities. And by exhausting the possibilities of metaphysics, he "brings to light what is decisive and essential" (*N1*, 20) about it. Because he stands at the end of a tradition, he can teach us things about it that no one else can. But why does Heidegger consider Nietzsche a metaphysician at all, let alone the last metaphysician of the West? The answer has to do with Nietzsche's reflections on will to power, which Heidegger sees as a theory about "the basic character of all beings" (*N1*, 3). Will to power is "*what* properly constitutes the being in beings" (*N1*, 31). The heart of Nietzsche's thought is that "any being which is, insofar as it is, is will to power. The expression stipulates the character that beings have as beings" (*N1*, 18). Nietzsche's writings abound with such statements about will to power. One of his unpublished notes declares that "this world is will to power – and nothing besides!"[43] Published works such as *Beyond Good and Evil* explore the idea that all phenomena can be understood as manifestations of will to power – though Nietzsche's language in these texts tends to be more tentative than in his unpublished work.[44] Works such as *Human, All Too Human* explain diverse psychological and moral phenomena in terms of power and willing.[45]

---

[42] In *Nietzsche, Volume IV*, Heidegger puts it this way: "But Being? Is it an accident that we scarcely grasp it, and that with all the manifold relations with beings we forget the relationship to Being? Or is metaphysics and its dominance the reason for the obscurity that enshrouds Being and man's relationship to it?" (*N4*, 153).

[43] Friedrich Nietzsche, *The Will to Power*, trans. R. J. Hollingdale and Walter Kaufmann, ed. Walter Kaufmann (New York: Random House, 1967), 550.

[44] Consider, for example, the following passage from §37 of *Beyond Good and Evil*: "Suppose nothing else were 'given' as real except our world of desires and passions, and we could not get down, or up, to any other 'reality' besides the reality of our drives …: is it not permitted to ask the question whether this 'given' would not be *sufficient* for also understanding on the basis of this kind of thing the so-called mechanistic (or 'material') world? … Then we would have gained the right to determine *all* efficient force univocally as – *will to power*. The world viewed from inside, the world defined and determined according to its 'intelligible character' – it would be 'will to power' and nothing else." See Friedrich Nietzsche, *Beyond Good and Evil*, in *Basic Writings of Nietzsche*, trans. and ed. Walter Kaufmann (New York: Random House, 1968), 238.

[45] See, for example, §44 of *Human, All Too Human*, which interprets gratitude and revenge from the perspective of the "man of power." See Friedrich Nietzsche, *Human, All Too Human*, trans. R. J. Hollingdale (Cambridge: Cambridge University Press, 1986), 36.

In Heidegger's view, Nietzsche's remarks add up to a "fundamental metaphysical position" (*N2*, 184). Nietzsche asks us to see beings as a whole as dynamic, as a play of forces. Heidegger claims that "[a]ll Being is for Nietzsche a Becoming. Such Becoming, however, has the character of action and the activity of willing. But in its essence will is will to power" (*N1*, 7). Heidegger goes to great lengths to show that a metaphysics of force is also at work in Nietzsche's thinking about eternal return and the revaluation of all values. But will to power is the key that unlocks Nietzsche's view of beings as a whole.

Why does Nietzsche's position occupy such an important place in the history of metaphysics? As Heidegger sees it, Nietzsche's contribution is to bring together two views that had been opposed for most of this history. Heidegger explains that the question of what character beings have as beings has traditionally been answered in one of two ways:

> The *one* answer – roughly speaking, it is the answer of Parmenides – tells us that *beings are* … [T]hat very response determines for the first time and for all thinkers to come, including Nietzsche, the meaning of *is* and *Being* – permanence and presence, that is, the eternal present. The *other* answer – roughly speaking, that of Heraclitus – tells us that *beings become*. The being is in being by virtue of its permanent becoming, its self-unfolding and eventual dissolution. (*N2*, 200)[46]

Nietzsche's doctrine of will to power brings these notions together. It teaches that "being *is* as fixated, as permanent; and that it *is* in perpetual creation and destruction … The essence of being is Becoming, but what becomes is and has Being only in creative transfiguration" (*N1*, 200). Nietzsche teaches that what is fixed and unchanging about beings is precisely their dynamic character, their "perpetual creation and destruction." Being and becoming turn out to be two ways of characterizing the same thing. In Heidegger's view, this "permanentizing of surpassment" (*N3*, 167) brings together all the possibilities for thinking that the metaphysical tradition contains. Once reality has been grasped as becoming, there are no new metaphysical positions left to create. This does not mean that later figures will stop thinking about beings as a whole. But there will be no new possibilities for "*essential* inquiry into the guiding question" (*N1*, 205, my emphasis). This is a significant development because of what it shows about the forgetfulness of Being. Nietzsche shows that metaphysical thinking can develop in the most radical way imaginable and *still* not pose the question of Being. He turns metaphysics on its head, equating beings

---

[46] I have altered the translation of this passage, rendering *das Seiende* as "beings" rather than "being" (which is Stambaugh's translation).

with what becomes and becoming with what is. But throughout all of this the *Seinsfrage* remains unasked: "[t]he question as to where the truth of this first and last metaphysical interpretation of Being is grounded, the question as to whether such a ground is ever to be experienced within metaphysics, is now so far away that it cannot be asked as a question at all" (*N3*, 157). Nietzsche shows definitively that the question of Being cannot be raised within the metaphysical tradition.

Heidegger's lectures on Nietzsche are an impressive achievement. But they are clearly not a piece of Nietzsche scholarship.[47] And as in *The Essence of Truth*, Heidegger admits as much. He does not claim to be accurately reconstructing Nietzsche's thought. On the contrary, he dismisses the attempt to do so as trivial. "We shall never," he claims, "experience who Nietzsche is through a historical report about his life history, nor through a presentation of the contents of his writings" (*N3*, 3). Instead of understanding the content of Nietzsche's writings, Heidegger wants to assess their significance for the history of Being. He grants that this agenda colors his engagement with Nietzsche. But this engagement, he argues, "can only have as its goal consciously to draw nearer to what is 'happening' in the history of the modern age" (*N3*, 8). So it is no surprise that Heidegger spurns the techniques of conventional Nietzsche scholarship. He pays little attention to the works Nietzsche published, claiming that the unpublished notes show us the real Nietzsche. Heidegger claims that if "*our knowledge were limited to what Nietzsche himself published, we could never learn what Nietzsche knew perfectly well, what he carefully prepared and continually thought through, yet withheld*. Only an investigation of the posthumously published notes in Nietzsche's own hand will provide a clearer picture" (*N2*, 15). Heidegger also ignores Nietzsche's perspectivism – that is, his strategy of saying different and often incompatible things about the same topic. Rather than considering a passage in the context of others that seem to contradict it, Heidegger is content to treat a single passage as the definitive statement of Nietzsche's view. He also pays disproportionate attention to what look like minor themes in Nietzsche's work. For example, he attaches great importance to the topic of revenge, claiming that the doctrine of eternal return must be seen as an attempt to redeem humanity from revenge. "Revenge," Heidegger says,

---

[47] This has not stopped some Nietzsche scholars from dismissing them as *bad* scholarship. Walter Kaufmann, for example, damns them with faint praise when he says that they are "important for those who want to understand *Heidegger*." See Walter Kaufmann, *Nietzsche: Philosopher, Psychologist, Antichrist*, 4th edn. (Princeton: Princeton University Press, 1974), 500, my emphasis.

is the will's ill will towards time and that means towards passing away, transiency … For Nietzsche, the most deepseated revenge consists in that reflection which posits supernatural ideality as absolute. Measured against it, the temporal must perforce degrade itself to nonbeing proper … If it is a matter of rescuing the earth as earth, then the spirit of revenge will have to vanish beforehand. (*N2*, 224–225)

As intriguing as this discussion is, it is oddly out of step with the letter of Nietzsche's texts. Nietzsche simply does not say much about revenge, and when he does discuss the topic, it is almost always in relation to ethical themes – as in the discussion of *ressentiment* in *The Genealogy of Morals*. Heidegger's infatuation with this theme shows that he is no conventional historian of philosophy.

So what *is* Heidegger doing in the Nietzsche lectures? As I have argued, he is evaluating the picture that he calls metaphysics, in the hope of explaining why we have forgotten the question of Being. But this task requires him to *diagnose* the metaphysical picture, since the conclusions he draws about metaphysics are far from obviously true. It is not at all obvious that Nietzsche is a metaphysical thinker at all, let alone the thinker who consummates the history of metaphysics. "At first," Heidegger concedes, "there seems to be not a trace of truth in [this] claim" (*N3*, 161). Nietzsche is best known as the thinker who abolishes the supersensible and dismisses the "true world" as a fable.[48] To the extent that Nietzsche is seen as a metaphysical thinker at all, it is as a modern version of Heraclitus, someone who rejects stable identities and emphasizes the transitory nature of all things. But if we look beneath the surface of Nietzsche's thought, Heidegger claims, we will see that his real metaphysical position is quite different. This position actually seeks "redemption from the eternal flux," in so far as "permanence – that is, when understood in Greek fashion, Being – is injected into *Becoming*" (*N2*, 147). Only a diagnostic reading of Nietzsche shows that he exhausts the last possibilities of metaphysical thinking by grasping becoming as the substance of things. Only a diagnostic reading shows that the question of Being remains unasked even in Nietzsche's radicalized metaphysics, and by extension in metaphysics as a whole. Only a diagnostic reading shows that Nietzsche's failure to ask this question is bound up with deeply rooted assumptions about the link between Being and time. Heidegger's central claim, as we have seen, is that philosophers since Plato have "defined the Being of beings as the permanence of presence" (*N3*, 155). The diagnostic thinker sees that Nietzsche is no exception,

---

[48] Friedrich Nietzsche, *Twilight of the Idols*, in *The Portable Nietzsche*, trans. and ed. Walter Kaufmann (New York: Penguin, 1976), 485.

his elevation of becoming notwithstanding. "Certainly," Heidegger claims, "Nietzsche wants Becoming and what becomes, as the fundamental character of beings as a whole; but he wants what becomes precisely and before all else as *what remains*, as 'being' proper" (*N3*, 156). Nietzsche conceives of becoming as what is permanent about beings, as what truly *is* with respect to them. As he does so, "the primordial interpretation of Being as the permanence of presencing is now rescued by being placed beyond questioning" (*N3*, 157).

FORGETFULNESS AS ONTO-THEOLOGY: *IDENTITY AND DIFFERENCE*

Let us now consider a final text of Heidegger's: *Identity and Difference*. This text dates from 1957, and, like the Nietzsche lectures, it investigates the picture that Heidegger calls metaphysics. But it gives a different and in some ways more precise account of this picture. It characterizes metaphysics as *onto-theology*: a type of thinking that sees all beings as unified by virtue of their common origin in a divine ground.[49] *Identity and Difference* explains how metaphysics leads to the forgetfulness of Being, and describes what it sees as the proper response to this forgetfulness. It does all of this by engaging with a different historical figure: Hegel. Heidegger sets out to diagnose Hegel's thought: to bring to light the assumptions about beings that animate it, and to develop an alternative to these assumptions.

Heidegger's remarks on Hegel appear in a part of the text called "The Onto-Theo-Logical Constitution of Metaphysics," which originally served as the conclusion to a seminar on Hegel that Heidegger conducted during the 1956/57 academic year. The text begins with a general characterization of Hegel's philosophy, and an account of how it differs from Heidegger's own work. An obvious similarity is that both Hegel and Heidegger claim that philosophy must start with a consideration of Being. Hegel's *Science of Logic* begins with the Doctrine of Being, which examines "nothing but *Being* in general: Being, and nothing else, without any further specification and filling."[50] Heidegger obviously approves of this approach, and says that for him "the matter of thinking is the Same, is Being" (*ID*, 53). But

---

[49] The Nietzsche lectures already toy with the idea that metaphysics is essentially onto-theological. See, for example, *N4*, 154–155, as well as *N4*, 207–211. But the theme of onto-theology is nowhere near as central to *Nietzsche* as it is to *Identity and Difference*.

[50] G. W. F. Hegel, *Science of Logic*, trans. A. V. Miller (Atlantic Highlands, NJ: Humanities Press International, 1989), 69. To make this passage consistent with my quotations from Heidegger, I have rendered *Sein* as "Being" (with a capital "B"), though Miller does not do so.

Heidegger's eye is caught by a parenthetical remark that Hegel makes in the introduction to the Doctrine of Being. If, Hegel says, philosophy begins with Being, then it should pay particular attention to the highest of all beings, God. "*God,*" he adds, "has the absolutely undisputed right that the beginning be made with him."[51] Heidegger concludes from this remark that Hegel sees philosophy as essentially theological – not because it is committed to "any creed or ecclesiastical doctrine," but because it is inseparable from "statements of representational thinking about God" (*ID*, 54). "If science must begin with God," Heidegger claims, "then it is the science of God: theology" (*ID*, 54). Whether this is an accurate reading of Hegel's text is clearly not the point. Heidegger uses Hegel's remark about God as a springboard to a larger discussion of what he sees as the essentially theological nature of metaphysical thinking.

Identity and Difference defines "metaphysics" in the same way as the Nietzsche lectures, calling it "the question about beings as such *and* as a whole" (*ID*, 54). Metaphysics inquires into the character all beings have, the character they have simply because they are beings. But Heidegger now insists that this inquiry is at bottom a theological one – that "Western metaphysics … since its beginning with the Greeks has eminently been both ontology and theology, still without being tied to these rubrics" (*ID*, 54). Ontology, as Heidegger uses the term here, is the attempt to understand beings as a whole in terms of what is "universal and primal" (*ID*, 61) in them. It tries to "account for them within the whole" (*ID*, 59). In other words, it conceives of beings as making up a class, membership in which is determined by their possession of some specific property. Theology, on the other hand, inquires into "the *ground* of beings as such" (*ID*, 59, my emphasis). It conceives of this ground as a cause, claiming that the highest being causes other entities to be through its creative act. Understanding beings is therefore a matter of viewing them in relation to their ground. Theological thought may be explicitly religious, but it need not be. Plato's conception of an unchanging Good to which all other things owe their Being would be theological in Heidegger's sense, as would Aristotle's account of the unmoved mover. Onto-theology, then, is the attempt to grasp beings in a way that is both ontological and theological – or rather, in a way that is ontological *because* it is theological, and vice versa.[52]

---

[51] Hegel, *Science of Logic*, 78.
[52] "Metaphysics," Heidegger argues, "is neither only the one nor the other *also*. Rather, metaphysics is theo-logic because it is onto-logic. It is onto-logic because it is theo-logic" (*ID*, 60). He insists, however, that the unity of the two aspects of metaphysics is "still *unthought*" (*ID*, 55).

Onto-theology maintains that what all beings have in common is their dependence on the ultimate being, on "the unifying One in the sense of the All-Highest" (*ID*, 69).

It should be clear why Heidegger objects to onto-theology. Like other versions of metaphysical thinking, onto-theology ignores the difference between beings and Being. It is concerned only with beings and their common character. When onto-theology views beings in relation to a divine ground, it thinks it has uncovered what is most basic and most important about them. It does not pose the truly fundamental question of what it means to be. In fact, it cannot pose this question. Ontological thinking draws us away from the *Seinsfrage*, leading us to think there is nothing to be learned about the Being of entities besides the nature of their ground. Onto-theology equates the Being of beings with their relation to one particular being – a divine being, perhaps, but a particular being nonetheless. It does not think "Being with respect to its difference from beings" (*ID*, 47). *Identity and Difference* makes some strikingly original suggestions about the proper way of understanding this difference. Reluctant to use more traditional philosophical language, Heidegger coins a new way of describing the ontological difference, one that relies on the notion of "coming-over" (*Überkommnis*) (*ID*, 64). He claims that in order to grasp the difference between Being and beings, we must see that

Being here becomes present in the manner of a transition to beings. But Being does not leave its own place and go over to beings, as though beings were first without Being and could be approached by Being subsequently. Being transits (that), comes unconcealingly over (that) which arrives as something of itself unconcealed only by that coming-over. Arrival means: to keep concealed in unconcealedness – to abide present in this keeping – to be a being. (*ID*, 64)

Being may be thought of as an "unconcealing overwhelming" (*entbergende Überkommnis*), beings as an "arrival that keeps itself concealed" (*in die Unverborgenheit sich bergenden Ankunft*) (*ID*, 65). Being "comes over" into beings in the sense that it lets us recognize them *as* beings, as things that are. Beings – that which is unconcealed by this coming-over – are what allow us to see that the unconcealment has taken place.

What is at stake in this extraordinarily difficult discussion is an attempt to understand the ontological difference as an event – not a mere "relation which our representing has added to Being and to beings" (*ID*, 62), but a process of differentiation. In the same way that the later Heidegger understands the forgetting of Being as something that happens rather than something we do, *Identity and Difference* thinks of the difference between Being and beings as something that unfolds rather than an act for which we are solely responsible. "That differentiation alone," Heidegger insists, "grants and holds apart the 'between'" (*ID*, 65) – what we naively call the difference *between* Being and beings. Heidegger refers to this event of differentiation as an *Austrag*, claiming that "[t]he difference of Being and beings, as the differentiation of overwhelming and arrival, is the *Austrag* of the two in *unconcealing keeping in concealment*" (*ID*, 65). *Austrag* is a neologism related to the verb *austragen*, which means "to deliver" or "to carry away." It therefore has connotations of causing something to arrive by sending it away, or of bringing something to its proper place by removing it. In her translation of *Identity and Difference*, Stambaugh renders *Austrag* as "perdurance"; elsewhere, she translates it as "settlement."[53] Heidegger seems to use the term as a placeholder for that event which discloses or opens up the difference between Being and beings. We might therefore think of it as a sort of ground for the ontological difference, or as an "origin of the difference" (*ID*, 71) between Being and beings. The problem is that a ground is often taken to be *a* being, an entity. Grounding in that sense presupposes the *Austrag* and cannot be used to explain it. As Heidegger puts it, "[g]rounding itself appears within the clearing of *Austrag* as something that *is*, thus itself as a being that requires the corresponding accounting for through a being, that is, causation, and indeed causation by the highest cause" (*ID*, 70). Seen in this light, onto-theological thinking is what prevents us from understanding the *Austrag*, the process of differentiation between Being and beings. Onto-theology reduces grounding to a relation among entities. The real challenge is to conceive of a more fundamental sort of ground or quasi-ground: the "ground" that makes it possible for us to speak of entities at all.[54] At the end of the day, however, talk of grounding and relations may serve as a helpful starting point, but is clearly inadequate to Heidegger's task. So it is no surprise that he claims that *Austrag* "can no longer be thought of within the scope of metaphysics" (*ID*, 71). We are in uncharted waters.

But why does Heidegger embed all of this in a discussion of Hegel? He could very well have discussed the *Austrag* and the ontological difference without referring to earlier thinkers. What purpose is served by approaching

---

[53] See, for example, *N4*, 155.

[54] To be sure, there are other differences between the type of ground described by onto-theological thinking and the quasi-grounding effected through *Austrag*. For onto-theology, grounding is unidirectional: entities depend on the highest being, but not the reverse. The "grounding" of *Austrag*, by contrast, is reciprocal: it is "the circling of Being and beings around each other" (*ID*, 70). Each reveals the other and accounts for the other, or as Heidegger puts it, "Being grounds beings, and beings, as what *is* most of all, account for Being. One comes over the other, one arrives in the other" (*ID*, 69).

these topics historically? The answer seems to be that Heidegger develops his approach to the ontological difference in opposition to Hegel. Heidegger's observations about metaphysics and its shortcomings emerge most clearly when contrasted with Hegel's reflections on Being. An obvious example is the way Heidegger frames his discussion of onto-theology with Hegel's remark about God. Hegel's remark is clearly an offhand one, since the topic of God does not play a major role in the Doctrine of Being. Heidegger pays special attention to this remark in order to highlight a distinctive feature of metaphysical thinking: its tendency to collapse the question of Being into the question of how entities relate to the highest being. But there are also subtler examples of Heidegger's strategy. One is the way he characterizes his method. *Identity and Difference* proposes a new way of thinking about the difference between Being and beings. This is difficult to do, since our existing philosophical vocabulary – even the term "difference" – tends to distort what we are trying to understand. So what *can* Heidegger say about his radically new approach? Perhaps the only strategy available to him is to contrast it with a method with which we are already familiar: Hegel's. Early in his discussion, Heidegger does precisely this. He claims that for Hegel, "the conversation with the earlier history of philosophy has the character of an *Aufhebung*, that is, of the mediating concept in the sense of an absolute foundation. For us, the character of the conversation with the history of thinking is no longer *Aufhebung*, but the step back [*Schritt zurück*]" (*ID*, 49). Whereas an *Aufhebung* seeks "the completely developed certainty of self-knowing knowledge," the step back "points to the realm which until now has been skipped over, and from which the essence of truth becomes first of all worthy of thought" (*ID*, 49). What has been "skipped over" is the unthought, a possibility for thinking that Hegel opens up but does not exploit. It is the ontological difference understood as *Austrag*, a ground that is not a ground, an event that makes possible the presence of entities without being an entity itself. And Heidegger's step back does not stop with what has been unthought. It moves beyond it to "what gives us thought. That is the forgetting of the difference. The forgetting here to be thought is the veiling of the difference as such" (*ID*, 50).[55] Forgetting defines the metaphysical picture. It is the veiling of the difference that leads us to think that we can exhaustively understand entities by tracing them back to a divine ground. But if we describe this forgetting using a traditional philosophical vocabulary, we will just reinforce the forgetting. Another approach

---

[55] I have altered Stambaugh's translation here, rendering *Vergessenheit* as "forgetting." Stambaugh translates it as "oblivion."

is necessary: a contrast with a historical example. History alone lets Heidegger diagnose the metaphysical picture and describe his alternative to it.

History also plays a crucial role in Heidegger's warnings about how *not* to think about Being. We have already seen how his discussion of the *Austrag* responds to the difficulties with onto-theology. Since we cannot think of the Being of beings as an entity that grounds them, we must see them as "grounded" in an event that is not itself an entity. Indeed, one of the reasons we must grasp the nature of this quasi-ground is so we may understand what has really been at stake in onto-theological discussions of grounding. This notion can help "clarify to what extent the onto-theological constitution of metaphysics has its essential origin in the *Austrag* that begins the history of metaphysics, governs all of its epochs, and yet remains everywhere concealed" (*ID*, 68). But it is striking that even Heidegger's criticisms of the metaphysical tradition draw on examples from this tradition. Consider his discussion of Hegel's fruit example. In a famous passage in the *Encyclopedia Logic*, Hegel warns us not to think about universals in ways appropriate only to particulars. He writes:

Taken formally, and put *side by side* with the particular, the universal itself becomes something particular too. In dealing with the ob-jects of ordinary life, this juxta-position would automatically strike us as inappropriate and awkward; as if someone who wants fruit, for instance, were to reject cherries, pears, raisins, etc., because they are cherries, pears, raisins, but *not* fruit.[56]

Fruit is not itself a type of fruit; it is a general category to which all fruit belongs. Similarly, universals are not particulars, and we must recognize them as belonging to a fundamentally different category. According to Heidegger, however, a failure to distinguish fundamentally different categories is what defines metaphysical thinking. Metaphysics treats Being as *a* being. Metaphysics as onto-theology equates the Being of entities with the divine being that causes them. But if it is a mistake to speak of universals as though they were particulars, then how much more mistaken is it to speak of Being as though it were an entity? If we must not think of fruit as though it were a type of fruit, then it is "still infinitely more impossible to represent 'Being' as the general characteristic of particular beings. There is Being only in this or that particular historic character … But these historic forms cannot be found in rows, like apples, pears, peaches, lined up on the counter of historical representational thinking" (*ID*, 66). Heidegger does not accuse

---

[56] Hegel, *Encyclopedia Logic*, 38.

Hegel of confusing fruit with raisins and pears. But he does accuse onto-theology of confusing Being with a general property of things. Whenever we think of Being in its "general meaning, we have thought of Being in an inappropriate way" (*ID*, 66). Again, we can imagine Heidegger making this point without referring to any historical figure. By advancing it in a discussion of Hegel, he sheds light on a new pitfall by contrasting it with a familiar one.

Identity and Difference is not a piece of Hegel scholarship. It is a diagnosis of metaphysics as onto-theology. But what it shows about this picture can be seen only in contrast with Hegel. As Heidegger might say, it reveals itself "only in the light that cleared itself for Hegel's thinking" (*ID*, 67).

THE BIGGER PICTURE

Taken together, these three texts give an instructive look at Heidegger's attempts to do philosophy historically. We could have chosen other examples: his readings of Leibniz and Kant, for example, or his studies of Platonic dialogues other than the *Republic*.[57] But the texts we have considered show a great deal about Heidegger's approach to philosophical pictures. They show him diagnosing the pictures that govern Western thought, uncovering the ways in which these pictures lead us to forget the question of Being. Platonism makes us think that only what is permanently present – the supersensible standard mirrored by our thoughts – truly is. It therefore blinds us to the more basic disclosive event that lets beings emerge into presence in the first place. Metaphysics in general causes us to think there is nothing to learn about Being besides the character of beings as a whole. Metaphysics as onto-theology leads us to think we know all there is to know about entities once we have discovered their ground. Heidegger diagnoses these pictures in a series of sweeping narratives about the history of Being, narratives that make us see familiar philosophers in strikingly new ways. They lead us to see Nietzsche as the last metaphysician of the West, Hegel as a quasi-theologian, and Plato as the figure who concealed the crucial pre-Socratic discoveries about Being. Of course, Heidegger constructs these

---

[57] For Heidegger's reading of Leibniz, see Martin Heidegger, *The Metaphysical Foundations of Logic*, trans. Michael Heim (Bloomington: Indiana University Press, 1984). On Kant, see Martin Heidegger, *Kant and the Problem of Metaphysics*, trans. Richard Taft (Bloomington: Indiana University Press, 1990). For an interesting look at Heidegger's approach to another Platonic dialogue, see Martin Heidegger, *Plato's Sophist*, trans. Richard Rojcewicz and André Schuwer (Bloomington: Indiana University Press, 1997).

narratives in the service of the *Seinsfrage*. He does not simply want to trigger a change in how we see Plato, Nietzsche, and Hegel. His main goal is to reawaken our perplexity in the face of Being. But even those who do not share Heidegger's commitment to this project have much to learn from his diagnostic readings of these figures. His investigations of their work, and of the types of thinking they embody, are a provocative reassessment of the history of philosophy.

But what can Heidegger teach us about the enterprise of doing philosophy historically? To start, he teaches an important lesson about its motivation and its value. Human beings are forgetful creatures, and we are particularly forgetful about the most basic assumptions that govern our thinking. Heidegger, of course, is concerned with the forgetfulness of Being: our tendency to forget the assumptions we have made about the relation between Being and time, coupled with our habit of forgetting that the *Seinsfrage* is a legitimate question at all. But this is not the only type of forgetfulness that taints our thinking. As I argued in Chapter 3, we also tend to forget the assumptions at work "in our manner of doing natural science, in our technology, in some at least of the dominant ways in which we construe political life …, and in other spheres too numerous to mention."[58] There is no reason to think that human beings will ever be less forgetful about the views of reality that structure their existence. It is crucial that they have a systematic way of addressing this forgetfulness. Given our need for philosophical pictures – what Gary Gutting calls our "ineradicable urge to act out of a comprehensive understanding of our situation"[59] – we must be prepared to diagnose them. We must be willing and able to uncover those aspects of pictures that we have overlooked. Heidegger offers a powerful example of how to do so. He has much to teach us about the art of diagnosis, even if we do not accept his specific claims about the history of philosophy. We might not agree that Platonism obscures the nature of truth, or that metaphysical thinking is essentially onto-theological. But most of us would agree that philosophy is a reflective discipline that involves self-criticism and self-justification. Philosophers must be able to explain, to themselves and others, what they are doing, and why, and why it is important. They must be aware of their own assumptions and of the effects those assumptions have on their work. In short, they must be capable of diagnosing their own thought. Heidegger offers valuable instruction in how such diagnosis proceeds.

---

[58] Taylor, "Philosophy and its History," 20.
[59] Gutting, *Pragmatic Liberalism and the Critique of Modernity*, 191.

Something else Heidegger demonstrates is that the enterprise called doing philosophy historically should be suspicious of itself. We have looked in great detail at Heidegger's suspicions of Platonism, metaphysics, and onto-theology. He does philosophy historically as a way of responding to these suspicions. But as I pointed out at the beginning of the chapter, Heidegger is just as suspicious of the basic concepts employed in doing philosophy historically. He is leery of the notion of a philosophical picture. He argues that the very idea of a "picture" of reality is a uniquely modern one, and one that rests on dubious metaphysical and epistemological assumptions. No doubt he would raise similar objections to the understanding of history that is taken for granted when we do philosophy historically. Heidegger is a fierce critic of conventional "historiological" (*historisch*) thinking, claiming that it makes questionable assumptions about time and is blind to its roots in Dasein's lived historicality (*Geschichtlichkeit*).[60] Heidegger would surely claim that my interpretation of his diagnostic project is itself in grave need of diagnosis. And this is all to the good. Philosophers need critical self-awareness. That is one of the best reasons for them to do philosophy historically. It makes perfect sense for them to be critically self-aware about their search for critical self-awareness – even if it means questioning the basic tools of that search.

The question is whether this search for self-awareness can, on Heidegger's account, ever go deep enough. If we are constantly in the grip of deceptive pictures, and if the very attempt to free ourselves from these pictures is itself badly deceived, then how confident can we ever be of anything? Are we doomed to do nothing but endlessly question our assumptions, forever undercutting all that is positive in our thinking? Perhaps. Perhaps no concept, method, or thesis is immune to Heideggerian doubt. If we can be radically deceived about the meaning of the word "is," then surely nothing is safe. Again, this may be a good thing. Philosophy is essentially critical, and none of its concepts, methods, or theses *should* be entirely exempt from criticism. But it does raise the question of whether philosophers can ever stop their endless self-undercutting long enough to build on their accomplishments. Heidegger's narratives about the history of Being sometimes look like examples of precisely this undercutting. The villain of his story is constantly changing. First it is Platonism that is responsible for our forgetfulness about Being. Later it is the tradition of metaphysical thinking, consummated by Nietzsche, that is to blame. Later still it is metaphysics as onto-theology. We should not be surprised by

---

[60] See, for example, *BT*, 424–455.

this changing cast of characters, given that we can use indefinitely many pictures to interpret the history of philosophy. And of course, Heidegger's various claims may be shown to be compatible, if we construct a narrative about the history of Being that is sufficiently detailed and comprehensive. But the spirit of Heidegger's thought, with its need for endless self-criticism, seems to undermine the construction of detailed and comprehensive narratives. Surely that is a problem.

In short, the diagnostic approach faces a special challenge. It encourages endless self-criticism at the price of constructiveness. We may not want it any other way. We may agree with Heidegger that "[t]o be preparatory is the essence of such thinking."[61] But if we wish to do philosophy historically in a way that is not just endlessly preparatory, we will need to consider this. Perhaps we should see the diagnostic approach as an invaluable supplement to other approaches, rather than an approach that stands on its own.

---

[61] Heidegger, "Nietzsche's Word: God is Dead," 158.

CHAPTER 6

The synthetic approach: Ricoeur

This chapter deals with the third major approach to doing philosophy historically: what I have called the *synthetic* approach. The synthetic approach involves bringing together a number of different philosophical pictures, typically ones that are in tension with each other. It involves trying to reconcile these pictures, in the hope of developing an approach to philosophy that draws on the resources of both. The desire to synthesize pictures is widespread and understandable. Unlike philosophical theories, pictures are not the sorts of things that can be proved or refuted. An indefinite number may seem plausible and attractive. As a result, philosophers are often drawn to several major pictures at once, and they may find themselves unwilling to abandon any of them. Those who can show these pictures to be compatible by synthesizing them in their own work provide a valuable service.

The practitioner of the synthetic approach with whom I will be concerned is Paul Ricoeur. This should not be a surprising choice. Ricoeur is widely recognized as an unusually synthetic thinker, one whose work draws on an exceptionally broad range of influences. I will not try to discuss all of these influences. Instead, I will focus on Ricoeur's attempts to reconcile two of them: the pictures of reality articulated by Kant and Hegel. Ricoeur often calls himself a "post-Hegelian Kantian,"[1] and his readers have long recognized that this notion is a valuable key for unlocking his work.[2] I will argue that Ricoeur's post-Hegelian Kantianism is best seen as an example of the synthetic approach to doing philosophy historically, and a particularly fruitful one at that. I will begin by examining the term "post-Hegelian Kantian." I will discuss Ricoeur's uses of this term, and I will argue that his readers have overlooked a crucial feature of it – that it is primarily concerned

---

[1] See, for example, *CI*, 412; *FS*, 207–216; *TA*, 200; and *TN3*, 215.
[2] See, for example, the following: Bernard Dauenhauer, *Paul Ricoeur: The Promise and Risk of Politics* (Oxford: Rowman and Littlefield, 1998), 3; François Dosse, *Paul Ricoeur: Les sens d'une vie*, 2nd edn. (Paris: La Découverte, 2001), 586–598; and David Kaplan, *Ricoeur's Critical Theory* (Albany: SUNY Press, 2003), 12–13.

with the philosophical pictures articulated by Kant and Hegel, not their theories. I will also argue that Ricoeur's post-Hegelian Kantianism is tied to a specific content, in that it is above all a way of understanding the three Kantian ideas: self, world, and God. Next, I will examine Ricoeur's approach to each of these ideas, and show that his views of self, world, and God all involve a synthesis of the Kantian and Hegelian pictures of reality. Finally, I will ask what this synthesis shows about the enterprise of doing philosophy historically.

There is one respect in which Ricoeur might seem a poor fit with the discussion so far. I have argued that we do philosophy historically by constructing a certain sort of narrative, one that seeks to trigger a change in our way of seeing earlier thinkers. MacIntyre and Heidegger clearly construct such narratives. Works such as *After Virtue* and *The Essence of Truth* relate long and detailed stories about philosophy's past, stories that directly advance original philosophical agendas. Ricoeur does not seem to write narratives of this sort. To be sure, he has a great deal to say about the history of philosophy. But there is no single work in which he learns from Kant and Hegel by telling a comprehensive story about the development of their thought. Does this make Ricoeur a counterexample to my claim that doing philosophy historically involves narratives? I do not think so. Despite appearances, Ricoeur does try to learn from Kant and Hegel by constructing a narrative. The problem is that this narrative is scattered throughout several different works. As I will argue, in essays such as "Freedom in the Light of Hope," Ricoeur offers a general account of how Kant and Hegel are related. These essays, however, do not try to synthesize their insights on specific topics in any detailed way. For that, we must look to other works by Ricoeur: *Oneself as Another*, for example, and his essays on narrative and religion. These works synthesize the Kantian and Hegelian pictures on specific topics, but lack the sweeping story told in essays such as "Freedom in the Light of Hope." When we read these more focused works alongside Ricoeur's programmatic remarks about Kant and Hegel, we are left with a very comprehensive narrative that is perfectly consistent with other attempts to do philosophy historically. But to some extent, we must piece it together ourselves. Appropriately enough, Ricoeur's synthetic narrative must itself be synthesized.

WHAT'S IN A NAME?

The term "post-Hegelian Kantian" was coined not by Ricoeur, but by Éric Weil. Weil uses this label to characterize his own approach to philosophy. In works such as *Philosophie politique* and *Philosophie morale*, Weil explores how the universal and essential features of human experience (the "Kantian" features) might be reconciled with the concrete and historical (or "Hegelian") features. Weil calls himself a Kantian and not a Hegelian because he privileges the universal side, seeing it as more fundamental than the historical. But his Kantianism is "post-Hegelian" in its insistence that the universal has meaning only in its concrete historical instantiations, and in its claim that studying these instantiations is a properly philosophical task.[3]

Even early in his career, Ricoeur was quite taken with Weil's label, and found it helpful to apply it to himself. His first use of the term in print seems to be in "Freedom in the Light of Hope."[4] In this essay, Ricoeur tries to come to terms with a theological trend instigated by Jürgen Moltmann, Albert Schweitzer, and Johannes Weiss – namely, the view that Christianity is primarily a religion of promise and hope, a faith "centered on the preaching of the Kingdom to come" (*CI*, 404).[5] In opposition to "liberal exegetes" who "make of discourse on the last things a sort of more or less optional appendix to a theology of revelation centered on a notion of *logos*," (*CI*, 404) Moltmann and his cohort read the New Testament in more eschatological terms. But if we are to join them, Ricoeur argues, we must be prepared to revise our theological concepts radically – to "readjust all theology in accordance with the norm of eschatology" (*CI*, 404). Foremost among these is the concept of religious freedom, a multifaceted concept that "can be approached in several ways and on several levels" (*CI*, 402). In "Freedom in the Light of Hope," Ricoeur sets out to give a "philosophical approximation" (*CI*, 411) of the idea of religious freedom – that is, to give a philosophical account of freedom that is compatible with a theology of

---

[3] For example, in both *Philosophie politique* and *Philosophie morale*, Weil characterizes morality as the process through which individuals become universalized, or more capable of identifying broadly with others. See Éric Weil, *Philosophie politique* (Paris: Vrin, 1956), and Éric Weil, *Philosophie morale* (Paris: Vrin, 1961). For a detailed discussion of Weil's views on this topic, see Elizabeth McMillan, "The Significance of Moral Universality: The Moral Philosophy of Éric Weil." *Philosophy Today* 21 (1977), 32–42.

[4] Though "Freedom in the Light of Hope" was published in 1969, it is a modified version of a lecture ("Approche philosophique du concept de liberté religieuse") delivered in 1968. It should also be noted that Ricoeur seems to have thought of himself as a post-Hegelian Kantian well before the late 1960s, even if he did not use the label in print before then. Bernard Dauenhauer tells the following story: "I recall hearing Ricoeur say some years ago at a professional meeting that Gabriel Marcel, one of his main philosophical mentors, had admonished him early in his career that he could not continue to try to build upon the heritages of both Kant and Hegel. He would have to opt for one and leave the other aside. Nevertheless, Ricoeur said smilingly, he has spent his career resisting making such a decision." See Dauenhauer, *Paul Ricoeur: The Promise and Risk of Politics*, 3.

[5] In the essay "Hope and Structure of Philosophical Systems," Ricoeur also mentions Martin Buber as an example of this trend (*FS*, 204).

hope. And he suggests that the most promising way to do so is to draw on the work of Kant.

But what would it mean to endorse a Kantian account of religious freedom *today*, given the criticisms Kant has faced over the last two hundred years? Ricoeur recognizes that we cannot give a Kantian account of freedom in the sense of endorsing Kant's precise conclusions about this topic. These conclusions have been found wanting by Kant's critics, and above all by Hegel. As Hegel has shown, Kant's view of freedom – not to mention many other topics – is insufficiently fluid. It tends to see our experience as fragmented into moments that are opposed and unbridgeable, rather than as continuous parts of larger processes. Ricoeur cites the following example of this tendency:

> I abandon the ethics of duty to the Hegelian critique with no regrets; it would appear to me, indeed, to have been correctly characterized by Hegel as an abstract thought, as a thought of understanding. With the *Encyclopedia* and the *Philosophy of Right*, I willingly concede that formal "morality" is simply a segment of a larger trajectory, that of the realization of freedom. (*CI*, 413)

Ricoeur goes so far as to say that Hegel's account of this trajectory is "*the* philosophy of the will," and that "[a]ll the philosophies of the will, from Aristotle to Kant, are there assumed and subsumed" (*CI*, 414). But according to Ricoeur, it does not follow that a Kantian account of freedom is impossible. After all, Hegel's critique of Kant has been subject to critique of its own, some of it decidedly Kantian in flavor. For contemporary philosophers, Ricoeur claims, "something of Hegel has vanquished something of Kant; but something of Kant has vanquished something of Hegel, because we are as radically post-Hegelian as we are post-Kantian" (*CI*, 412).

The "something of Hegel" that has been vanquished is a hasty desire to totalize – a wish to mediate that which cannot be mediated. In Ricoeur's view, Hegel is too quick to leave behind genuine tensions in experience, and to submerge inconvenient oppositions into higher unities. For Hegel, as Ricoeur reads him, nothing can withstand dialectical mediation; even the most stubborn oppositions can in principle be *aufgehoben*. "The Hegel I reject," Ricoeur says, "is the philosopher of retrospection, the one who not only accompanies the dialectic of the Spirit but reabsorbs all rationality in the already happened meaning" (*CI*, 414).[6] This Hegel embodies a hubristic

---

[6] This criticism is strikingly similar to one that Ricoeur would advance many years later in *Time and Narrative*. There, Ricoeur accuses Hegel of attempting an "impossible totalization," of believing that "the history of the world may be thought of as a completed whole." See Ricoeur, *TN3*, 205. In opposition to this "impossible totalization," Ricoeur seeks only an "open-ended, incomplete, imperfect mediation … with no *Aufhebung* into a totality where reason in history and its reality would coincide" (207). An intriguing difference between these two texts is that *Time and Narrative* seems

"philosophy of system," to which Ricoeur prefers "a philosophy of limits" (*CI*, 415). Interestingly enough, this philosophy of limits is best embodied by Kant – not, to be sure, the Kant whom Hegel rightly criticized, but "a Kant who, in his turn, understands Hegel … [T]his is the Kant of the dialectic" (*CI*, 414). Ricoeur's Kant is the Kant who reins us in when we presume to know the unconditioned. He is the Kant who offers a critique of our transcendental illusions, while at the same time reminding us of the importance of the ideas of God, self and world in regulating experience.[7] For Ricoeur, then, Hegel's critique of Kant stands – "[a]nd yet, Kant remains. What is more, he surpasses Hegel from a certain point of view" (*CI*, 414). For this reason, Ricoeur does not hesitate to call himself a Kantian. But he is adamant that "the Kantianism that I wish to develop now is, paradoxically, more to be constructed than repeated; it would be something like a post-Hegelian Kantianism, to borrow an expression from Éric Weil" (*CI*, 412). A post-Hegelian Kantian need not accept the letter of Kant's or Hegel's texts, but tries "to think them always better by thinking them together – one against the other, and one by means of the other" (*CI*, 412).

If we wish to understand Ricoeur's post-Hegelian Kantianism, "Freedom in the Light of Hope" is a good place to start. The approach to philosophy described here is one that is sensitive to the fragmented character of our experience. Like the "analytical" Kant – that is to say, the Kant of the analytical parts of the first two critiques – Ricoeur is aware of the oppositions and dualisms that haunt experience: freedom and determinism, duty and inclination, phenomena and noumena. Like Hegel, however, he recognizes that we must not be too quick to reify such oppositions. Rather than taking their poles as static givens, we should try to think them dialectically, as moments of fluid processes.[8] At the same time, we must not simply steamroll over them. Not every tension can be resolved, and not every opposition can be transcended. It is sometimes necessary to constrain reflection by treating ideas such as God and world as ideal limits, rather than as objects we can know speculatively. Ricoeur associates this modesty with the "dialectical" Kant – that is, the Kant of the transcendental dialectic

---

more modest in its criticism of Hegel. In "Freedom in the Light of Hope," Ricoeur speaks as if it is possible to "reject" Hegel (*CI*, 413), or to refute his views by means of argument. In *Time and Narrative*, however, Ricoeur scrupulously avoids saying that Hegel can or should be refuted. He says only that "we have abandoned … Hegel's work site" (*TN3*, 205). This abandonment is not the triumph of an argument, but an "event in thinking" (*TN3*, 203).

[7] For an extended and very valuable discussion of the ways in which Ricoeur's work makes use of the Kantian notion of limit, see Patrick Bourgeois, *Philosophy at the Boundary of Reason* (Albany: SUNY Press, 2001).

[8] In the essay "Practical Reason," Ricoeur puts it like this: "the Kantian moment of the problematic cannot be eliminated but neither should it be hypostatized" (*TA*, 197).

and the dialectic of pure practical reason, the Kant who offers a "critique of absolute objects" (*CI*, 416). According to "Freedom in the Light of Hope," then, Ricoeur's post-Hegelian Kantianism amounts to a resolution to treat philosophical problems from three successive standpoints: an openness to dualisms; a desire to overcome these dualisms by seeking totality; and a modesty about our ability to do so.

But "Freedom in the Light of Hope" does not tell the whole story. For one thing, it describes Ricoeur's approach to just one philosophical topic: the nature of freedom. But when Ricoeur calls himself a post-Hegelian Kantian, he clearly intends to say something general about his approach to many different philosophical problems. As we have seen, he applies this label to his views on a number of topics, not just his views on freedom. *Time and Narrative*, for instance, gives what Ricoeur calls a post-Hegelian Kantian account of history,[9] while *Oneself as Another* gives a similar account of moral and ethical obligation.[10] Given the many contexts in which this label appears, we cannot understand it with the help of "Freedom in the Light of Hope" alone. Furthermore, while Ricoeur calls himself a post-Hegelian Kantian with respect to a number of different topics, there seem to be a few with which the label is a particularly good fit. Ricoeur seems most inclined to use this label while discussing the very topics on which Kant and Hegel disagree most sharply – the nature of freedom and moral obligation, for example. This is not surprising, given Ricoeur's claim to be a follower of the "dialectical" Kant. After all, in the transcendental dialectic, Kant does not just claim that we tend to seek knowledge of unconditioned totalities beyond possible experience. He claims that there are three specific ways in which we do so, and that as a result, there are exactly three ideas of pure reason.[11] These are the ideas of God, self, and world, and it is with respect to these specific ideas that Kant warns us not to seek unachievable totalities. If

---

[9] See Ricoeur, *TN3*, 215.

[10] See *OAA*, Chapters 7, 8, and 9. Chapter 7 sketches what might be called a Hegelian approach to ethics, one in which *Sittlichkeit* is primary and agents formulate life plans in accordance with a communal sense of what is good. Chapter 8 argues that this Hegelian ethic of *Sittlichkeit* must be subordinated to a Kantian ethic of duty – that one's communally formed virtues and values must "pass through the sieve" of a Kantian formalism (*OAA*, 170). Finally, in Chapter 9, Ricoeur shows how the conflicts to which this formalism inevitably leads can only be addressed through incomplete, open-ended mediation.

[11] See, for example, the following passage from the first *Critique*: "[A]ll relation of representations, of which we can form either a concept or an idea, is then threefold: (1) the relation to a subject; (2) the relation to the manifold of the object in the field of appearance; (3) the relation to all things in general ... All transcendental ideas can therefore be arranged in three classes, the *first* containing the absolute (unconditioned) *unity of the thinking subject*, the *second*, the absolute *unity of the series of conditions of appearance*, the *third* the absolute *unity of the condition of all objects of thought in general*" (*KRV*, 323, A334/B391).

Ricoeur's post-Hegelian Kantianism were simply a resolution to treat philosophical problems from three standpoints, then it could be applied indifferently to any topic. But Ricoeur, far from applying it to just any topic, usually restricts it to the very topics Kant recommends. An interpretation of Ricoeur's post-Hegelian Kantianism must reflect this. It must show that the label is flexible, but that it applies more fruitfully to some topics than others.

So how do Ricoeur's readers interpret this label? Some take a deflationary approach, treating it merely as evidence of Ricoeur's breadth and his willingness to learn from different traditions. Bernard Dauenhauer, for example, seems to understand the label in this way. He writes:

Ricoeur's way of appropriating Kant and Hegel is typical of his catholic way of appropriating a large number of important figures in the history of philosophy. He is the exponent of the "both-and," and the opponent of the "either-or." Thus he finds instruction not only in both Kant and Hegel but also in both Plato and Aristotle, Augustine and Benedict de Spinoza, and Karl Marx and Freud.[12]

Dauenhauer is surely right that Ricoeur is an unusually catholic thinker, and that his willingness to learn from both Kant and Hegel is a good example of this tendency. But there must be more to his post-Hegelian Kantianism than this. Many well-known philosophers – Heidegger and Habermas come to mind – display a willingness to learn from both Kant and Hegel. But few, if any, claim that this willingness is central to their work in the way Ricoeur does. Moreover, as Dauenhauer notes, Ricoeur is willing to learn from quite a few opposed figures in the history of philosophy, to say nothing of contemporary philosophy. Yet he does not call himself a post-Aristotelian Platonist or a post-Freudian Marxist. Ricoeur singles out the term "post-Hegelian Kantian" and gives it a special prominence. That he does so shows that it means more than a vague willingness to learn from a wide range of thinkers.

Another reason to reject the deflationary approach is that there is a very precise sense in which Ricoeur tries to learn from Kant and Hegel. As we have seen, Ricoeur's willingness to accept elements of their work does not lead him to endorse the letter of their views. On the contrary, in "Freedom in the Light of Hope," he suggests that learning from Kant and Hegel might require one to reject the letter of their views. The task, he argues, "is to think them always better by thinking them together – one against the other, and one by means of the other … [T]his 'thinking Kant and Hegel better'

---

[12] Dauenhauer, *Paul Ricoeur: The Promise and Risk of Politics*, 3.

pertains, in one way or another, to this 'thinking differently from Kant and Hegel,' 'something other than Kant or Hegel'" (*CI*, 12). Ricoeur does not hesitate to reject large and central parts of their philosophical theories. His Kantianism and his Hegelianism are more subtle than the conviction that Kant or Hegel got certain things right. What is at stake in them is the desire to adopt the *spirit* or *orientation* of Kant and Hegel's work without endorsing their precise conclusions. The point is that Ricoeur's post-Hegelian Kantianism has much more to do with philosophical pictures than with theories. Indeed, he sometimes comes close to saying this explicitly. In the essay "Hope and the Structure of Philosophical Systems," for example, he says of Kant and Hegel that "I do not take them as individual systems but precisely as types" (*FS*, 208). Thus when Ricoeur says that "something of Hegel has vanquished something of Kant" (*CI*, 412), but that "Kant remains" (*CI*, 414), he must mean that although Hegel has refuted certain elements of Kant's theories, the Kantian picture of the world is still viable. Ricoeur's goal is to synthesize the Kantian and Hegelian pictures in a productive way – to fuse the resources of two general types of thinking in order to respond to philosophical problems in novel ways.

The deflationary approach, as I have called it, looks unpromising. Another common strategy among Ricoeur's readers is to interpret his post-Hegelian Kantianism in more procedural terms – to identify it with a certain *method* or *way* of doing philosophy. François Dosse, for example, seems to understand the label in this way. He argues:

> The philosophical gesture common to both Éric Weil and Ricoeur consists in posing antinomies without overcoming them dialectically in a reconciliation of contraries, as in Hegel. They maintain the tension of the contradiction up to the point of crisis. This leads not to the overcoming of the terms of the contradiction, but to their overflowing, in a shift that allows thought to rebound.[13]

Note that Dosse makes no reference here to *which* antinomies Ricoeur treats in this way. He does not suggest that Ricoeur's dialectical method is best applied to certain philosophical problems. Dosse presents it as a general method, one that could be fruitfully applied to topics other than the three Kantian ideas. David Kaplan interprets Ricoeur's post-Hegelian Kantianism in a similarly general way. He also takes it to be an open-ended method that might be applied to any number of topics.[14] Kaplan describes this method as follows:

---

[13] Dosse, *Paul Ricoeur: Les sens d'une vie*, 586. The translation is mine.
[14] Kaplan does recognize that there is a close link between Ricoeur's post-Hegelian Kantianism and his treatment of the three Kantian ideas. He says, for example, that Ricoeur "retains a Kantian reluctance

A post-Hegelian Kantian recognizes the importance of the concept of totality but not to the point where social, political, and religious integration become the conditions for rational reflection. At this point, it is important to limit the scope of reflection for the sake of critique. Totality, unity, and absolute mediation are only limit ideas that, in principle, cannot be attained.[15]

How exactly does a post-Hegelian Kantian limit reflection for the sake of critique? Kaplan continues:

Evidence of Ricoeur's post-Hegelian Kantianism appears throughout his career in each of his philosophical meditations. The third term he creates mediates without reconciling … Ricoeur's "third way" recognizes the aporetic quality of human experience and respects the plurality of voices and conflicting interpretation while at the same time affirming the ability of philosophy to find reason. Instead of resolving an *aporia* or succumbing to it, he proposes another option.[16]

So for Kaplan, as for Dosse, being a post-Hegelian Kantian is primarily a methodological matter. It consists in having a dialectical procedure for addressing philosophical problems, a procedure that is not restricted to any particular subject matter.[17]

There is a great deal that seems right in Dosse's and Kaplan's accounts. Ricoeur's post-Hegelian Kantianism does involve a specific method. It is clear from texts such as "Freedom in the Light of Hope" that Ricoeur does pose antinomies without overcoming them dialectically, and that he does respond to contradictions by positing a third term that mediates without reconciling. Ricoeur does approach philosophical problems with a distinctive dialectical method, and Dosse and Kaplan describe it accurately. Nevertheless, being a post-Hegelian Kantian cannot be just a methodological matter. As we have seen, Ricoeur does not present his dialectical method as being neutral with respect to content. He does not

---

to reconcile the dualism that haunts our understanding of *self, nature, and God*" (Kaplan, *Ricoeur's Critical Theory*, 12, my emphasis). Still, when Kaplan describes Ricoeur's dialectical method, he presents it as a general one that could be applied to any number of topics – not just the Kantian ideas. Consider Kaplan's list of the topics to which Ricoeur has applied this method: "Each subject he takes up – the will, evil, the subject, meaning, narrative, ethics, politics, the law – he finds *aporias* and creative, practical responses to them" (13). Clearly, this list contains topics not obviously related to the three Kantian ideas. In opposition to Kaplan, I argue that Ricoeur does not just happen to apply his dialectical procedure to the topics of God, self, and world, as well as to a host of others. Ricoeur's preoccupation with these ideas is inseparable from that procedure.

[15] Kaplan, *Ricoeur's Critical Theory*, 12.   [16] Kaplan, *Ricoeur's Critical Theory*, 13.
[17] Another discussion of Ricoeur's method is Michel Philibert, "The Philosophic Method of Paul Ricoeur," in *Studies in the Philosophy of Paul Ricoeur*, ed. Charles Reagan (Athens: Ohio University Press, 1979), 133–139. Philibert, however, makes only passing reference to Ricoeur's post-Hegelian Kantianism.

suggest, as Dosse and Kaplan seem to do, that this method could be applied to any philosophical problem whatsoever. He is most inclined to use this method when discussing the three Kantian ideas – God, self, and world. As I have argued, this is not surprising, given that Ricoeur calls himself a follower of the dialectical Kant. The dialectical Kant argues that the three ideas of reason correspond to the three specific ways in which we are tempted to overstep the bounds of experience. Thus the three Kantian ideas are the topics most in need of Ricoeur's incomplete, open-ended mediation, and it is only natural for Ricoeur to focus his dialectical method on them.

In addition to all this, we should remember that Ricoeur calls himself a *post-Hegelian* Kantian – that is, a Kantian who takes seriously Hegel's criticisms of Kant. Without a doubt, the criticism that Hegel directs most frequently and most passionately at Kant is that he is a formalist whose theories lack content. He attacks Kant's ethics, for example, as entirely abstract. The categorical imperative, Hegel tells us, is an empty testing procedure that offers no concrete guidance in how to act, because it has been implausibly separated from all actual practices and institutions.[18] In short, it seems obvious that a *post-Hegelian* Kantian would be sensitive to the charge that Kant's thought is formalistic and lacking in content.[19] So it would be strange indeed if Ricoeur's post-Hegelian Kantianism were just a methodological affair. True, it leads him to adopt a certain philosophical method. But this method cannot be entirely content-neutral.

Ricoeur's post-Hegelian Kantianism, then, is not just a desire to learn from two different philosophical traditions. Nor is it just a willingness to use a distinctive philosophical method, important as this method might be. But what *is* it? To answer this question, we must look beyond Ricoeur's programmatic statements. Rather than focusing on what he *says* about his post-Hegelian Kantianism, we should see what he actually *does* with the three Kantian ideas. We should begin with the idea of self, and with Ricoeur's most ambitious (though still "exploratory" (*OAA*, 297)) discussion of self-hood – the tenth study of *Oneself as Another*.

---

[18] The best example of Hegel's critique of Kantian morality is found in the *Phenomenology of Spirit*. See Hegel, *Phenomenology*, 364–409.

[19] To be fair, Kaplan recognizes this. He says that "Hegel adds content to Kantian reflection, transforming a hermeneutics of the *cogito* into a hermeneutics of embodied existence" (*Ricoeur's Critical Theory*, 13). But Kaplan does not seem to think that this fact will lead Ricoeur to apply his dialectical method mainly or exclusively to the Kantian ideas.

SELF

A number of Ricoeur's works deal with the nature of the self. *Freedom and Nature* gives a lengthy phenomenological description of the self's experience as an agent who wills.[20] And as we have seen, essays such as "Freedom in the Light of Hope" deal with certain aspects of the self, such as the kind of freedom it enjoys. But what is Ricoeur's ontology of selfhood? What kind of thing does he take the self to be, and how are his views on this matter both post-Hegelian and Kantian? Obviously, a post-Hegelian Kantian ontology of the self would reject the "analytical" Kant's approach to the self, and would take seriously Hegel's criticisms of this approach. But it would also find Hegel's alternative unacceptable, favoring a more modest and less totalizing ontology of selfhood. So how does the "analytical" Kant approach the ontology of the self? Though Kant argues that it is impossible to give a metaphysical description of the self – that there can be no "rational doctrine of the soul" (*KRV*, 329, A342/B400) – he has a great deal to say about what such an account would look like if it were possible.[21] It would view the self as a *substance*, and more specifically as a substance that is "an object of inner sense" (*KRV*, 329, A342/B400). As an object of inner and not outer sense, the self would have to be seen as an *immaterial* substance (*KRV*, 331, A345/B403). The rational doctrine of the soul would also view the self as a simple substance, and therefore as incorruptible (*KRV*, 331, A345/B403). Finally, it would assert "the absolute unity of this subject itself" (*KRV*, 328, A340/B398) – it would claim that "[a]s regards the different times in which it exists, it is numerically identical" (*KRV*, 330, A344/B402). Of course, Kant does not endorse any of these claims about the self, at least not from the standpoint of theoretical reason. Since the soul is not an object of possible experience, any attempt to show that it is a simple, numerically identical substance must be a "pseudo-rational inference" (*KRV*, 328, A340/B398). But while Kant does not think that a rational doctrine of the soul can succeed, he is clear about what form it would have to take. For Kant, an ontology of selfhood must be an ontology of substance.

It is well known that Hegel rejects this approach to selfhood. He denies that we should view the self as a simple, immaterial substance. Not

---

[20] Paul Ricoeur, *Freedom and Nature*, trans. Erazim Kohak (Evanston: Northwestern University Press, 1966).

[21] Actually, there has been considerable controversy in recent Kant scholarship about whether Kant should be seen as a non-metaphysical thinker. Karl Ameriks, for example, has argued that Kant should be seen as offering "modest" or "moderate" metaphysical accounts of self, God, and world, rather than as refusing to address these topics from the standpoint of theoretical reason. See Karl Ameriks, *Kant and the Fate of Autonomy* (Cambridge: Cambridge University Press, 2000).

coincidentally, he is more optimistic than Kant about the prospects of developing an ontology of selfhood. For Hegel, the self must be understood not as a simple or discrete entity, but as essentially relational. It exists not only in itself, but *for* itself. In other words, a self exists *as* a self only in a certain kind of social context. More specifically, selfhood exists as such only when it is *recognized* by other selves.[22] It requires that one be recognized by other free, self-conscious beings through a complex web of social relations. So for Hegel, as John Russon puts it, "truthfully saying 'I' is not something that can be done directly and easily, but is a process that can be fulfilled only through the support of others; … that is, it is a social act."[23] Moreover, the simple social acts through which we initially seek our sense of selfhood – the recognition of one individual by another, for example – are typically too full of contradictions to accomplish what they intend.[24] True recognition requires the richer social context offered by institutions such as a state with a system of morality and laws.[25] So for Hegel, the self must not be taken to be a substance, let alone Kant's simple, immaterial substance. It exists in, or as, an array of social practices, practices that essentially involve others and that evolve according to a complex dialectical logic.

It is not surprising that Ricoeur prefers the Hegelian approach to self-hood to that of the "analytical" Kant. After all, Ricoeur often warns us that Kant's thought can be too static, too prone to reify oppositions. When possible, he prefers to view seemingly opposed terms, such as self and other, as moments of dynamic processes. Hegel's view of selfhood does exactly that. Where Kant sees a discrete entity, Hegel sees a fluid social process, and Ricoeur would approve of this dialectical approach to selfhood. But there is also something in Hegel's account that would worry Ricoeur. If selfhood exists in, or as, a series of social acts, then in principle, there is no reason the acts in question could not be carried out in a perfectly satisfying way. If selfhood involves the dialectical process of being recognized by others, there is nothing that rules out the possibility of others recognizing the self in an entirely adequate way. It is unlikely, of course, that the acts and institutions that constitute selves could ever function perfectly. But there is no way to rule it out, and it seems inevitable that as our institutions progress, selfhood

[22] Hegel puts the point this way: "Self-consciousness exists in and for itself when, and by the fact that, it so exists for another; that is, it exists only in being acknowledged." See Hegel, *Phenomenology*, 111.

[23] John Russon, *Reading Hegel's* Phenomenology (Bloomington: Indiana University Press, 2004), 157.

[24] The most obvious example is the chapter of the *Phenomenology* entitled "Independence and Dependence of Self-Consciousness: Lordship and Bondage." Here, Hegel shows that the process of recognition essential to selfhood is bound to fail as long as it is taken to involve only individual persons.

[25] For a more detailed discussion of this point, see Russon, *Reading Hegel's Phenomenology*, 158.

moves asymptotically towards this ideal. In this respect, Hegel's view of selfhood contains a tendency towards totalization that Ricoeur would find troubling. It leaves open the possibility of the self, under ideal conditions, becoming an "exalted subject" (*OAA*, 16) – an entirely stable and homogeneous entity suffering no fragmentation at all. Hegel's account might be preferable to Kant's, but it risks steamrolling over the tensions and contradictions that Ricoeur considers an ineliminable feature of selfhood.

A post-Hegelian Kantian ontology of selfhood would have to avoid the pitfalls of both approaches. It would reject Kant's substance ontology by viewing the self as essentially relational, and as constituted by a dialectical encounter with otherness. At the same time, it would deny that this dialectic could ever be completed once and for all, or that it could ever take place in an entirely adequate way. In short, a post-Hegelian Kantian would adopt an ontology that makes the self *dependent* on otherness without being able to *triumph* over otherness. It would understand the self's integrity as partial and incomplete – as a limit that must be sought but that can never be fully achieved. Not surprisingly, this is precisely how Ricoeur understands the self. One can find glimmers of this view in many different texts from all stages of Ricoeur's career.[26] But it is presented most clearly in the tenth study of *Oneself as Another*, and it is to this study that we should now turn.

Ricoeur's project in *Oneself as Another* is to develop a "hermeneutics of the self" (*OAA*, 16). He presents this approach as an alternative to two views of selfhood that are clearly unsatisfactory: the "exalted subject" (*OAA*, 16) of classical modern philosophers such as Descartes, and the "shattered cogito" (*OAA*, 11) of Nietzsche and his followers. Ricoeur seeks a third way between these extremes. He acknowledges that the self is fragmented and in some ways opaque to itself, but he does not see it as totally devoid of unity and intelligibility. His hermeneutical approach to selfhood seeks a compromise that is "characterized by [an] indirect manner of positing the self" (*OAA*, 17). The word "indirect" is meant to suggest that the self's unity and intelligibility

---

[26] An obvious example is the theory of narrative identity presented in Volume III of *Time and Narrative*. Ricoeur offers this theory as a solution to the following dilemma: "Either we must posit a subject identical with itself through the diversity of its different states, or, following Hume and Nietzsche, we must hold that this identical subject is nothing more than a substantialist illusion." According to Ricoeur, this dilemma disappears if we view the self's identity as an identity accomplished by narrative – that is, if we see that "[t]o answer the question 'Who?' is to tell the story of a life" (*TN3*, 246). A little later in this discussion, Ricoeur describes narrative identity in terms very similar to the ones I have used in describing Ricoeur's post-Hegelian Kantian ontology of selfhood. He says that "narrative identity is not a stable and seamless identity. Just as it is possible to compose several plots on the subject of the same incidents (which, thus, should not really be called the same events), so it is always possible to weave different, even opposed, plots about our lives" (*TN3*, 248).

are real but limited, and that they result from a series of "detours" (*OAA*, 17) in which the self encounters that which is other than itself. If this talk of encounters and otherness sounds dialectical, then it is also sharply opposed to Hegel's dialectic of selfhood.[27] For Ricoeur, the dialectic of self and other is not a straightforward encounter between one self and another, or even between a self and a society. It is much more diffuse – "the otherness joined to selfhood," Ricoeur says, "is attested to only in a wide range of dissimilar experiences, following a diversity of centers of otherness" (*OAA*, 318). While Hegel sees this dialectic as a process that could, in principle, be completed, Ricoeur denies that the self could ever emerge whole from its encounter with otherness. This is because the otherness in question is not just something found outside the self, but something *in* the self. As Ricoeur puts it, "otherness is not added on to selfhood from outside, as though to prevent its solipsistic drift, but … belongs instead to the tenor and meaning and to the ontological constitution of selfhood" (*OAA*, 329). Since otherness is not simply opposed to selfhood, but is internal to it, there is no way for the self to overcome it altogether.[28]

Ricoeur presents his views on this matter in the final study of *Oneself as Another*, entitled "What Ontology in View?" It is a tentative study, more "exploratory" (*OAA*, 297) than the rest of the book. Yet its guiding question is unapologetically ambitious: "What mode of being … belongs to the self, what sort of entity is it?" (*OAA*, 297). As we have seen, Ricoeur's general answer is that the self exists as a dialectical interaction between a certain type of identity and a certain type of otherness. But he does not leave it at that. He also considers it important to highlight several specific ways in which otherness resides in the self. The first concerns what Ricoeur calls "the flesh," or "the enigmatic nature of the phenomenon of one's own body" (*OAA*, 319). A self exists as embodied, as a physical being. My body is the locus of my selfhood. But it is also something foreign to me, because as a physical substance among other physical substances, the body belongs "to the domain of things" (*OAA*, 319). It is capable of being objectified by empirical science,

---

[27] Ricoeur expresses this idea by saying that there is a "change of orientation of the celebrated dialectic of the Same and the Other when it comes in contact with the hermeneutics of the self. In fact, it is the pole of the Same that is the first to lose its univocity, through the fragmentation that occurs when the identical is split" (*OAA*, 318).

[28] The term "otherness" is not entirely appropriate here. Ricoeur takes "otherness" to be a "metacategory" (*OAA*, 298), much like the "great kinds" in Platonic dialogues such as the *Sophist*. Strictly speaking, the term "otherness" should be restricted to the "second-order discourse" (*OAA*, 298) of speculative philosophy. In a first-order discourse about "persons and things" (*OAA*, 298), Ricoeur prefers the term "passivity," which he describes as an ontic attestation of otherness. Nevertheless, in what follows, I will use the term "otherness" in referring to persons and things, since doing so makes it easier to compare Ricoeur with Kant and Hegel.

and of being understood in a way that makes no reference to my interior sense of self. My body acts on other physical things and is acted on by them. Many of my most vivid experiences – my sensations and moods, for example – clearly result from the ways in which my body is affected by others. Indeed, as Husserl shows in the *Cartesian Meditations*, it is only because my body is other to me that I am able to constitute the sense "other ego," and thus come to understand what a self is in the first place (*OAA*, 324). My own sense of self, far from being more basic than my relation to otherness, is a function of it. To be a self is to be embodied, and to be embodied is to be alienated from oneself through the otherness of the flesh. Since this alienation is essential to embodied existence, it is impossible for the self to rid itself of it.

A second way in which otherness permeates the self concerns my dependence on other people. Though I am distinct from other people, I exist among them, and I have always already been affected by them. Indeed, some of the experiences that I think of as being most intimately my own are residues of the actions of other people. My use of language is a clear example – "every participant," Ricoeur writes, "is affected by the speech addressed to him or her" (*OAA*, 329). My ability to speak, and therefore to have conversations with myself in thought, is instilled in me by others. So is my ability to act and to understand myself as an agent. This ability, Ricoeur claims, is "inseparable from the ascription by another, who designates me in the accusative as the author of my actions" (*OAA*, 329). In much the same way, my experiences of ethical and moral obligation involve encounters with other people. I experience such obligations because I find myself "aiming at the 'good life,' with and for others, in just institutions" (*OAA*, 172). My behavior is subject to norms because my actions affect others, and because they take place in a social setting. Even in answering deeply personal questions about what I value or which sort of life I wish to pursue, I find myself affecting and being affected by other people. Ricoeur takes great pains to emphasize the reciprocal character of my relations to other people. "Acting and suffering," he claims, "seem to be distributed among two different protagonists: the agent and the patient, the latter appearing as the potential victim of the former. But because of the reversibility of the roles, each agent is the patient of the other" (*OAA*, 330).[29]

---

[29] Interestingly, Ricoeur argues that the reciprocity involved in the self's relation to other people has rarely been noticed. He claims that the best-known accounts of this relation are one-sided: they either reduce the self to a mode of the existence of others, or they reduce other people to a mode of the self. He sees Levinas as an example of the former approach, Husserl as an example of the latter (*OAA*, 331–341). Ricoeur repeats this claim about Levinas and Husserl in *The Course of Recognition*, trans. David Pellauer (Cambridge, MA: Harvard University Press, 2005), 153–161. In opposition to both figures, Ricoeur claims that "there is no contradiction in holding the movement from the Same toward the Other and that from the Other toward the Same to be dialectically complementary" (*OAA*, 340).

The self's dependence on other people does not make it completely passive. But like the otherness of my body, the otherness of other people ineluctably precedes my explicit sense of self, and makes it possible. I could not understand what a self is, or what kind of self I take myself to be, without affecting and being affected by other people. The presence of other people is thus an ineliminable feature of selfhood.

A third way in which otherness appears in the self concerns experiences of conscience (*Gewissen*). These are experiences in which I feel myself to be guilty of something, to stand accused of something, or to be indebted to someone or something. According to Ricoeur, Heidegger "described perfectly" (*OAA*, 342) the experience of conscience in *Being and Time*.[30] Heidegger likens conscience to a voice that calls out to me and finds me guilty. But it is a paradoxical voice, because it is "at once inside me and higher than me" (*OAA*, 342). It is *my* conscience that speaks to me; the experience is most intimately my own. Yet the peculiar authority of conscience derives from the way it presents itself as higher than me, as more important than my whims and desires. Conscience, then, presents the self with a unique kind of otherness. It "presents a remarkable dissymmetry, one that can be called vertical, between the agency that calls and the self called upon. It is the vertical nature of the call, equal to its interiority, that creates the enigma of the phenomenon of conscience" (*OAA*, 342). To be sure, the enigmatic character of conscience gives rise to a number of challenges. The notions of "bad" and "good" conscience, for example, are "suspect" (*OAA*, 341), and must be subjected to a hermeneutics of suspicion. We must also address Freud's claim that the otherness of conscience can be reduced to the otherness of other people – that "conscience is another name for the superego" (*OAA*, 353).[31] But nothing changes the fact that in conscience, the self confronts an aspect of itself that is foreign to itself. It is a particularly vivid example of the otherness internal to the self.

Ricoeur's ontology of selfhood is obviously quite different from either Kant's or Hegel's. But as *Oneself as Another* makes clear, his overall approach

---

[30] That said, later in his discussion, Ricoeur expresses some reservations about Heidegger's account of conscience. He suggests that "one can no longer concur with the Heidegger of *Being and Time* that the voice says nothing but is restricted to directing Dasein back to its ownmost potentiality for being" (*OAA*, 352).

[31] Briefly, Ricoeur's response is that Freud begs the question. Freud argues that the superego is formed as the self internalizes the demands of authority figures. But in order for the self to encounter authority figures at all, it must first be capable of recognizing otherness. And as Husserl has shown, this encounter with otherness is made possible by the self's own proper otherness. Or as Ricoeur puts it: "If … the self were not constituted primordially as a receptive structure for the sedimentation of the superego, the internalization of ancestral voices would be unthinkable" (*OAA*, 354).

to the topic of selfhood is both Kantian and Hegelian. It is Kantian, in the sense of the analytical Kant, in that it recognizes the dualisms and opposed moments involved in selfhood. Though he rejects Kant's substance ontology, Ricoeur sees that the self possesses an irreducible identity, and that it is opposed to otherness. His view of the self is Hegelian in that he does not see this opposition as unbridgeable. He grasps the opposition dialectically, and understands the self's identity as a result of its relation to otherness. Finally, Ricoeur's account is Kantian in the sense of the dialectical Kant in its insistence that the self's encounter with otherness can never come to an end, and can never conclude in an entirely satisfying way. Otherness – in the form of the flesh, the traces of other people, and conscience – is *in* the self. No social act or institution can remove it once and for all. The self's own otherness is, as Kaplan puts it, a "third term [that] mediates without reconciling."[32] It mediates the self's substantiality with its relation to otherness, its character as an in-itself with its character as a for-itself. And it does so in a resolutely non-totalizing way.

A particularly clear sign of this appears in the final sentences of *Oneself as Another*. Ricoeur notes that he has placed three very different kinds of otherness in the self, and asks – with "a tone of Socratic irony" (*OAA*, 355) – whether they should be described in a more unified way. But he concludes that it is "necessary to leave in such a state of dispersion the three great experiences of passivity," because "[t]his dispersion seems to me on the whole well suited to the idea of otherness" (*OAA*, 356). Ricoeur refuses to give a totalizing description of the ways in which selfhood resists totalization. An account of the self's fragmented character must itself remain fragmented.

WORLD

Let us now consider the second Kantian idea: the idea of the *world*. Kant argues that this idea, like the idea of the self, is a product of reason's attempt to unify appearances into a totality. The idea of the self, however, arises from reason's attempt to unify the objects of *inner* sense – that is, the states of our own consciousness. The idea of the world, by contrast, unifies the objects of *outer* sense – spatiotemporal objects, or in other words, physical things. Since space and time are the forms of sensible intuition, all objects of outer sense are given as extended in space and time. But in encountering particular spatiotemporal objects, we inevitably try to go beyond them. We

---

[32] Kaplan, *Ricoeur's Critical Theory*, 13.

form the idea of a totality of such objects – that is, of *all* particular physical things thought of as a whole. We are inevitably tempted to think that "if *the conditioned is given, the entire sum of conditions, and consequently the absolutely unconditioned* (through which alone the conditioned has been possible) *is also given*" (*KRV*, 386, A409/B436). We therefore conceive of particular appearances as belonging to a totality, and as given against the backdrop of this totality. This totality – the world – is the idea of "the absolute *unity of the series of conditions of appearance*" (*KRV*, 323, A334/B391). It lets us think of our experiences of particular spatiotemporal objects as unified, as making up an "absolute totality in the synthesis of appearances" (*KRV*, 385, A407/B434).

But like a self that underlies all objects of inner sense, the world is not an object of possible experience. We never do, and never could, encounter "the entire sum of conditions," so we can know nothing positive about such a totality. But this has not stopped philosophers from trying to demonstrate certain facts about the world using reason alone. Accordingly, most of Kant's discussion of this idea is devoted to showing that any attempt to know the world theoretically involves fallacious reasoning. It leads to antinomies – inconclusive debates between two positions that are incompatible but equally plausible. For example, if we ask whether the world is finite or infinite in time and space, we find equally compelling arguments on both sides. Reason can prove *both* that "[t]he world has a beginning in time, and is also limited as regards space" (*KRV*, 396, A426/B454), *and* that "[t]he world has no beginning, and no limits in space" (*KRV*, 396, A427/B455). Such antinomies are a sign that reason has overstepped its bounds. Kant argues that the proper response to them is not to endorse either side of the debate, but to reject the premise shared by both – what Henry Allison calls the "initially plausible but ultimately incoherent conception of the sensible world as a whole existing in itself."[33] But while we must reject the assumption that the sensible world is an object of possible experience, we must also recognize that the idea of the world plays an indispensable regulative role. Conceiving of physical things as parts of a whole helps make our experience of them systematic. Consequently, we must view spatiotemporal objects *as if* they belonged to a totality, even as we recognize that this totality could never be given as the objects are.

Hegel is sharply critical of Kant's approach to the idea of the world. He agrees that this idea plays a crucial role in regulating experience, and that we

---

[33] Henry Allison, *Kant's Transcendental Idealism: An Interpretation and Defense* (New Haven: Yale University Press, 1983), 38.

must see spatiotemporal objects as belonging to a larger whole. Unlike Kant, however, he believes that reason can demonstrate certain things about this whole. According to Hegel, the reason that Kant is unable to say anything positive about the world is that Kant understands this idea in an excessively abstract way. Kant divorces this idea from all content, viewing it as nothing more than an empty "principle of totality."[34] Hegel claims that it is the abstractness of this approach, and not the notion of worldhood as such, that leads to antinomies. So while we must, in Hegel's view, make use of the idea of the world, "it is above all necessary not to cling to the abstract determinations of the understanding as if they were ultimate – as if each of the two terms of an antithesis could stand on its own."[35] But this, he claims, is precisely what Kant's cosmological discussions do. They therefore miss the phenomenon of the world. According to Hegel, instead of abandoning the attempt to know the world theoretically, we should approach this idea in a way that transcends "the one-sidedness of the abstract determinations of the understanding."[36] This means viewing the world dialectically, since dialectical thought alone can grasp its opposed aspects as moments of something fluid. It also means seeing the world as a "*concrete* whole," and not "according to abstract determinations."[37] To understand the world concretely is to say that the backdrop of our experiences of spatiotemporal objects is not just an empty principle of totalization, but has a specific content. For Hegel, this content is described by his theory of objective spirit. Objective spirit plays much the same role in Hegel's thought that the idea of the world plays in Kant's. It lets us see particular spatiotemporal objects as belonging to a larger context. But this larger context takes a number of concrete forms: natural phenomena, historical events, and particular social and political institutions. The "objective world," Hegel maintains, "has distinction in it; as objective *world* it falls apart inwardly into [an] undetermined manifoldness – and each of these *isolated* [bits] is also an object, or something-there that is inwardly concrete, complete, and independent."[38] Moreover, Hegel's theory of objective spirit gives a comprehensive account of how these different forms are related. It explains why objective spirit must take the particular forms it does; it also explains how these forms evolve, with one form giving rise to another in a necessary order. In short, the theory of objective spirit allows Hegel to claim not just that particular objects are given as parts of a whole, but that "the true *is* the whole."[39] And it allows him to see this whole as something concrete.

---

[34] Hegel, *Encyclopedia Logic*, 70.   [35] Hegel, *Encyclopedia Logic*, 72–73.
[36] Hegel, *Encyclopedia Logic*, 70.   [37] Hegel, *Encyclopedia Logic*, 72. My emphasis.
[38] Hegel, *Encyclopedia Logic*, 268–269.   [39] Hegel, *Phenomenology*, 11. My emphasis.

What would Ricoeur make of these approaches? He would surely agree that the idea of the world plays a crucial role in regulating experience. He would grant that our experiences of particular spatiotemporal objects are always given against a wider context, and that it is philosophy's task to shed light on this context. From the beginning of his career, Ricoeur's work has explored the larger contexts in which human experience unfolds: nature, history, and political communities, for example. He has also frequently claimed that we cannot do without the unity provided by such contexts, and that our experiences of spatiotemporal objects are intelligible only when seen as elements of a larger whole. *Time and Narrative*, for example, argues that we cannot experience an object as temporal unless we situate it in a narrative – that "time becomes human time to the extent that it is organized after the manner of a narrative" (*TN1*, 3). Ricoeur would also agree with Hegel that Kant's view of worldhood is too abstract, too dependent on empty dualisms. Our account of the world must therefore be made concrete by being given a specific content. "The unequalled genius of Hegel," Ricoeur claims, "is to have employed the *Darstellung* with unprecedented richness, exhibiting our historical experience in all its social, political, cultural, and spiritual dimensions" (*TA*, 244).[40] But it is also clear that Ricoeur would be uneasy with some of the claims Hegel makes about this content. He would be uncomfortable with Hegel's theory of objective spirit, seeing it as unacceptably totalizing. In Ricoeur's view, Hegel tends to "hypostatize" (*TA*, 245) objective spirit. He tends to claim that the collective entities described by the theory of objective spirit – for example, the state and the movement of history – are more real than the individuals that comprise them.[41] On this view, an individual human being is a sort of abstraction, and has less reality – and perhaps less importance – than the wholes of which it is a part. Ricoeur finds this consequence unacceptable. He therefore distances himself from Hegel's account of the world as well as from Kant's:

[40] While Ricoeur credits Hegel with recognizing the need to understand the world concretely, he has doubts about Hegel's particular strategy for doing so. He suggests that "Hegel's superiority in the order of content is ... not overwhelming," and that other thinkers do a better job of understanding worldhood concretely. Max Weber, for example, "at times outdoes Hegel himself, in the area of the economy, certainly; in the political idea, probably; and in the field of comparative history of religions, assuredly" (*TA*, 244).

[41] Of course, not all readers of Hegel would accept Ricoeur's interpretation. Many would insist that in Hegel's view, collective entities such as the state have no reality apart from the acts of individuals. A good example is Robert Pippin; see his *Idealism as Modernism* (Cambridge: Cambridge University Press, 1997).

The point at which the Hegelian attempt becomes, in my mind, a temptation to be vigorously avoided is this: one can fundamentally doubt whether, in order to be elevated from the individual to the State, it is necessary to distinguish ontologically between subjective spirit and objective spirit, or rather between consciousness and spirit.[42] (*TA*, 203–204)

What would it mean to refrain from distinguishing ontologically between subjective spirit and objective spirit? It would involve putting individual human beings and their acts at the center of our understanding of the world. It would mean insisting that the collective entities described by Hegel's theory of objective spirit – the state, for example – may always be reduced to individuals and explained in terms of them. On this view, collective entities such as the state are products of "composition" (*TA*, 188). They are constituted through the acts of individuals, and have no reality apart from these acts. Ricoeur is led to this approach by his views on the philosophy of action. It is part of the "the minimal criteria of human action," he argues, that we be able "to identify this action through the projects, intentions, and motives of agents capable of imputing their action to themselves" (*TA*, 245). In other words, it must be possible to describe an action accurately using terms that the agent performing the action would recognize and accept. But when we view individuals as abstract determinations of some hypostatized collective entity, we describe their actions in terms they would *not* recognize or accept – for example, in terms of a "cunning of reason" that puts the individual "to work for itself."[43] In doing so, we "[l]et these minimal criteria be abandoned," and we begin "to hypostatize social and political entities, to raise power to the heavens, and to tremble before the State" (*TA*, 245). Ricoeur also seems to have ethical reasons for favoring an account based on composition. "One may wonder," he says, "whether [Hegel's] hypostasis of spirit, elevated in this way above individual consciousness and even above intersubjectivity, is not responsible for another hypostasis, that of the State itself" (*TA*, 204). It is a short leap from the claim that the state is somehow more real than individuals to the conclusion that individuals have less value or importance than the state.[44] To

---

[42] In this passage, and in similar passages following it, I translate Ricoeur's term *esprit* as "spirit." Blamey and Thompson render it as "mind."

[43] Hegel, *Philosophy of History*, 33.

[44] And it is hard to dismiss Ricoeur's worry, given passages such as the following one from Hegel's *Philosophy of History*: "In contemplating the fate which virtue, morality, even piety experience in history, we must not fall into the Litany of Lamentations, that the good and pious often – or for the most part – fare ill in the world, while the evil-disposed and wicked prosper … In speaking of something which in and for itself constitutes an aim of existence, that so-called well or ill-faring of these or those isolated individuals cannot be regarded as an essential element in the rational order of the universe." See G. W. F. Hegel, *Philosophy of History*, trans. J. Sibree (New York: Dover, 1956), 34.

the extent that our account of worldhood refers to collective entities, it must reduce these entities to "a network of interactions" (*TA*, 245). In Ricoeur's view, the philosopher who has articulated the most promising account of this sort is Husserl. Comparing Hegel's and Husserl's views on social phenomena, Ricoeur muses:

[I]f one refuses to hypostatize objective spirit, then one has to explore the other alternative in depth, namely, that it must always be possible, according to Husserl's working hypothesis in the fifth *Cartesian Meditation*, to generate all the higher-level communities, such as the State, solely on the basis of the constitution of others in an intersubjective relation. All the constitutions have to be derivative: first, those of the common physical world, then those of the common cultural world, conducting themselves in their turn in relation to one another as higher-order selves confronting others of the same order. (*TA*, 204)

The task is to combine the best parts of Hegel's account of worldhood with Husserl's reliance on composition. We must conceive of the world as made concrete in collective entities such as history and the state. But if we are to avoid hypostatizing these entities, we must see them as constituted by individual agents, all the way down.

It is not surprising, then, that Ricoeur's account of the world owes a great deal to phenomenological discussions of this idea, as well as to Kant and Hegel. Phenomenological accounts of the world typically see it not as a thing – much less a thing that is more real than any individual – but as a web of meanings essentially linked to subjectivity. For phenomenological thinkers, as Dan Zahavi puts it, "[t]he world is not something that simply exists. The world appears, and the structure of this appearance is conditioned and made possible by subjectivity."[45] Husserl certainly conceives of the world in this way. In early texts such as the *Ideas*, he describes it as an environment or setting in which consciousness finds itself situated. In his later work, talk of this sort is replaced by talk of the lifeworld – that is, the pre-theoretical sphere that always precedes reflection and that can never be fully thematized.[46] But in all of these discussions, Husserl resists thinking of the world as a mind-independent object. The world is always the world that appears to some conscious subject, and no other sort of world is even imaginable. "The attempt," Husserl writes, "to conceive the universe of

---

[45] Dan Zahavi, *Husserl's Phenomenology* (Stanford, CA: Stanford University Press, 2003), 52.

[46] One of the differences between Husserl's early discussions of the world and his later discussions of the lifeworld is that in the latter, he emphasizes the lifeworld's concreteness. This is very much in keeping with the post-Hegelian approach to worldhood endorsed by Ricoeur. For a good discussion of this point, see Rudolf Bernet *et al., An Introduction to Husserlian Phenomenology* (Evanston: Northwestern University Press, 1993), 222.

true being as something lying outside the universe of possible consciousness, possible knowledge, possible evidence, … is nonsensical. They belong together essentially."[47] Heidegger develops a similar but even more radical account of worldhood. Of course, Heidegger no longer speaks of a world constituted by "subjectivity," preferring instead to speak of Dasein. But he is just as hostile as Husserl to the claim that the world is a thing or an object. Heidegger conceives of a world as "that '*wherein*' a factical Dasein as such can be said to 'live'" (*BT*, 93).[48] Dasein's world is the set of meaning relations that link it to other entities. My pen and my desk, for example, are given as equipment that I may use in my various practical projects. They therefore "refer back" to me, and have specific meanings in virtue of the role they play in my existence.[49] My world is the totality of such meanings. So for Heidegger, as for Husserl, the world is a structure of meanings constituted by the acts of a subject – or in Heidegger's case, by something *like* a subject. Like Kant and Hegel, these thinkers insist that spatiotemporal objects are always encountered against the backdrop of a larger context. Unlike Kant and Hegel, however, they see this context as dependent on the meaning-giving acts performed by a subject. These phenomenological understandings of the world show Ricoeur a strategy for thinking about this idea, a strategy that will meet the demands of his post-Hegelian Kantianism. Following Husserl and Heidegger, Ricoeur will conceive of the world as a set of meanings *disclosed* or *opened up* by the subject. He will, however, take special care to show that this set of meanings is concrete without being totalizing.

Ricoeur's most explicit discussions of worldhood appear in his writings on narrative from the 1970s and 1980s. In *Time and Narrative*, as well as in a number of essays dealing with related themes, Ricoeur offers the idea of the world as a way of thinking about the relation between narrative and reference. Ricoeur is adamant that narratives refer to reality. Contrary to certain developments in recent French philosophy, he insists that there is a *hors-texte*. But in the case of narrative, the notion of reference must be

---

[47] Husserl, *Cartesian Meditations*, 84. Zahavi points out that statements like this one sound idealistic, contrary to Husserl's intentions. They are less misleading when "formulated negatively. It is basically a rejection of a realistic and naturalistic objectivism that claims that the nature of meaning, truth, and reality can be understood without taking subjectivity into account." See Zahavi, *Husserl's Phenomenology*, 52.

[48] Heidegger does distinguish four different uses of the term "world," one of which is "the totality of entities which can be present-at-hand within the world" (*BT*, 93). But he also makes clear that this is not what he means by the term.

[49] Heidegger calls this type of meaning an "assignment," and claims that it has the structure of "in-order-to." See *BT*, 97.

separated "from the limits of ostensive reference" (*TA*, 149). Narratives refer to reality, but they do not simply point out some aspect of reality that exists independently of them. They refer to something "beyond the sense of the work" (*TN3*, 172), something that is not merely described by the narrative in question. Ricoeur calls this "something" a world. He claims, for example, that the type of reference effected by narrative is "a second-order reference, which reaches the world not only at the level of manipulable objects but at the level that Husserl designated by the expression *Lebenswelt* and Heidegger by the expression *being-in-the-world*" (*TA*, 85–86). In other words, narratives refer not to specific objects or states of affairs, but to the contexts or meaning networks in which objects and states of affairs are encountered. These networks are worlds, in the phenomenological sense of the term. Ricoeur elaborates on his claim as follows:

> For us, the world is the ensemble of references opened up by the text. Thus we speak about the "world" of Greece, not to designate any more what were the situations for those who lived them, but to designate the non-situational references that outline the effacement of the first and that henceforth are offered as possible modes of being, as symbolic dimensions of our being-in-the-world. For me, this is the referent of all literature: no longer the *Umwelt* of the ostensive references of dialogue, but the *Welt* projected by the nonostensive references of every text that we have read, understood, and loved. (*TA*, 149)

Note Ricoeur's mention of "non-situational references." Narratives refer not to past or present states of affairs – "situations" – but to something that is "projected" or "opened up" by them. Specifically, a narrative projects "possible modes of being" for its reader, "symbolic dimensions of [the reader's] being-in-the-world." It refers to *ways in which the reader might exist*, and it refers to them by uncovering them, showing them to us for the first time. A narrative's referent is "a *proposed world* that I could inhabit and wherein I could project one of my ownmost possibilities" (*TA*, 86).

In some ways, Ricoeur's point is a simple one. When I read a story, I make sense of it by appropriating it, bringing it to bear on my own situation. Ricoeur follows Gadamer in claiming that understanding is completed in application, and that to understand a text is to let it speak to something specific in me – to allow it to fuse with the horizons of my existence, as Gadamer would say. This is first and foremost a matter of seeing how a possibility described by the text might manifest itself in my own existence, and this in turn is a matter of imagining ways in which I might act out the existential possibilities described by the text. In reading *Hamlet*, for example, I see the protagonist wrestle with the reality and the inevitability of death. I watch as Hamlet is paralyzed by this insight, but

ultimately accepts it and learns to act in the face of it. Ultimately, understanding *Hamlet* is a matter of asking whether this insight should be
incorporated into my own existence, and of imagining the different ways
in which it might be. It involves experiencing the text as issuing a challenge
to me – a challenge that I might accept, reject, or dismiss, but that in any
case I respond to *by existing*. A narrative, then, refers not to something
actual, but to a *possible* way of existing. Surely this is what Ricoeur has in
mind when he says that "[t]o understand is not to project oneself into the
text but to expose oneself to it; it is to receive a self enlarged by the
appropriation of the proposed worlds that interpretation unfolds" (*TA*,
301). Gerald Bruns calls this view a "magical looking glass theory of textual
meaning."[50] For Ricoeur, a narrative is a "magical looking glass" in the sense
that it lets us see a potential mode of our own existence that would otherwise
have remained invisible. Bruns elaborates on Ricoeur's view as follows:

Texts *mean* not by corresponding to states of affairs, not by satisfying truth
conditions, but by manifesting or opening up a region of existence whose reality
is not simply matter for analysis but is, on the contrary, matter for appropriation,
for intervention and action. The task of discourse in this sense would be not merely
to picture reality but to throw light on the situation in which we find ourselves
historically and open up a path for us to follow in the way of action and conduct.[51]

In short, a "region of existence" whose reality is a "matter for appropriation"
is what Ricoeur means by "world."[52]

But Ricoeur's "magical looking glass theory" is richer and more complex
than it first seems. For Ricoeur, the world is not just an idea connected with
the interpretation of written texts.[53] It is of much broader significance,
because for Ricoeur, the notion of narrative is of much broader significance.
Written texts are not the only sorts of narratives. In fact, it is misleading to
use the term "narrative" at all, since it suggests that the sorts of structures

---

[50] Gerald Bruns, *Hermeneutics Ancient and Modern* (New Haven: Yale University Press, 1992), 238.
[51] Bruns, *Hermeneutics Ancient and Modern*, 238. Bruns goes on to call Ricoeur's view an "Aristotelian"
     one, since it involves many of the same functions that, according to Aristotle, are performed by
     mimesis.
[52] Rudolf Bernet has argued that this view of interpretation implicitly criticizes a popular account of
     subjectivity. According to Bernet, continental philosophy since Heidegger has believed in a minimal
     subject, a "subject without qualities." The looking glass theory of meaning requires a richer subject:
     "[S]uch a subject cannot be confused with the pure Ego or a transcendental subject which deserted its
     post in a particular historical world and which sheltered itself from the events of concrete life, about
     which, moreover, he understands nothing … [H]e will be able to attain his goals only by plunging
     himself into empirical life without reservation, rather than evading it." See Rudolf Bernet, "The
     Subject's Participation in the Game of Truth." *Review of Metaphysics* 58 (2005), 805.
[53] The wider implications of Ricoeur's view are not always seen. Bruns, for example, seems to regard him
     as concerned with written texts alone. See *Hermeneutics Ancient and Modern*, 238–239.

found in written and spoken stories are found only there. Ricoeur denies this. He puts the point this way:

I fight against the claim that texts constitute by themselves a world or a closed world. It is only by methodological decision that we say that the world of literature, let us say, constitutes a world of its own. It is only in libraries that texts are closed on themselves – and even then only when nobody reads them. So then, we have a closed world of texts in a library, but literature is not a big library. It is by the act of reading that I follow a certain trajectory, a trajectory of meaning of the text. Then I reenact in a certain sense the dynamic course of the text and I prolong this dynamic beyond the text itself.[54]

The narrative function is, to use Gadamer's phrase, "universal in scope."[55] Narration – the process of situating objects into organized structures with beginnings, middles, and ends – is a general feature of human awareness.[56] As we have already seen, *Time and Narrative* argues that it is through narrative that we experience time, to the extent we can – that to experience an object as temporal *just is* to situate it in some narrative structure. Time "becomes human time to the extent that it is organized after the manner of a narrative" (*TN1*, 3), and as a result, "there can be no thought about time without narrated time" (*TN3*, 240). Since all human experience unfolds in time, it also involves narrative ordering.[57] Ricoeur therefore denies that there is "any experience that is not already the fruit of narrative activity" (*TN3*, 248). There are also more specific reasons to think that the significance of narrative goes well beyond the sphere of written texts. In his essay "The Model of the Text," for example, Ricoeur argues that human action

---

[54] Quoted in Charles Reagan, *Paul Ricoeur: His Life and Work* (Chicago: University of Chicago Press, 1996), 108.

[55] Hans-Georg Gadamer, *Philosophical Hermeneutics*, trans. David E. Linge (Berkeley: University of California Press, 1976), 3.

[56] For a more detailed, albeit critical, discussion of Ricoeur's views on this matter, see Hans Kellner, "'As Real as it Gets …:' Ricoeur and Narrativity." *Philosophy Today* 34:1 (1990), 229–242.

[57] David Carr has raised questions about just how pervasive narrative structure is, on Ricoeur's view. According to Carr, Ricoeur unduly limits the scope of narrative by describing it as an order that the human mind *imposes* on the real world, rather than as part of the real world itself. Ricoeur thinks that the real world has a "'pre-narrative' structure of elements that lend themselves to narrative configuration"; but, as Carr points out, "this prefiguration is not itself narrative structure." See David Carr, "Narrative and the Real World: An Argument for Continuity." *History and Theory* 15 (1986), 119. It is worth noting that Ricoeur rejects this characterization of his view. In an interview with Charles Reagan, for example, he denies that narrative simply "redescribes" the world – a view that Carr attributes to him on p. 120 of his article. See Reagan, *Paul Ricoeur: His Life and Work*, 106. For my purposes, it is not necessary to choose sides in this dispute. All that my argument requires is that narrative structure be a universal feature of the world *as humans experience it*. Whether it is universal because it is part of the "real world" itself, or because it is imposed on certain aspects of that world by the human mind, does not matter for my purposes. The universality is what is important; how it comes about is irrelevant.

has a narrative structure. Actions display the same essential features as written texts. They have meanings and effects that may escape the intentions of their authors, and they are "open works" (*TA*, 155) that may be interpreted and reinterpreted by audiences of indefinite size and makeup. In this way as well, narrative structure is a pervasive feature of human experience. It follows that the opening up of worlds through narrative is also a pervasive feature of human experience. Since we are always narrating, we are always disclosing new worlds – new networks of meaning that act as backdrops for the objects of experience. For Ricoeur, as for Kant and Hegel, we are always unifying experience by situating its elements in the context of a world. Ricoeur simply has a different view of what sort of context a world is.

Despite appearances to the contrary, then, Ricoeur does give a general account of what the world is – the same sort of account offered by Kant and Hegel. Though he presents this account through discussions of literary texts, and though it is heavily influenced by Husserl's and Heidegger's phenomenology, it performs the same functions as Kant's and Hegel's treatments of this idea. More importantly for our purposes, it is an account that is both post-Hegelian and Kantian. It is Kantian, in the sense of the analytical Kant, in its acknowledgement of the oppositions and dualisms inherent in the idea of the world. Ricoeur recognizes, for example, that a world is a fundamentally different type of phenomenon than the particular objects encountered within it. Particular objects are *things*, and are met with in experience; worlds are networks of meaning, and are the contexts of experience rather than possible objects of experience. Ricoeur's account is therefore open to dualisms. Like Hegel, however, Ricoeur tries to overcome these dualisms as much as he can, by understanding the world concretely. For Ricoeur, the world is not an empty principle of totality. It is a set of existential possibilities that are disclosed through the application of a narrative to a highly specific situation. *Hamlet* opens up a world for me when I let it speak to my own situation and my own concerns, ones that might be very different from those of other readers. And the existential possibilities opened up in this process are always *my* existential possibilities. There is no world in general. There are only concrete worlds disclosed to particular subjects by specific narratives. But Ricoeur's account is concrete without being totalizing, and it therefore meets the requirements of a "dialectical" Kantianism. It does not totalize because it does not swamp individuals in collective entities that are alleged to be more real or more valuable than they are. In Ricoeur's view, a world is constituted through an act of projection performed by an individual. What is projected in this act does not precede the act or exist independently of it. So while a world may make reference to collective entities – as when a novel asks us to reflect on our relations to society or history, for example – it does not hypostatize these entities. It views them as "derivative" (*TA*, 204), or as made up of individual acts all the way down. It therefore leaves ample room for freedom and indeterminacy, room for individuals to re-imagine society and history in new ways. For Ricoeur, individuals are never mere puppets of the cunning of reason.

Indeed, it is striking that when Ricoeur describes the process of situating objects in a larger context, he takes great care to show that these contexts are concrete but not totalizing. A good example is his discussion of tradition. Like most hermeneutical philosophers, Ricoeur argues that belonging to a tradition helps make thought possible – that as Gadamer says, "being situated within an event of tradition, a process of handing down, is a prior condition of understanding."[58] Individual thinkers must situate themselves within a tradition by identifying with it and adopting some attitude towards it. This process is one of the concrete ways in which one relates one's experiences to a larger context. Furthermore, it is a process that opens up a world for the individual in question. To identify with a tradition is above all to uncover certain existential possibilities for oneself – the possibility of endorsing one's tradition or of rejecting it, for example. At the same time, Ricoeur resists thinking of tradition as a collective entity that swallows individuals and tramples their individuality. There is not just one valid tradition. The fact that we must situate ourselves in some tradition or other does not mean that any single tradition trumps all others. Ricoeur is careful to distinguish *traditionality* – our need to belong to some tradition or other – from *traditions*, or the particular cultural heritages to which we might belong.[59] The former concept is "a transcendental for thinking about history" (*TN3*, 219), but its transcendental status implies nothing about the legitimacy or illegitimacy of any particular tradition. Ricoeur also insists that even particular traditions are not monoliths that merely constrain individuals. They are constituted through the acts of individuals, and their reality is "derivative" (*TA*, 204). "Before being an inert deposit," Ricoeur says, "tradition is an operation that can only make sense dialectically through the exchange between the interpreted past and the interpreting present" (*TN3*, 221). He is even more adamant about this when

[58] Gadamer, *Truth and Method*, 309.
[59] For Ricoeur's views on this matter, see *TN3*, 219–227. For a more detailed discussion of Ricoeur's view of tradition, see my "Ricoeur's Account of Tradition and the Gadamer-Habermas Debate." *Human Studies* 27:3 (2004), 259–280.

discussing particular communities and concrete traditions. When discussing the future of Europe, for example, he insists that "[t]he identity of a group, culture, people, or nation, is not that of an immutable substance, nor that of a fixed structure, but that, rather, of a recounted story."[60] As a result, "[a] tradition remains living ... only if it comes to be held in an unbroken process of reinterpretation. It is at this point that the reappraisal of narratives of the past and the plural reading of founding events come into effect."[61] Tradition is a concrete expression of worldhood, and thus it is something we help shape.

GOD

Having considered the first two Kantian ideas, let us turn to the third: God. God is a constant concern of Ricoeur's work, a fact that may strike some of his readers as audacious. The idea of God is the idea of an infinite being, and such a being, by definition, would exceed the ability of human reason to comprehend it. But the idea of God plays such an important role in the work of both Kant and Hegel that there is no way for a post-Hegelian Kantian to avoid it. So what would a post-Hegelian Kantian approach to the idea of God look like? First of all, how does Kant understand this idea?[62] The short answer is that he understands it in a manner analogous to the other two ideas of reason. Like the ideas of self and world, the idea of God is primarily a means through which reason seeks to unify experience. Just as the self is the idea of "the absolute (unconditioned) *unity of the thinking subject*," and the world is the idea of "the absolute *unity of the series of conditions of appearance*," God is the idea of "the absolute *unity of the condition of all objects of thought in general*" (*KRV*, 323, A334/B391). To think of God is to think of a ground for all things, a single being to which everything else owes its existence. It is to see all the objects of experience as making up an unconditioned totality due to their common source. The idea of God is therefore a sort of synthesis of the other two Kantian ideas. Self

---

[60] Paul Ricoeur, "Reflections on a New Ethos for Europe." *Philosophy and Social Criticism* 21:5/6 (1995), 7.

[61] Ricoeur, "Reflections on a New Ethos for Europe," 8. The idea that no tradition has just one meaning can be found even in Ricoeur's earliest work. See, for example, the 1954 essay "The History of Philosophy and the Unity of Truth," in *History and Truth*, trans. Charles Kelbley (Evanston: Northwestern University Press, 1965), 41–56.

[62] Ricoeur distinguishes two different approaches to the idea of God in Kant's work. Some of Kant's works, such as the first two critiques, give philosophical accounts of God's nature. Such accounts ask what sort of being God is, and what sort of knowledge we may have of this being. Some of Kant's other works – notably *Religion Within the Limits of Reason Alone* – study religion in its "historical, 'positive' character" (*FS*, 75).

and world are both totalities, but in a sense, conditioned totalities. They are the ways in which we unify certain aspects of experience – respectively, our experiences of ourselves as thinking subjects, and of objects in the spatio-temporal world. But these experiences are of things that we recognize might not have existed. In order to seek a truly *unconditioned* totality of our experiences, we must strive to see self and world as owing their existence to a *necessary* being, a being not conditioned by anything outside itself. This is the idea of the most real being, the *ens realissimum* (*KRV*, 492, A578/B606). The idea of an *ens realissimum* plays a crucial role in regulating experience. It lets us fulfill "the purpose of deriving from an unconditioned totality of complete determination the conditioned totality, that is, the totality of the limited" (*KRV*, 491–492, A578/B606).

As is well known, Kant argues that the idea of God plays very different roles for theoretical and practical reason. From the standpoint of theoretical reason, the most salient feature of this idea is that it is impossible to prove the existence of such a being. This is not to say that we should, or could, do without the idea. Since reason inevitably seeks unconditioned totalities, we must view all other beings as though they originated in a necessary being. But it is impossible to demonstrate that God exists: "arguments of speculative reason in proof of the existence of a supreme being" (*KRV*, 495, A583/B611) are specious. All such arguments fail, and must fail. But while theoretical reason cannot prove God's existence, practical reason must assume it. This assumption is the only way to overcome a tension in our experience as moral agents. Practical reason, in Kant's view, commands us to act out of duty. We must act not just *in accordance with* the moral law, but *for the sake* of it. The only genuinely moral act is one performed out of reverence for the law as such. Of course, there is no guarantee that performing such acts will make us happy – "there is," Kant claims, "not the slightest ground in the moral law for a necessary connection between the morality and proportionate happiness of a being who belongs to the world."[63] At the same time, to act out of reverence for the law is to seek "to further the *highest good*."[64] It therefore implies that the highest good is possible. And the highest good, just because it *is* the highest, cannot involve an ultimate gap between duty and inclination. In acting morally, we must assume that our duty and our inclination will somehow, at some point, be bridged. But to assume this is to assume the existence of a being powerful enough to bring

---

[63] Immanuel Kant, *Critique of Practical Reason*, 3rd edn., trans. Lewis White Beck (New York: Macmillan, 1993), 131.

[64] Kant, *Critique of Practical Reason*, 131. My emphasis.

them together. It is to assume "the existence … of a cause of the whole of nature, itself distinct from nature, which contains the ground of the exact coincidence of happiness with morality."[65] To be a moral agent is to postulate the existence of God.

It should be clear from all of this that Kant's approach to God is heavily dualistic. Kant sees human beings as torn between several different ways of looking at God, and these ways of looking themselves involve oppositions between different sides of our nature. The way in which theoretical reason approaches God is opposed to the way in which practical reason does so. For theoretical reason, God is a regulative idea, and it is impossible to prove the existence of a being that corresponds to this idea. Yet practical reason must postulate the existence of such a being. This postulate is not a theoretical proof, but it compels all the same. These different ways of viewing God involve further oppositions. In thinking about God, theoretical reason is forced to observe a distinction between its regulative and speculative employments. Reason must continually remind itself that, although it must view all things as though they derived from God, this is purely a way of bringing unconditioned totality to experience. It is not a way of extending our knowledge of what exists. For its part, practical reason is forced to assume God's existence in order to bridge an otherwise unbridgeable gap between duty and inclination. In all of these respects, Kant sees our thinking about God as deeply fragmented.

Hegel, of course, finds this fragmentation unacceptable. At all stages of his career, he criticizes the Kantian approach to God for being too dualistic, too quick to reify oppositions that should instead be grasped dynamically. In the *Encyclopedia Logic*, for example, Hegel says the following about Kant's understanding of God:

In any dualistic system, but in the Kantian system particularly, its fundamental defect reveals itself through the inconsistency of *uniting* what, a moment earlier, was declared to be independent, and therefore *incompatible*. Just as, a moment before, what is united was declared to be what is genuine, so now it is said that *both moments* … have truth and actuality only by being separate – and this, therefore, is what is genuine instead. What is lacking in a philosophizing of this kind is the simple consciousness that, in this very to-ing and fro-ing, each of the simple determinations is declared to be unsatisfactory; and the defect consists in the simple incapacity to bring two thoughts together.[66]

The opposition between duty and inclination is the clearest example of Kant's to-ing and fro-ing. If duty and inclination really are separate, then no

---

[65] Kant, *Critique of Practical Reason*, 131.   [66] Hegel, *Encyclopedia Logic*, 105.

postulate can bring them together. The unity that Kant envisions "is determined as something merely *subjective* – as what only *ought* to be; i.e. what does *not* at the same time have reality."[67] According to Hegel, instead of trusting that an external force will somehow unite duty and inclination, we must strive to see these moments as not really separate to begin with.

In Hegel's view, this is precisely what Christianity contributes to the understanding of God. Christianity teaches us to see God as embodying a *fusion* or *synthesis* of duty and inclination, rather than as an external agency that brings the two together. Christianity does so through "the spirit of Jesus, a spirit raised above morality."[68] The morality taught by Christianity, and embodied by Jesus, "does not teach reverence for the laws; on the contrary, it exhibits that which fulfils the law but annuls it as law and so is something higher than obedience to law and makes law superfluous."[69] In the Sermon on the Mount, Jesus criticizes traditional Jewish law – not to condone breaking the law, but to show that a person who truly loves God and his neighbors fulfills his obligations freely and gladly, and is to that extent beyond law. In other words, Christianity transcends the opposition between duty and inclination. It teaches us to see God, in the figure of Christ, as fusing these moments, as embodying a synthesis of them. It follows that for Hegel, the idea of God should be approached through a specific content. If, like Kant, we take God to be a mere ideal of reason, we will be forced to see the different aspects of God's being as wholly abstract determinations, and we will be unable to understand how these aspects might actually co-exist. But if we approach the idea of God concretely – through the figure of Christ, for example – then we can see how these different aspects might be united in a being that embodies both. For Hegel, the remedy to Kant's dualistic approach to the idea of God is to see this idea as embodied in something concrete.[70]

---

[67] Hegel, *Encyclopedia Logic*, 104.

[68] G. W. F. Hegel, *Early Theological Writings*, trans. T. M. Knox (Philadelphia: University of Pennsylvania Press, 1992), 212. It should be clear that when Hegel says that Christianity is "above morality," he means morality in the Kantian sense – that is, morality identified with the ethics of duty.

[69] Hegel, *Early Theological Writings*, 212.

[70] According to Ricoeur, this difference in Kant's and Hegel's approaches to the idea of God helps explains their different attitudes to the historical Jesus. For Kant, Ricoeur argues, the circumstances of Jesus's life are of absolutely no interest. Jesus simply represents a certain moral ideal, and since this ideal is already available to practical reason as such, we need not be acquainted with a historical example of it. For Hegel, by contrast, the historical Jesus is extremely important, since it is precisely the "positivity" of the Christian religion that makes it an alternative to the dualisms that plague Kant's approach. See *FS*, 83.

What does Ricoeur make of these approaches? Like Kant and Hegel, he considers the idea of God indispensable, something of which philosophy must speak. He does so for a variety of reasons, including his own religious beliefs. Ricoeur calls himself a "listener to Christian preaching" (*FS*, 217), someone who is personally committed to Christianity and who takes this faith seriously in his philosophical work. His work makes certain presuppositions about Christian preaching: "I assume that this speaking is meaningful, that it is worthy of consideration, and that examining it may accompany and guide the transfer from the text to life where it will verify itself fully" (*FS*, 217). But while Ricoeur agrees with Kant and Hegel about the indispensability of the idea of God, he does not find either of their approaches to this idea adequate. He rejects Kant's approach as too dualistic, too torn by oppositions. In particular, he rejects Kant's claim that we must distinguish several different ways of relating to the idea of God – that we must distinguish the theoretical view of God from the practical, for example, or the regulative view from the speculative. Ricoeur admires the humility of these Kantian distinctions. But he claims that they contain a hidden danger:

[T]his letting go of the knowledge of God through the resources of critical philosophy has no apologetic value, even in its negative form. For if a first hubris is knocked down, that of metaphysical knowledge, a second one replaces it, that of a knowledge that is no longer metaphysical but transcendental. This knowledge makes the "I think" the principle of everything that is valid … The idea of a subject that posits itself therefore becomes the unfounded foundation, or, better, the foundation that founds itself, in relation to which every rule of validity is derived. In this way, the subject becomes the supreme "presupposition." (*FS*, 223–224)

To distinguish several ways of thinking about God, and to limit oneself to only one of them, is to valorize the thinking subject in a way Ricoeur finds unpalatable. It is to make this subject the arbiter of what can and cannot be known, of what is and is not within its abilities. Such "second hubris" is no doubt preferable to the "first hubris" of claiming to know God speculatively. But it is still to be resisted. It must be replaced by "a second letting go, the abandoning of a more subtle and more tenacious pretension than that of onto-theological knowledge. It requires giving up the human self in its will to mastery" (*FS*, 224).

Interestingly enough, for Ricoeur, this "giving up" results in an understanding of God that is in some ways similar to Hegel's. Like Hegel, Ricoeur argues that in order to overcome the dualisms of the Kantian approach, we must view the idea of God as concrete. We must understand this idea not as an abstract ideal of reason, but as tied to a specific content. For Ricoeur's part, this means understanding God using the resources of some concrete religious tradition.[71] It means that philosophical reflection about God "is linked in a contingent way to individual events and particular texts that report them" (*FS*, 217). But while Ricoeur agrees with Hegel about the need to link the idea of God to a specific content, he does not connect the two in the way Hegel does.[72] In particular, Ricoeur does not claim that understanding God through a specific content amounts to an *Aufhebung* of the more abstract Kantian approach to this idea. It does not result in more complete knowledge of God. For Hegel, the person who grasps God through the figure of Christ understands God better than the person who does not. For Ricoeur, on the other hand, to approach God by means of a specific symbol or tradition is precisely to abandon all claims to onto-theological knowledge. It is not to totalize the idea of God or to presume to grasp it speculatively.

Furthermore, Ricoeur argues that although concrete symbols such as the figure of Christ are necessary, they do not abolish the need for a more abstract discourse about God. They complement and enrich this more abstract discourse, but do not replace it. This fact is particularly important in the Christian context, where the appearance of Christ might be seen as obviating all talk of God the father. Ricoeur thinks this would be a mistake. He rejects "the formula of Christian atheism that God is dead in Jesus Christ, with the consequence that the referent 'God' recedes to the rank of a simple cultural given that needs to be neutralized … [T]he New Testament *continues* to name God" (*FS*, 230). The figure of Christ, far from eliminating the need to reflect on God the father, is inseparable from God the father. As Ricoeur points out, "what Jesus preaches is the kingdom *of God*" (*FS*, 230). If we treat the symbol of Christ as a way of leaving behind all talk of the

---

[71] Though Ricoeur thinks that the idea of God is best understood through the resources of a concrete religious tradition, he does not think that any one tradition is uniquely qualified to shed light on this idea. His view of religious tradition seems similar to the more general account of tradition given in *Time and Narrative*. (See *TN3*, Chapter 10.) There, Ricoeur carefully distinguishes traditions from what he calls traditionality. Traditions are the specific sets of cultural and symbolic resources that we inherit by virtue of our historical situation. Traditionality, on the other hand, is a general feature of human understanding. It is the need that all humans have to inherit *some tradition or other*, although people living at different times and in different places inherit very different ones. So in Ricoeur's view, everyone must inhabit some concrete tradition, but no one tradition can claim to be uniquely correct. Ricoeur seems to see religious traditions in much the same way. They are indispensable because we must understand God in *some* concrete way, but no particular concrete way can claim a monopoly on truth. Ricoeur's approach to God is therefore compatible with religious pluralism.

[72] For a wide-ranging discussion of Hegel's philosophy of religion, and of Ricoeur's agreements and disagreements with it, see Paul Ricoeur, "The Status of *Vorstellung* in Hegel's Philosophy of Religion," in Leroy Rouner (ed.), *Meaning, Truth, and God* (Notre Dame: University of Notre Dame Press, 1982), 70–88.

kingdom of God, we will distort the meaning of this symbol. After all, Ricoeur asks, "[w]hat is the cross without the cry, '*My God, My God*, why have you forsaken me?' inscribed into the naming of God by the psalmist? And what is the resurrection if it is not an act of God homologous to that of the exodus?" (*FS*, 230). A Christianity without God is "as unthinkable as Israel without Yahweh … Jesus of Nazareth cannot be understood apart from God, apart from his God" (*FS*, 230–231). The more general point is that approaching the idea of God through a specific symbol or tradition does not allow us to abandon a more abstract understanding of God. Nor does it allow us to abandon all that a more abstract approach entails, such as a tendency towards dualism and fragmentation. To be sure, our understanding of God must not be needlessly abstract or dualistic. But neither should we expect it to overcome abstractions and dualisms altogether. Ricoeur insists that our view of God, like our views of the other two Kantian ideas, must be concrete without being totalizing. We must approach the idea of God through a specific set of symbolic resources, but we must not turn it into a particular object that we claim to know speculatively. And we must not expect to grasp this idea in a manner totally free of tension.

Not surprisingly, this is precisely the approach to God that we find in Ricoeur's theological writings. A good example is the remarkably rich and dense essay "Naming God." While displaying Ricoeur's characteristic desire to avoid hubris, this essay comes as close as any of his works to summarizing his thinking about God. It is not, Ricoeur warns, an answer to the question "What I Believe"; rather, it belongs with the attempts of "more than one listener of Christian preaching … to describe the ways they understand what they have heard" (*FS*, 217). Ricoeur's understanding of what he has heard also goes beyond a mere list of statements about God. It involves reflection on the nature of religious language, particularly on the fact that this language is less descriptive than it is poetic, and aims to "manifest and thereby reveal a world we might inhabit" (*FS*, 223). It also involves reflection on the role of tradition in religious experience – on the fact that, as Ricoeur puts it, "I can name God in my faith because the texts preached to me have already named God" (*FS*, 218). But Ricoeur's essay does make claims about how the idea of God should be understood. Its central claim is that the naming of God is essentially narrative in character. To reflect meaningfully on the idea of God is not to ponder this idea armchair-style. It is to think in a way that is tied to the construction and interpretation of concrete narratives. To reflect on God just is to see how God is named in specific texts, institutions, and practices.[73] Narrative form is not added to the reflection, but is essential to it. Not surprisingly, Ricoeur is especially interested in the ways in which God is named in the narratives that make up Christianity. In many ways, narrative is central to this religious tradition:

The theology of the Old Testament is first established as a "theology of traditions" revolving around several kernel events: the call of Abraham, the exodus, the anointing of David, and so forth. The naming of God is thus first of all a narrative naming. The theology of traditions names God in accord with a historical drama that recounts itself as a narrative of liberation. God is the God of Abraham, Isaac, and Jacob and is, therefore, the Actant of the great gesture of deliverance. And God's meaning as Actant is bound up with the founding events in which the community of interpretation recognizes itself as enrooted, set up, and established. It is these events that name God. In this regard, the naming of God in the resurrection narratives of the New Testament is in accord with the naming of God in the deliverance narratives of the Old Testament: God called Christ from the dead. Here, too, God is designated by the transcendence of the founding events in relation to the ordinary course of history. (*FS*, 224–225)

What does Christianity take God to be? First and foremost, it sees God as the subject of those stories that a certain "community of interpretation" tells itself. God is the constant concern of a set of narratives through which a certain tradition establishes and understands itself. The narratives in question do more than that, of course. "The naming of God," Ricoeur claims, "is not simple but multiple. It is not a single tone, but polyphonic" (*FS*, 224). In addition to the stories that found and sustain a community, Christianity involves "narration that recounts the divine acts, prophecy that speaks in the divine name, prescription that designates God as the source of the imperative, wisdom that seeks God as the meaning of meaning, and the hymn that invokes God in the second person" (*FS*, 227). What is common to all of these narratives, however, is that they do not envision God as a being that could be approached through reason alone. The naming of God is inseparable from a group of specific practices and texts.

So far, Ricoeur's account of the naming of God looks consistent with Hegel's. Like Hegel, he insists that we must understand God concretely, not through an abstract thinking prone to dualisms. But unlike Hegel, he wants to avoid the onto-theological temptation of saying that the person who

---

[73] It is worth remembering that for Ricoeur, the term "narrative" denotes something broader than written or spoken stories. It refers to all the ways in which we humanize time by structuring our temporal experiences into coherent wholes with beginnings, middles, and ends. Human action, for example, is a sort of narrative – see *TA*, 144–167. For a fuller discussion of what narratives are, see *TN1*, 3–87.

grasps God concretely understands God better than the person who does not. So he adds an intriguing twist to his account. Christianity, according to Ricoeur, names God through a series of narratives. But paradoxically, what these narratives say about God is that God is hidden. These stories describe a God who cannot be adequately described through *any* story. In this way, God is both the constant concern of these stories and that "which escapes each of them" (*FS*, 228). God is "not just the index of the mutual belonging together of the originary forms of the discourse of faith. It is also the index of their incompleteness" (*FS*, 228). The story of the burning bush has exemplary significance here. In one respect, this story is "the revelation of the divine name" (*FS*, 228). But the name it reveals – "Yahweh," or "I am" – is "precisely unnamable" (*FS*, 228). The story of the burning bush is both a way of naming God, and a reminder that God is "the being whom humanity cannot really name, that is, hold at the mercy of our language" (*FS*, 228). Ricoeur sees this idea as a recurring theme of the Christian narratives. It is found, for example, in the way Jesus describes God using "parables, proverbs, and paradoxes" (*FS*, 228). Parables and proverbs are valuable ways of speaking about God precisely because "no literal translation can exhaust their meaning" (*FS*, 229). They are not theories or claims to onto-theological knowledge. A God who is understood through parables and proverbs is a God who resists our every attempt to grasp Him through a specific story. And paradoxically, this lesson is one that Christianity expresses by means of a specific story. The Christian narrative, far from containing "a positive ontology capable of capping off the narrative …, protects the secret of the 'in itself' of God" (*FS*, 228).

What is Ricoeur doing here? Simply put, he is offering an account of God that is remarkably similar to his accounts of self and world. Like these accounts, it is a dialectical account that passes through three stages. The first stage is comparable to the type of thinking practiced by the analytical Kant. It is a recognition that our thinking about God involves tensions and dualisms. The opposition between aspiring to onto-theological knowledge of God and being a "listener" to a certain type of preaching is an obvious example. Ricoeur is reluctant to let these oppositions stand unchallenged, so like Hegel, he tries to approach God using the resources of a concrete religious tradition. This is the second stage of his account, the stage at which he claims that the naming of God is essentially an exercise in narrative. Unlike Hegel, however, Ricoeur insists that to name God by means of narrative is not to attain better knowledge of God's nature. Thus the third stage of his account is his insistence that the God described by the Christian narratives is a hidden God. In these stories, the word "God" functions as a "limit expression" (*FS*, 228), a name for that which is both the *telos* and the blind spot of our religious stories.[74] In moving from the first stage to the second, Ricoeur grants that we should overcome some of the clumsier dualisms in our thinking about God. But in moving from the second stage to the third, he insists that our thinking about God must be concrete without being totalizing. In short, Ricoeur seeks to think about God in a way that is both post-Hegelian and Kantian. It is post-Hegelian in the importance it attaches to content; it is Kantian in its treatment of God as a "limit-expression."

"Naming God" articulates a way of thinking about God that is deeply consistent with some of Ricoeur's other religious writings. It is similar, for example, to the understanding of God expressed in a pair of essays dealing with the notion of hope: "Freedom in the Light of Hope" and "Hope and the Structure of Philosophical Systems." We have already considered the first of these essays. It explores what freedom might look like if we take Christianity to be primarily a religion of hope and promise. It argues that Christians should view God as an eschatological object of hope – that "[t]he God who is witnessed to is not … the God who is but the God who is coming" (*CI*, 406). The Resurrection, for example, should not be understood as a sign that God is *in* the world, or as a "temporal manifestation of eternal being and the eternal present" (*CI*, 406). It should be seen as the extension of a promise. It is "the sign that the promise is henceforth for all; the meaning of the Resurrection is in its future, the death of death, the resurrection of all from the dead" (*CI*, 406). Ricoeur opposes this eschatological view of God to the onto-theological one of the "Greek Christologies" (*CI*, 406). The latter view believes in a God who reveals, who makes Himself *present* to reason. The former view believes in a God who withdraws and conceals, a God of whom a proper understanding is always to come. In approaching God through the narratives of Christianity, and especially through the narrative of the Resurrection, Ricoeur understands the idea of God concretely. But in claiming that the God of these narratives is always to come, Ricoeur refuses to totalize this idea.

Ricoeur does something similar in "Hope and the Structure of Philosophical Systems," an essay concerned with the relation of reason to faith. It denies that there is an unbridgeable gap between proving and believing, between the God of the philosophers and the God of the theologians. What links faith and reason is the notion of hope. Hope, properly understood, plays as important a role in philosophical reflection

---

[74] That said, Ricoeur does not think that limit-expressions exhaust religious language. See *FS*, 233.

as it does in theology. Not all philosophers see this. In particular, philosophers who share Hegel's understanding of their enterprise tend not to recognize the philosophical importance of hope.[75] Their thinking is "retrospective," in that its goal is "a system written from the end toward the beginning, from the standpoint of the totality toward the partial achievements of the system" (*FS*, 208). In other words, this type of thinking seeks to reconcile us to the real by tracing the ways in which reason has gradually appeared in it. According to Ricoeur, this is "the contrary of a philosophy of hope. It is a philosophy of reminiscence" (*FS*, 208). But another major approach to philosophy attaches greater importance to hope. This is the philosophy of Kant, and specifically the dialectical Kant – the Kant who reins in our claims to absolute knowledge. On this view, the aim of philosophy is a proper understanding of the limits of knowledge, and a deepened understanding of the status of the ideas of reason. In Kant's case, reason is compelled to seek a totality that it knows it cannot achieve. It must regulate its experience using the ideas of God, self, and world, though it knows that it cannot acquire theoretical knowledge of them. Thus it is forced to adopt a new attitude towards these ideas, an attitude that Ricoeur characterizes as a type of hope. This hope "has exactly the same extension as that of transcendental illusion. I hope at the very place where I am deceived by the so-called absolute objects: 'I' as a substance, 'freedom' as an object in the world, 'God' as a supreme being" (*FS*, 212). Reason hopes in the sense that it believes in certain things – especially the existence of God – even as it renounces all knowledge claims about them. So again, we see Ricoeur's thinking about God follow a dialectical pattern. It begins by expressing dissatisfaction with a certain dualism – in this case, the opposition between having faith in God and understanding God philosophically. It next tries to overcome this dualism by means of the concrete notion of religious hope. But to avoid the temptation of totalizing – a temptation he explicitly connects to Hegel – Ricoeur argues that a God to whom we relate through hope is a God we cannot know theoretically. This approach is very much in keeping with the approach to God articulated in "Naming God," and Ricoeur's approach to the other two Kantian ideas.

THE BIGGER PICTURE

Ricoeur's discussions of self, world, and God are an extraordinarily powerful contribution to three of the most important inquiries in philosophy. At first

---

[75] Ricoeur claims that he is here treating Hegel not as an individual thinker but as a "type" (*FS*, 208).

glance, Ricoeur's contribution looks theoretical. He appears to be advancing new *theories* of self, world, and God. But while Ricoeur has a great deal to teach those doing theoretical work in these areas, his real contribution is to fuse two pictures, two general approaches to philosophy. Ricoeur even suggests that the two are *the* fundamental pictures available to us – that at bottom, there are "two philosophical styles, that of a philosophy of absolute knowledge and that of a philosophy of limits" (*FS*, 209). Ricoeur's goal is to understand these pictures "not only one against the other but one through the other" (*FS*, 209). He seeks to synthesize two pictures that are invaluable but one-sided, in the hope of articulating a more flexible and more complete view of reality. "Synthesize," of course, does not just mean "combine." Ricoeur does not wish to tack one set of theories onto another – to combine Kant's and Hegel's claims about God into a new super-theory, for example. His goal is to explore *possibilities* for thinking: to articulate a new way of approaching philosophical questions that learns from two older approaches while avoiding their limitations. Interestingly, Ricoeur's discussion of worldhood provides a helpful way of understanding this synthesis. Narratives, Ricoeur argues, disclose new worlds. They reveal a set of existential possibilities that might be incorporated into our own lives. But before they can reveal anything to us, they must be applied to our specific situations. Similarly, synthesizing two pictures is a way of opening up new possibilities for thinking, new ways of approaching philosophical questions. But synthesis depends on application. We cannot learn what a picture offers until we let it speak to our own set of concerns. Ricoeur's concerns often have sources that would be foreign to Kant and Hegel. His insistence on seeing collective entities such as objective spirit as "composed" of intersubjective acts derives from Weber and from the phenomenological tradition. His belief that the self is alienated from itself by virtue of the body comes from phenomenology as well. Neither of these concerns appears in the writings of Kant or Hegel. But the fact that Ricoeur has these concerns leads him to notice resources in Kant and Hegel that these thinkers themselves may not have recognized. Ricoeur shows that seeing what a picture can do involves letting it speak to something in *us*.

What does all of this show about doing philosophy historically? I believe Ricoeur can teach us two main lessons here. The first has to do with the nature of philosophical pictures. As I discussed in Chapter 1, it is easy to reify pictures. It is easy to think of the Kantian or the Hegelian pictures as unchanging bodies of dogma, sets of claims endorsed by every Kantian or Hegelian thinker. As I have argued, it is more plausible to think of pictures as dispositions, or as tendencies to approach philosophical problems in certain characteristic ways. Ricoeur's example helps us to see pictures in this non-reifying way. Though Ricoeur is drawn to both Kantianism and Hegelianism, he is adamant that these are not doctrines, much less doctrines embraced without question by a great many thinkers. One can be a Kantian while rejecting Kant's position on specific issues. In fact, one's allegiance to the spirit of Kant's thought may *require* one to reject the letter of his views. If pictures were simply doctrines or bodies of dogma, it would be hard to see how one could be a Kantian while rejecting Kant's specific views. Ricoeur's use of the Kantian and Hegelian pictures helps show that they are more dynamic and more flexible than we might think. It also shows that asking what a picture can do may be quite a complex process. If Hegelianism were an unchanging doctrine, it would be relatively easy to determine what it can and cannot do. But because it is a fluid style of thinking, matters are much less straightforward. As Ricoeur shows, it may take a great deal of digging, and a great deal of application, to determine what the Hegelian picture is really capable of. It may require us to separate the spirit of Hegel's thought from what he explicitly says. It may require us to ask what Hegelianism could learn from more recent developments in philosophy – from the phenomenological tradition, for example. Above all, it may require us to reject the conventional wisdom about Hegel and to reassess his thought radically. In short, doing philosophy historically involves a great deal more than revisiting familiar, potted histories of the discipline. When done well, the enterprise spurs innovation and creativity in our view of the past.

Second, Ricoeur shows that learning from a picture is compatible with our having new and distinctive philosophical concerns. To put it crudely, he shows that the student of Kant and Hegel can explore topics other than the ones these figures explicitly address. Ricoeur does this through his emphasis on application. For Ricoeur, to see what a picture can do is to ask what it says *to us*: what it reveals about the topics and debates that concern us. These topics and debates may be ones that were familiar to the thinkers who first articulated the picture, but they need not be. Even if they are, we may frame them in ways that would have been unthinkable for earlier thinkers. Consider Ricoeur's discussion of God. He articulates a way of thinking about God that is both Hegelian and Kantian: Hegelian in its insistence on giving content to the idea of God, Kantian in its rejection of the claim to know God theoretically. In developing this view of God, Ricoeur draws on resources that were not available to Hegel or Kant. His eschatological vision of God draws on Moltmann, Schweitzer, and Weiss; his reflections on naming God draw on Gadamerian hermeneutics and his own work on narrative. But these later influences do not make his discussion of God un-Hegelian or un-Kantian. On the contrary, it is because Ricoeur occupies the unique perspective he does that he can see new possibilities for thinking about God in Hegelian or Kantian ways. Ricoeur shows that determining what a picture can do is often a matter of bringing it into a new context. When we read past philosophers with an eye to present debates, we are not necessarily distorting them. We may be understanding them in deeper, truer ways.

Consequences

This book has argued that philosophy can be done historically. It has tried to explain what is involved in doing so, and it has learned about this enterprise by studying it in action. Now, to conclude, I would like to ask what all of this implies. What can we learn about philosophy from the fact that it may be done historically? How does this fact force us to rethink the nature of the discipline? These are large questions, and I cannot hope to say the last word about them here. But I would like to make some suggestions about how to begin thinking about them, suggestions that are best seen as signposts to further inquiry.

The general answer to all of these questions should already be familiar. The fact that philosophy can be done historically shows that the discipline is concerned not just with theories, but with pictures. Philosophers are not just in the business of giving specific, detailed answers to specific, detailed questions. They are also in the business of articulating, developing, and assessing pictures of reality, general conceptions of what the world is like and how we fit into it. This fact is not often recognized. We often describe philosophy with reference to theories and arguments alone, depicting it as a search for answers to perennial questions. But philosophy also strives to offer synoptic visions, comprehensive understandings of ourselves and our situation. Some of these visions prove better than others. Some can do things that others cannot; some advance our projects more effectively than their competitors. We need a way to assess philosophical pictures, a systematic way of probing their nature, their strengths, and their weaknesses. This is what historical inquiry offers. Pictures are not the sorts of things that can be proved or refuted. Unlike arguments, they cannot be shown to be valid or invalid, sound or unsound. But they have track records. They can therefore be shown to have fared well or badly in certain ways over the course of their development. That philosophy can be done historically shows that it is a broader enterprise than we might think – but an enterprise that is still defined by criticism and rational justification.

What else does it show? I suggest that it asks us to widen our view of philosophy in three specific ways. The first concerns the relation between philosophy and the humanities. Philosophers have long been vexed by the question of whether their discipline is a humanistic one – that is, whether philosophy has more in common with the physical (and perhaps social) sciences, or with the study of literature, history, and culture. Those who see it as more scientific than humanistic tend to think that its purpose is to find universal answers to timeless questions. As Rorty puts it, they think that philosophers "use reason to discover how things really are."[1] Those who see philosophy as one of the humanities tend to think it pursues something else: Dilthey's *Verstehen*, for example, or some other form of understanding that does not seek universal answers to timeless questions. Philosophers, on this view, "use imagination to transform themselves."[2] An important part of this task is the construction of synoptic visions, comprehensive accounts of our condition and its significance. Both views have some intuitive appeal. Both describe figures who unquestionably belong to the canon of great philosophers. But both views raise problems. Those who see philosophy as nothing but a problem-solving enterprise risk making it dispensable, as the questions it asks – how the mind relates to the body, for example – are increasingly taken over by specialized sciences. Those who see it as a purely humanistic discipline risk depriving it of arguments and rational criticism – of making philosophy "just one more literary genre,"[3] as Rorty puts it. Which view is right?

In my view, both are. Philosophy is both a quasi-scientific discipline and a humanistic enterprise. It seeks both to solve problems and to offer a comprehensive understanding of our situation and its significance. It is a problem-solving enterprise in so far as it is concerned with theories. When philosophers develop theories about the nature of knowledge, reference, or consciousness, they are trying to solve problems. Historians of philosophy are also concerned with theories when they try to give correct reconstructions of the views of earlier thinkers. But when historically minded philosophers examine our more general pictures of reality, they are concerned with synoptic visions. When a MacIntyre, or a Heidegger, or a Ricoeur probes a picture by tracing its development, he is concerned with the comprehensive understanding of our situation and its significance. This is

---

[1] Richard Rorty, "Grandeur, Profundity, and Finitude," in *Philosophy as Cultural Politics: Philosophical Papers, Volume IV* (Cambridge: Cambridge University Press, 2007), 74.
[2] Rorty, "Grandeur, Profundity, and Finitude," 74.
[3] Richard Rorty, "Deconstruction and Circumvention," in *Essays on Heidegger and Others: Philosophical Papers, Volume II* (Cambridge: Cambridge University Press, 1991), 105.

a task usually assigned to the humanities. The crucial point here is that philosophy's humanistic side and its scientific side do not conflict. Theories are not second-rate pictures, and pictures are not second-rate theories. It would be wrong to dismiss the best theoretical work in epistemology or philosophy of mind as just another literary genre. It would be equally wrong to dismiss the narratives of MacIntyre, Heidegger, and Ricoeur for failing to solve timeless problems. Each activity has a legitimate and even an indispensable role to play. But each must be recognized for what it is and assessed in appropriate ways.

Something similar holds for a second topic: the nature of "good" philosophy. We routinely evaluate philosophers and their work, saying that one argument, theory, or book is better than another. What standards are we invoking here? What does it mean to say that a piece of philosophy is good or bad? It is common to claim that there is no one thing that makes someone a good philosopher. Hilary Putnam has said that if we have to generalize, a good philosopher is one who has both "vision *and* arguments."[4] Putnam's point is that there is "something disappointing about a philosophical work that contains arguments, however good, which are not inspired by some genuine vision, and something disappointing about philosophical work that contains a vision, however inspiring, which is unsupported by arguments."[5] It is surely true that most philosophers care about vision as well as arguments. But what exactly *are* visions and arguments? How does each matter to philosophy, and how do they interact? Once we see that philosophy may be done historically, it is easier to answer these questions. Arguments matter to philosophy in so far as it is a problem-solving enterprise that constructs theories. Philosophers cannot answer theoretical questions satisfactorily without supporting their views with arguments. Vision matters to philosophy in that it is a humanistic discipline, one that seeks a comprehensive account of what reality is like and how we fit into it. Arguments matter to the construction of theories; vision matters to the articulation of pictures.

---

[4] Hilary Putnam, "Hilary Putnam: The Vision and Arguments of a Famous Harvard Philosopher." *Cogito* 3 (1989), 85.

[5] Putnam, "Vision and Arguments," 85. W. H. Walsh also argues that philosophy involves both vision and arguments, though he makes this claim only about metaphysics. Walsh argues that "vision is important as well as argument when it comes to appreciating and criticizing metaphysical thought," and that the metaphysician "needs, in fact, to argue as well as to have a vision." See W. H. Walsh, *Metaphysics* (London: Hutchinson, 1963), 82. Interestingly, when Walsh describes what vision is, he explicitly uses the term "picture." He says that every metaphysical system is rooted in "a certain intuition, an imaginative picture which constitutes the metaphysician's primary insight; it is from this that he starts and to this that he constantly returns" (81). I am grateful to an anonymous reader for Cambridge University Press for drawing this text to my attention.

We care about vision *and* arguments because philosophy is not simply one or the other. It is both a search for answers and an attempt to understand ourselves and our situation. Recognizing this helps explain the sense many of us have that there is something important about Kierkegaard, even if we find his arguments disappointing, and that there is something important about Carnap, even if we find his vision uninspiring. More importantly, perhaps, it helps explain how the philosophers we revere most differ from the ones who are merely good. The list of indisputably great philosophers is quite short. It may extend no longer than Plato, Aristotle, Kant, and Hegel. What sets these thinkers apart? Their arguments, certainly; but also the way in which they articulate new and inspiring ways of looking at the world. What distinguishes Plato and Kant from lesser philosophers is their skill at both activities: the ability to develop a powerful new picture of reality, *and* to embed this picture in work of unrivaled theoretical sophistication. Recognizing that we can do philosophy historically helps explain what it means for philosophy to be good.

Finally, it helps explain what philosophy is good *for*. Philosophers have always had a hard time explaining why their discipline matters to those outside it, and what it contributes to the wider culture. Some claim that its contribution is the same as any other academic specialty. Like physics or economics, it seeks results: definitive answers to specialized questions. On this view, philosophy is at its best when it is most technical, when it discovers more and more about less and less. Others insist that philosophy is not just an academic specialty, but has a goal other than accumulating results. Jerry Fodor – himself an extremely accomplished specialist – has said the following about the state of philosophy today:

I can't shake off the sense that something has gone awfully wrong … There seems to be, to put it bluntly, a lot of earnest discussion of questions that strike my ear as frivolous. For example: "I have never crossed the Himalayas, though I might have done. So there is a non-actual (or, if you prefer, a non-actualized) possible world (or possible state of the world) in which someone crosses some mountains. Is that person me, and are those mountains the Himalayas?"… [C]ould that really be the sort of thing that philosophy is about? Is that a way for grown-ups to spend their time?[6]

Those sympathetic to Fodor's view often counter that the discipline's mission is different. Philosophy, they suggest, is really a synoptic enterprise. Its point is "to see how everything hangs together,"[7] as Rorty puts it. For

---

[6] Jerry Fodor, "Water's Water Everywhere." *London Review of Books* 26:20 (21 October 2004).
[7] Richard Rorty, "How Many Grains Make a Heap?" *London Review of Books* 27:2 (20 January 2005).

their part, more technically minded philosophers find such talk unbearably vague and lacking in rigor. Which side is right? Is philosophy valuable because it seeks specialized results, or because it offers a more general account of how things hang together?

It is valuable for both reasons. Philosophy makes two contributions to a culture: it seeks definitive answers to highly technical questions, *and* it offers a synoptic vision of how things hang together. It does the former in so far as it constructs theories, and it does the latter in so far as it articulates pictures. These roles are not in conflict. Philosophers who try to solve specialized problems are not ignoring their discipline's true calling. They are doing something essential to that calling. At the same time, philosophers who are more interested in synoptic accounts of how things hang together are not offering poor substitutes for "real" philosophy – that is, narrowly technical philosophy. Articulating and assessing pictures of reality is just as much a part of the discipline as anything that the specialized problem-solvers do. And this is a good thing. We should be glad that philosophy is concerned with pictures as well as theories, synoptic visions as well as definitive results. If philosophy were simply the search for definitive answers to specialized questions, it might appear quite pointless, and of little value to the wider culture. We need not be relativists to see that philosophy has a poor record of finding definitive answers to its central questions. Nearly two centuries ago, Hegel observed that

the most various thoughts arise in numerous philosophies, each of which opposes, contradicts, and refutes the other. This fact, which cannot be denied, seems to contain the justification, indeed the necessity for applying to philosophy the words of Christ: "Let the dead bury their dead; arise, and follow me." The whole history of philosophy becomes a battlefield covered with the bones of the dead; it is a kingdom not merely formed of dead and lifeless individuals, but of refuted and spiritually dead systems, since each has killed and buried the other.[8]

If we see philosophers as concerned with results alone, we may well wonder whether the discipline is worthwhile. If, on the other hand, we see them as engaged in the development and refinement of pictures, then their failure to find definitive results does not undermine their enterprise. Pictures play a number of critically important roles in a culture. They address "an ineradicable urge to act out of a comprehensive understanding of our situation,"[9] and they provide alternatives to which we may turn when a dominant picture of reality collapses. That pictures are central to

[8] Hegel, *Lectures on the History of Philosophy*, 17.
[9] Gutting, *Pragmatic Liberalism and the Critique of Modernity*, 191.

philosophy helps explain why the discipline matters, and what its cultural function is.

None of this means that those who do philosophy historically should scorn those who develop theories. They may even be more optimistic about the possibility of theoretical progress than Hegel was.[10] But we can grant that philosophers achieve theoretical progress without claiming that this is their only achievement, or even their main achievement. We can admire this progress and still see pictures as a crucial instrument of philosophical understanding. Doing so helps explain why the past is philosophically significant. More importantly, it helps explain why philosophy has an important role to play in what Gadamer calls "the conversation that we are."

---

[10] Gutting puts the point this way: "When philosophers are doing their job properly, each new formulation will be superior to the extent that it resolves the difficulties that defeated its predecessors. And, in fact, there has been considerable philosophical progress over the centuries, and particularly in the twentieth century, through increasingly better theoretical formulations. It is fair to say that we have better *theories* of knowledge than Plato or Descartes did." See Gutting, *Pragmatic Liberalism and the Critique of Modernity*, 191. Randall echoes this point when he says that "there is actually much in the philosophic enterprise, as in science, that is cumulative and achieved." See Randall, *How Philosophy Uses Its Past*, 79.

References

Allison, Henry. *Kant's Transcendental Idealism: An Interpretation and Defense*. New Haven: Yale University Press, 1983.

Ameriks, Karl. *Kant and the Fate of Autonomy*. Cambridge: Cambridge University Press, 2000.

Annas, Julia. "MacIntyre on Traditions." *Philosophy and Public Affairs* 18:4 (1989), 388–404.

Aristotle. *Metaphysics*, trans. W. D. Ross. In *The Complete Works of Aristotle*, Volume II, ed. Jonathan Barnes. Princeton: Princeton University Press, 1984.

Barash, Jeffrey. *Martin Heidegger and the Problem of Historical Meaning*. New York: Fordham University Press, 2003.

Beistegui, Miguel de. *The New Heidegger*. London: Continuum, 2005.

Bennett, Jonathan. "Critical Notice of D. J. O'Connor (ed), *A Critical History of Western Philosophy*." *Mind* 75 (1966), 437.

Bernet, Rudolf. "On Derrida's 'Introduction' to Husserl's *Origin of Geometry*." In *Derrida and Deconstruction*, ed. Hugh Silverman. London: Routledge, 1989, 139–153.

   "The Subject's Participation in the Game of Truth." *Review of Metaphysics* 58 (2005), 785–814.

Bernet, Rudolf, Iso Kern, and Eduard Marbach. *An Introduction to Husserlian Phenomenology*. Evanston: Northwestern University Press, 1993.

Bourgeois, Patrick. *Philosophy at the Boundary of Reason*. Albany: SUNY Press, 2001.

Browning, Gary. *Lyotard and the End of Grand Narratives*. Cardiff: University of Wales Press, 2000.

Bruns, Gerald. *Hermeneutics Ancient and Modern*. New Haven: Yale University Press, 1992.

Campbell, Richard. *Truth and Historicity*. Oxford: Oxford University Press, 1992.

Carr, David. "Narrative and the Real World: An Argument for Continuity." *History and Theory* 15 (1986), 117–131.

   Time, Narrative, and History. Bloomington: Indiana University Press, 1986.

Cohen, Lesley. "Doing Philosophy is Doing its History." *Synthese* 67 (1986), 51–55.

Curley, Edwin. "Dialogues with the Dead." *Synthese* 67 (1986), 33–49.

Dancy, Jonathan. *Moral Reasons*. Oxford: Blackwell, 1993.

Danto, Arthur. *Narration and Knowledge*. New York: Columbia University Press, 1985.

Dauenhauer, Bernard. *Paul Ricoeur: The Promise and Risk of Politics*. Oxford: Rowman and Littlefield, 1998.

(ed.). *At the Nexus of Philosophy and History*. Athens: University of Georgia Press, 1987.

Davenport, John. "The Meaning of Kierkegaard's Choice Between the Aesthetic and the Ethical: A Response to MacIntyre." In *Kierkegaard After MacIntyre*, ed. John Davenport and Anthony Rudd. Chicago: Open Court, 2001, 75–112.

Derrida, Jacques. *Edmund Husserl's* Origin of Geometry: *An Introduction*, trans. John P. Leavey. Lincoln: University of Nebraska Press, 1978.

Margins of Philosophy, trans. Alan Bass. Chicago: University of Chicago Press, 1982.

"Structure, Sign and Play in the Discourse of the Human Sciences." In *Writing and Difference*, trans. Alan Bass. Chicago: University of Chicago Press, 1978, 278–293.

Dosse, François. *Paul Ricoeur: Les sens d'une vie*. Paris: Découverte, 2001.

Dupré, Louis. "Is the History of Philosophy Philosophy?" *Review of Metaphysics* 42 (1989), 463–482.

Passage to Modernity. New Haven: Yale University Press, 1993.

Fodor, Jerry. "Water's Water Everywhere." *London Review of Books* 26:20 (21 October 2004).

Gadamer, Hans-Georg. *Philosophical Hermeneutics*, trans. David E. Linge. Berkeley: University of California Press, 1976.

Truth and Method, 2nd edn., trans. Joel Weinsheimer and Donald Marshall. New York: Crossroads, 1992.

George, Robert. "Moral Particularism, Thomism, and Traditions." *Review of Metaphysics* 42 (1989), 593–605.

Gewirth, Alan. "Rights and Virtues." *Review of Metaphysics* 38 (1985), 739–762.

Gracia, Jorge. *Philosophy and its History: Issues in Philosophical Historiography*. Albany: SUNY Press, 1992.

Gutting, Gary. "Can Philosophical Beliefs Be Rationally Justified?" *American Philosophical Quarterly* 19:4 (1982), 315–330.

Pragmatic Liberalism and the Critique of Modernity. Cambridge: Cambridge University Press, 1999.

"Review of Brian Leiter (ed), *The Future for Philosophy*." *Notre Dame Philosophical Reviews*, Dec. 14, 2005 [Online]. Available: http://ndpr.nd.edu/review.cfm?id=5161

Haar, Michel. "The Doubleness of the Unthought of the Overman: Ambiguities of Heideggerian Political Thought." *Research in Phenomenology* 20 (1990), 87–111.

Hare, Peter (ed.). *Doing Philosophy Historically*. Buffalo: Prometheus, 1988.

Hegel, G. W. F. *Early Theological Writings*, trans. T. M. Knox. Philadelphia: University of Pennsylvania Press, 1992.

Encyclopedia Logic, trans. T. F. Geraets, W. A. Suchting, and H. S. Harris. Indianapolis: Hackett Publishing Company, 1991.

Lectures on the History of Philosophy, Volume I, trans. E. S. Haldane. Lincoln: University of Nebraska Press, 1995.

Phenomenology of Spirit, trans. A. V. Miller. Oxford: Oxford University Press, 1977.

Philosophy of History, trans. J. Sibree. New York: Dover, 1956.

Science of Logic, trans. A. V. Miller. Atlantic Highlands, NJ: Humanities Press International, 1989.

Heidegger, Martin. "The Age of the World Picture." In *Off the Beaten Track*, trans. and ed. Julian Young and Kenneth Haynes. Cambridge: Cambridge University Press, 2002, 57–85.

"Anaximander's Saying." In *Off the Beaten Track*, trans. and ed. Julian Young and Kenneth Haynes. Cambridge: Cambridge University Press, 2002, 242–281.

Basic Problems of Phenomenology, trans. Albert Hofstadter. Bloomington: Indiana University Press, 1988.

Being and Time, trans. John Macquarrie and Edward Robinson. San Francisco: Harper Collins, 1962.

"The End of Philosophy and the Task of Thinking." In *On Time and Being*, trans. Joan Stambaugh. New York: Harper and Row, 1972, 55–73.

The Essence of Truth, trans. Ted Sadler. New York: Continuum, 2002.

Identity and Difference, trans. Joan Stambaugh. New York: Harper and Row, 1969.

Kant and the Problem of Metaphysics, trans. Richard Taft. Bloomington: Indiana University Press, 1990.

"Kant's Thesis About Being," trans. Ted Klein and William Pohl. In *Pathmarks*, ed. William McNeill. Cambridge: Cambridge University Press, 1998, 337–363.

"Letter on 'Humanism,'" trans. Frank Capuzzi. In *Pathmarks*, ed. William McNeill. Cambridge: Cambridge University Press, 1998, 239–276.

The Metaphysical Foundations of Logic, trans. Michael Heim. Bloomington: Indiana University Press, 1984.

"My Way to Phenomenology." In *On Time and Being*, trans. Joan Stambaugh. New York: Harper and Row, 1972, 74–84.

Nietzsche, Volume I: The Will to Power as Art, trans. David Farrell Krell. San Francisco: Harper Collins, 1991.

Nietzsche, Volume II: The Eternal Recurrence of the Same, trans. David Farrell Krell. San Francisco: Harper Collins, 1991.

Nietzsche, Volume III: The Will to Power as Knowledge and as Metaphysics, trans. David Farrell Krell. San Francisco: Harper Collins, 1991.

Nietzsche, Volume IV: Nihilism, trans. David Farrell Krell. San Francisco: Harper Collins, 1991.

"Nietzsche's Word: God is Dead." In *Off the Beaten Track*, trans. and ed. Julian Young and Kenneth Haynes. Cambridge: Cambridge University Press, 2002, 157–199.

"On the Essence of Truth," trans. John Sallis. In *Pathmarks*, ed. William McNeill. Cambridge: Cambridge University Press, 1998, 136–154.

"The Origin of the Work of Art," trans. Albert Hofstadter. In *Basic Writings*, ed. David Farrell Krell. San Francisco: Harper Collins, 1971, 139–212.

Parmenides, trans. André Schuwer and Richard Rojcewicz. Bloomington: Indiana University Press, 1992.

"Plato's Doctrine of Truth," trans. Thomas Sheehan. In *Pathmarks*, ed. William McNeill. Cambridge: Cambridge University Press, 1998, 155–182.

Plato's Sophist, trans. Richard Rojcewicz and André Schuwer. Bloomington: Indiana University Press, 1997.

"The Question Concerning Technology." In *The Question Concerning Technology and Other Essays*, trans. William Lovitt. New York: Harper and Row, 1977.

Towards the Definition of Philosophy, trans. Ted Sadler. London: Athlone, 2000.

Husserl, Edmund. *Cartesian Meditations*, trans. Dorion Cairns. Dordrecht: Kluwer, 1991.

Kant, Immanuel. *Critique of Practical Reason*, 3rd edn., trans. Lewis White Beck. New York: Macmillan, 1993.

Critique of Pure Reason, trans. Norman Kemp Smith. London: Macmillan, 1927.

Lectures on Metaphysics, trans. and ed. Karl Ameriks and Steve Naragon. Cambridge: Cambridge University Press, 1997.

Kaplan, David. *Ricoeur's Critical Theory*. Albany: SUNY Press, 2003.

Kates, Joshua. *Essential History: Jacques Derrida and the Development of Deconstruction*. Evanston: Northwestern University Press, 2005.

Kaufmann, Walter. *Nietzsche: Philosopher, Psychologist, Antichrist*, 4th edn. Princeton, NJ: Princeton University Press, 1974.

Kellner, Hans. "'As Real as it Gets…:' Ricoeur and Narrativity." *Philosophy Today* 34:1 (1990), 229–242.

Kripke, Saul. *Naming and Necessity*. Oxford: Blackwell, 1980.

Kuhn, Thomas. *The Structure of Scientific Revolutions*, 2nd edn. Chicago: University of Chicago Press, 1970.

Levinas, Emmanuel. *Otherwise Than Being or Beyond Essence*, trans. Alphonso Lingis. Dordrecht: Kluwer, 1991.

Lutz, Christopher. *Tradition in the Ethics of Alasdair MacIntyre*. Lanham, MD: Lexington Books, 2004.

Lyotard, Jean-François. *The Postmodern Condition*, trans. Geoff Bennington and Brian Massumi. Minneapolis: University of Minnesota Press, 1984.

MacIntyre, Alasdair. *After Virtue*. 2nd edn. Notre Dame: University of Notre Dame Press, 1984.

Against the Self-Images of the Age. Notre Dame: University of Notre Dame Press, 1978.

"Contexts of Interpretation: Reflections on Hans-Georg Gadamer's *Truth and Method*." *Boston University Journal* 24: 1 (1976), 41–46.

Dependent Rational Animals. Chicago: Open Court, 1999.

"Epistemological Crises, Dramatic Narrative, and the Philosophy of Science." *Monist* 60 (1977), 453–472.

First Principles, Final Ends and Contemporary Philosophical Issues. Milwaukee: Marquette University Press, 1990.

"An Interview with Giovanna Borradori." In *The MacIntyre Reader*, ed. Kevin Knight. Notre Dame: University of Notre Dame Press, 1998, 255–266.

"Notes From the Moral Wilderness I." *New Reasoner* 7 (1958–1959), 90–100.

"A Partial Response to my Critics." In *After MacIntyre*, ed. John Horton and Susan Mendus. London: Polity, 1994, 283–304.

"The Relationship of Philosophy to its Past." In *Philosophy in History*, ed. Richard Rorty, J. B. Schneewind, and Quentin Skinner. Cambridge: Cambridge University Press, 1984, 31–48.

A Short History of Ethics, 2nd edn. Notre Dame: University of Notre Dame Press, 1998.

Three Rival Versions of Moral Enquiry. Notre Dame: University of Notre Dame Press, 1990.

Whose Justice? Which Rationality? Notre Dame: University of Notre Dame Press, 1988.

Macomber, W. B. *The Anatomy of Disillusion: Martin Heidegger's Notion of Truth*. Evanston: Northwestern University Press, 1967.

Makkreel, Rudolf. "An Ethically Responsive Hermeneutics of History." In *The Ethics of History*, ed. David Carr, Thomas Flynn, and Rudolf Makkreel. Evanston: Northwestern University Press, 2004, 214–229.

Marino, Gordon. "The Place of Reason in Kierkegaard's Ethics." In *Kierkegaard After MacIntyre*, 113–127.

Marx, Werner. *Heidegger and the Tradition*, trans. Theodore Kisiel and Murray Greene. Evanston: Northwestern University Press, 1971.

McMillan, Elizabeth. "The Significance of Moral Universality: The Moral Philosophy of Éric Weil." *Philosophy Today* 21 (1977), 32–42.

McMullin, Ernan. "The Shaping of Scientific Rationality: Construction and Constraint." In *Construction and Constraint: The Shaping of Scientific Rationality*, ed. Ernan McMullin. Notre Dame: University of Notre Dame Press, 1988, 1–47.

Mulhall, Stephen. *On Being in the World: Wittgenstein and Heidegger on Seeing Aspects*. London: Routledge, 1990.

Nietzsche, Friedrich. *Beyond Good and Evil*. In *Basic Writings of Nietzsche*, trans. and ed. Walter Kaufmann. New York: Random House, 1968.

Human, All Too Human, trans. R. J. Hollingdale. Cambridge: Cambridge University Press, 1986.

Twilight of the Idols. In *The Portable Nietzsche*, trans. and ed. Walter Kaufmann. New York: Penguin, 1976.

The Will to Power, trans. R. J. Hollingdale and Walter Kaufmann, ed. Walter Kaufmann. New York: Random House, 1967.

Nozick, Robert. *The Nature of Rationality*. Princeton: Princeton University Press, 1994.

Philibert, Michel. "The Philosophic Method of Paul Ricoeur." In *Studies in the Philosophy of Paul Ricoeur*, ed. Charles Reagan. Athens: Ohio University Press, 1979, 133–139.

Piercey, Robert. "Active Mimesis and the Art of History of Philosophy." *International Philosophical Quarterly* 43:1 (2003), 29–42.

"Ricoeur's Account of Tradition and the Gadamer-Habermas Debate." *Human Studies* 27:3 (2004), 259–280.

Pippin, Robert. *Idealism as Modernism*. Cambridge: Cambridge University Press, 1997.

Modernity as a Philosophical Problem. Cambridge, MA: Blackwell, 1991.

Plato. *Republic*, trans. G. M. A. Grube. Indianapolis: Hackett, 1992.

Pojman, Louis. *Philosophy: The Quest for Truth*, 4th edn. Belmont, CA: Wadsworth, 1999.

Porter, Jean. "Tradition in the Recent Work of Alasdair MacIntyre." In *Alasdair MacIntyre*, ed. Mark Murphy. Cambridge: Cambridge University Press, 2003, 38–69.

Putnam, Hilary. "Hilary Putnam: The Vision and Arguments of a Famous Harvard Philosopher." *Cogito* 3 (1989), 85–91.

Randall, John Herman. *How Philosophy Uses Its Past*. New York: Columbia University Press, 1963.

   Nature and Historical Experience. New York: Columbia University Press, 1958.

Raz, Joseph. *The Morality of Freedom*. Oxford: Clarendon Press, 1986.

Reagan, Charles. *Paul Ricoeur: His Life and Work*. Chicago: University of Chicago Press, 1996.

Reames, Kent. "Metaphysics, History, and Moral Philosophy: The Centrality of the 1990 Aquinas Lecture to MacIntyre's Argument for Thomism." *Thomist* 62 (1998), 419–443.

Ricoeur, Paul. *The Conflict of Interpretations*, ed. Don Ihde. Evanston: Northwestern University Press, 1974.

   The Course of Recognition, trans. David Pellauer. Cambridge, MA: Harvard University Press, 2005.

   Figuring the Sacred: Religion, Narrative, and Imagination, trans. David Pellauer, ed. Mark Wallace. Minneapolis: Fortress Press, 1995.

   Freedom and Nature, trans. Erazim Kohak. Evanston: Northwestern University Press, 1966.

   Freud and Philosophy: An Essay on Interpretation, trans. Denis Savage. New Haven: Yale University Press, 1970.

   From Text to Action, trans. Kathleen Blamey and John Thompson. Evanston: Northwestern University Press, 1991.

   History and Truth, trans. Charles Kelbley. Evanston: Northwestern University Press, 1965.

   The Just, trans. David Pellauer. Chicago: University of Chicago Press, 2000.

   Memory, History, Forgetting, trans. Kathleen Blamey and David Pellauer. Chicago: University of Chicago Press, 2004.

   Oneself as Another, trans. Kathleen Blamey. Chicago: University of Chicago Press, 1992.

   "Reflections on a New Ethos for Europe." *Philosophy and Social Criticism* 21:5/6 (1995), 3–13.

   "The Status of *Vorstellung* in Hegel's Philosophy of Religion." In *Meaning, Truth, and God*, ed. Leroy Rouner. Notre Dame: University of Notre Dame Press, 1982.

   Time and Narrative, Volume I, trans. Kathleen McLaughlin and David Pellauer. Chicago: University of Chicago Press, 1984.

   Time and Narrative, Volume II, trans. Kathleen McLaughlin and David Pellauer. Chicago: University of Chicago Press, 1985.

   Time and Narrative, Volume III, trans. Kathleen McLaughlin and David Pellauer. Chicago: University of Chicago Press, 1988.

Rorty, Richard. *Contingency, Irony, Solidarity*. Cambridge: Cambridge University Press, 1989.

"Deconstruction and Circumvention." In *Essays on Heidegger and Others: Philosophical Papers, Volume II*. Cambridge: Cambridge University Press, 1991, 85–106.

"Grandeur, Profundity, and Finitude." In *Philosophy as Cultural Politics: Philosophical Papers, Volume IV*. Cambridge: Cambridge University Press, 2007, 73–88.

"How Many Grains Make a Heap?" *London Review of Books* 27:2 (20 January 2005).

Philosophy and the Mirror of Nature. Princeton: Princeton University Press, 1979.

Rüsen, Jörn. "Responsibility and Irresponsibility in Historical Studies: A Critical Consideration of the Ethical Dimension in the Historian's Work." In *The Ethics of History*, 195–213.

Russell, Bertrand. "On Denoting." In *Logic and Knowledge*, ed. Robert Charles Marsh. London: Routledge, 1956, 41–56.

Russon, John. *Reading Hegel's* Phenomenology. Bloomington: Indiana University Press, 2004.

Schneewind, J. B. "MacIntyre and the Indispensability of Tradition." *Philosophy and Phenomenological Research* 51:1 (1991), 165–168.

Schrag, Calvin O. *The Resources of Rationality*. Bloomington: Indiana University Press, 1992.

Smith, P. Christopher. *The Hermeneutics of Original Argument*. Evanston: Northwestern University Press, 1998.

Taylor, Charles. "Philosophy and its History." In *Philosophy in History*, 17–30.

Veatch, Henry. *Aristotle: A Contemporary Introduction*. Bloomington: Indiana University Press, 1974.

Walsh, W. H. *Metaphysics*. London: Hutchinson, 1963.

Watson, Stephen. *Tradition(s) II: Hermeneutics, Ethics, and the Dispensation of the Good*. Bloomington: Indiana University Press, 2001.

Weil, Éric. *Philosophie morale*. Paris: Vrin, 1961.

Philosophie politique. Paris: Vrin, 1956.

White, Carol. "Ontology, the Ontological Difference, and the Unthought." *Tulane Studies in Philosophy* 32 (1984), 95–102.

White, David. "Truth and Being: A Critique of Heidegger on Plato." *Man and World* 7 (1974), 118–134.

Wittgenstein, Ludwig. *Philosophical Investigations*, trans. G. E. M. Anscombe. Oxford: Blackwell, 1953.

Wokler, Robert. "Projecting the Enlightenment." In *After MacIntyre*, 108–126.

Wrathall, Mark. "Heidegger on Plato, Truth, and Unconcealment: The 1931–32 Lecture on *The Essence of Truth*." *Inquiry* 47 (2004), 443–463.

Zagzebski, Linda. *Virtues of the Mind*. Cambridge: Cambridge University Press, 1996.

Zahavi, Dan. *Husserl's Phenomenology*. Stanford, CA: Stanford University Press, 2003.

Index